THE IMMIGRATION DEBATE

Kumarian Press Books for a World that Works

The Immigration Debate:
Remaking America
John Isbister

Multi-Track Diplomacy:
A Systems Approach to Peace,
Third Edition
*Louise Diamond and
John McDonald*

Bread, Bricks, and Belief:
Communities In Charge of
Their Future
Mary Lean

The Human Farm:
A Tale of Changing Lives and
Changing Lands
Katie Smith

HIV & AIDS:
The Global Inter-Connection
Elizabeth Reid, editor

When Corporations
Rule the World
David C. Korten

GAZA: Legacy of Occupation—
A Photographer's Journey
*Dick Doughty and
Mohammed El Aydi*

All Her Paths Are Peace:
Women Pioneers in
Peacemaking
Michael Henderson

Summer in the Balkans:
Laughter and Tears after
Communism
Randall Baker

Voices from the Amazon
Binka Le Breton

THE IMMIGRATION DEBATE

DEBATE

REMAKING AMERICA

John Isbister

Kumarian Press

Kumarian Press Books for a World that Works

Dedicated to my daughter
Victoria Wilkinson

THE IMMIGRATION DEBATE: REMAKING AMERICA
Published 1996 in the United States of America by
Kumarian Press, Inc.
14 Oakwood Avenue
West Hartford, Connecticut 06119-2127 USA

Production supervised by Jenna Dixon
Copyedited by Linda Lotz   *Proofread by Beth Richards*
Text design by Jenna Dixon   *Typeset by UltraGraphics*
Index prepared by Alan M. Greenberg
♻
Printed in the United States of America on recycled acid-free paper by Thomson-Shore, Inc. Text printed with soy-based ink.

Library of Congress Cataloging-in-Publication Data
Isbister, John, 1942–
    The immigration debate : remaking America / John Isbister.
        p.   cm. — (Kumarian Press books for a world that works)
    Includes bibliographical references and index.
    ISBN 1-56549-054-1 (cl. : alk paper). — ISBN 1-56549-053-3 (pbk. : alk. paper)
    1. United States—Emigration and immigration. 2. United States—Emigration and immigration—Government policy. I. Title. II. Series.
JV6455.5.I73   1996
325.73—dc20
                                                                95-20519

05 04 03 02 01 00 99 98 97 96   10 9 8 7 6 5 4 3 2 1   1st Printing 1996

Contents

Illustrations

Preface

My interest in international migration stems partly from my academic background in demography, third world economic development and poverty in the United States. All three areas come together in the subject of immigration. Rapid population growth and erratic patterns of economic growth and stagnation in the third world are causing immigration into the United States, immigration that in turn has an impact on America's poor and ethnic minority groups.

My interest is more than academic, however. When I was a teenager, my father, Claude M. Isbister, was Deputy Minister of Citizenship and Immigration in the government of Canada, so immigration was one of the principal topics of discussion around the family dinner table in Ottawa. Later I became an immigrant myself, entering the United States first on a student visa in 1964 and then as a permanent resident in 1968. As a professor and administrator in a public university in California, I work with a student body that is increasingly composed of immigrants and the children of immigrants. If the rate of immigration is maintained, my experience of working in a multicultural, increasingly immigrant environment will be repeated by more and more Americans. In part, therefore, this book is a personal essay, a series of attempts to locate my own experience in a broader context, written in the hope that these explorations will be relevant to others.

When one is dealing with issues of race, ethnicity and nationality, problems of terminology arise, and I have had to make some arbitrary decisions. I have reserved the term *American* for citizens of the United States of America, even though all citizens of the Western Hemisphere have a right to that name. I do so simply because it is conventional and because I cannot think of a better alternative. For the most part, I do not distinguish between whites and non-whites, but between Anglos and non-Anglos. The reason for this choice is that most Latinos are regarded by the U.S. Census Bureau as white. *Anglo* is not a very happy choice, since it includes white people of every European descent, not just the English. It serves, however, to distinguish between European Americans on the one hand and non-Europeans (Native Americans, Latinos and people of third world origins) on the other. When referring to people of Latin American background, I prefer *Latino* to *Hispanic*, since the latter logically includes people from Spain. The Census Bureau uses *Hispanic*, however, so when referring to census data, I use that term. When referring to descendents of the original inhabitants of the United States, I use *Native American* or *Native* (capitalized); when referring to all people born in the United States, I sometimes use *native* (lower case).

I would like to thank Peter Isbister, Susanne Jonas, Sherri Paris and Karen Woodrow-Lafield, all of whom helped me see my arguments more clearly. Thanks to the Chicano/Latino Research Center at the University of California, Santa Cruz, for its support. A special thanks to my wife, Roz Spafford, who gave the manuscript its first full editing. Finally, I would like to acknowledge a lifetime debt to my graduate-school mentor at the Office of Population Research, Princeton University, Ansley J. Coale, one of the world's most innovative and productive demographers, who taught me to take my subject seriously.

Introduction

At the end of the twentieth century, immigrants are coming to the United States in numbers seen only once before, at the beginning of the century. In earlier periods, most of the immigrants were white Europeans; today the great majority are Latino or non-white. Immigration is the most visible manifestation of the growing connection between the United States and the third world.

The arrival of these new immigrants is generating a backlash of opposition, for reasons that are both economic and cultural. The backlash is met in turn with a spirited defense of immigration. With each passing year, the debate grows more heated; immigration will probably be a major issue in the politics of the next decade and beyond.

This book defends immigration. Although I take serious account of the many reasons advanced for opposing immigration, I conclude that immigrants contribute positively to the quality of American life and that immigration is consistent with the moral values that Americans hold closest. The book is an attempt, therefore, to help stay the rising tide of anti-immigrant sentiment.

Chapter 1 begins with the debate itself. The chapter is not a description of the individual debaters; instead, it focuses on the reasoning. What are the many arguments for and against immigration?

The next seven chapters turn to an analysis of immigration. They answer the broad question: what do we need to know in order to make sense out of the debate? Chapter 2 surveys the history of immigration into the United States, showing how the current numbers compare with earlier waves, how immigration legislation has evolved and how the national backgrounds of the immigrants have shifted over time. Chapter 3 paints a portrait of today's immigrants: where they come from and what their skills and backgrounds are. Chapter 4 turns to the question of why they come: what combination of social forces at work in their home countries and in the United States, plus individual factors, leads people to make the decision to pull up stakes and make new lives for themselves in the United States?

Chapters 5 through 8 look at the impacts of immigration on the United States. Chapter 5 deals with demography. It shows how an increasing proportion of American population growth will be accounted for by immigration in the twenty-first century and how immigration will shift the ethnic composition of the population. If the current level of immigration is maintained, every ethnic group in the U.S. population will be a minority by the second half of the twenty-first century. Non-Latino whites, although still the largest group, will be less than half the population, and Latinos will be the next largest group by far.

Chapter 6 looks at the issues that have been the most hotly debated and in which the research literature is richest: the economic impact of immigration on wages, incomes, employment and government finances. I conclude that immigration presents some economic dangers to the country. Chapter 7 continues the discussion of economic impacts, this time looking at the long-run effects of immigration on the structure of the U.S. economy and its competitive position in the world, and on the quality of the natural environment. Here again, I conclude that continued high immigration may entail some dangers.

Chapter 8 turns to the social and cultural consequences of continued immigration, particularly the change in American ethnicity that it is producing. The central issue is whether a more intensely multiracial and multicultural population will lead to greater social conflict, or whether it will produce a mosaic of cultural diversity that enriches the citizenry and is an example to the rest of the world. Both tendencies will be with us for a long time; I argue that immigration will help the latter to prevail.

Some participants in the debate argue that immigration is a net economic benefit to the country but a cultural disaster, that the latter sphere is more important than the former and that immigration should therefore be cut back. I differ in my assessment. Continued high immigration is likely to create economic difficulties for the country but will also present important new social opportunities—and for that reason, immigration will contribute positively to the country.

Chapter 9 considers some of the moral issues connected with immigration. Most people who write and talk about immigration appear to believe that a national interest can be identified with respect to immigration and that policy should be designed to promote that national interest. A smaller group, myself included, believes that ethics compel us to look beyond the national interest. Two principal conclusions emerge from the chapter. First, immigration controls are hard to justify ethically. If they can be justified at all, higher rather than lower levels of immigration are called for. Second, if the United States is to restrict immigration, it should rethink the high priority it currently gives to family reunification and the correspondingly low priority it gives to refugees.

Some of the participants in the debate think that it is pointless to argue about whether immigration helps or hurts the United States and whether it should be expanded or contracted. Immigration is a massive fact of life, they think, and nothing much can be done to stem the inflow of newcomers even if a reduction were desired. What should be debated, they argue, is the reception given to the immigrants, particularly the human and political rights accorded to them. The perspective taken in this book is different. Although the laws of the land cannot completely control the number of immigrants into the United States, they have a significant effect. The current explosion in immigration has taken place in response to a major change in 1965 in the immigration law—and that law could be changed again, thereby changing the flow of immigration. This book concentrates, therefore, on the questions of how many immigrants, and what sorts of immigrants, should be admitted into the United States.

1

The Debate

Immigration has become one of the most contentious topics of debate in the United States. It is not surprising.

In 1965, Congress reformed the country's immigration law, removing the system of quotas based on national origins that had been in place since the 1920s. The architects of the 1965 act wanted to expunge what they saw as racial discrimination in the country's immigration legislation. They did not expect, however, that the new law would lead to much of a shift in either the number or the national origins of the country's immigrants.[3] Yet, since 1965, an enormous change has occurred in both. The amount of immigration has reached levels seen only once before, at the turn of the present century. The United States now accepts more immigrants than all other countries combined.[4] The principal sources of immigration have changed completely, from Europe with its white populations to the third world countries of Latin America and Asia. The pressure for immigration from foreign countries has grown faster than the legal gates have been opening, so the number of undocumented immigrants has increased too.

We should, as rapidly as possible, reduce net immigration into the United States . . . to zero.

—Garrett Hardin[1]

Our view is, borders should be open.

—*Wall Street Journal*[2]

As immigration has grown, opposition to it has grown as well. The country is flooded with proposals to reduce the flow of immigrants, to change the priority categories, to tighten controls at the border and to penalize immigrants, both legal and illegal. The Commission on Immigration Reform, headed by former Representative Barbara Jordan of Texas, recommended in 1995 that immigration be cut by one-third, and President Clinton endorsed the recommendation.[5] The opposition is similar to the resistance that built up against the great influx of immigrants at the beginning of the century. Public opinion against that wave became so strong that Congress passed a series of acts in the 1920s severely restricting the number of new entrants. Today's critics of immigration would like to see the same sort of policy response.

Public opinion polls show strong resistance to immigration, even among some ethnic groups that include a large proportion of recent immigrants. A Roper poll showed that 55 percent of the population is in favor of a temporary freeze on immigration. A poll that divided its respondents by ethnicity showed that 70 to 80 percent of not only Anglos but also Mexican Americans, Puerto Ricans and Cuban Americans agreed with the statement, "There are too many immigrants coming to the U.S."[6] A *Newsweek* poll found that 60 percent of Americans think that immigration is a "bad thing" for the country, and 62 percent think that immigrants take the jobs of American workers.[7] In 1994, Californians voted by a 59–41 margin for Proposition 187, to cut undocumented immigrants and their children off from all public expenditures except emergency medical care.[8] A Field poll showed that almost half of Californians favored a constitutional amendment to deny citizenship to the American-born children of undocumented immigrants.[9] Any number of other polls show the same thing: the majority of Americans are at least skeptical about the value of immigration and, for the most part, are hostile to it.

Little about the debate is new; most of the arguments, both pro and con, have surfaced many times in the past. In the thirteen colonies of the eighteenth century, for example, the predominant opinion was that immigration was essential to prosperity and that any attempt to restrict it was illegitimate. Among the grievances listed in the Declaration of Independence was that the king had:

> endeavoured to prevent the population of these States; for that purpose obstructing the Laws for Naturalization of Foreigners; refusing to pass others to encourage their migration hither.

It had to be a certain *type* of immigrant, however; non-English new-comers were suspect. In the *Federalist Papers*, John Jay wrote,

> Providence has been pleased to give this one connected country to one united people—a people descended from the same ancestors, speaking the same language, professing the same religion, attached to the same principles of government, very similar in their manners and customs.[10]

Benjamin Franklin, writing in 1775, was more explicitly racist:

> Why should the *Palatine Boors* be suffered to swarm into our settlements, and by herding together establish their language and manners to the exclusion of ours? Why should *Pennsylvania*, founded by the *English*, become a colony of *Aliens*, who will shortly be so numerous as to Germanize us instead of our Anglifying them, and will never adopt our language or customs, any more than they can acquire our complexion.
>
> Which leads me to add one remark: That the number of purely white people in the world is proportionably very small. All *Africa* is black or tawney. *Asia* chiefly tawney. *America* (exclusive of the new comers) wholly so. And in *Europe*, the *Spaniards, Italians, French, Russians* and *Swedes*, are generally of what we call swarthy complexion, as are the *Germans* also, the *Saxons* only excepted, who with the *English* make the principal body of white people on the face of the earth. I could wish their numbers were increased. And while we are, as I may call it *scouring* our planet, by clearing America of woods, and so making this side of our globe reflect a brighter light to the eyes of inhabitants in *Mars* or *Venus*, why should we in the sight of superior beings, darken its people? Why increase the sons of *Africa*, by planting them in *America*, where we have so fair an opportunity, by excluding all blacks and tawneys, of increasing the lovely white and red?[11]

The arguments today are only slightly less passionate. One of the proponents of increased immigration, economist Julian Simon, writes:

> I delight in looking at the variety of faces that I see on the subway when I visit New York, and I mark with pleasure the range of costumes and the languages of the newspapers the people are reading. When I share a cab from the airport to that city with two visiting high school girls from Belfast, Ireland, and I tell them about the Irish in New York—and about the other groups, too—I get tears in my eyes, as I again do now in recalling the incident."[12]

To which a restrictionist, Peter Brimelow, replies,

This is obviously somewhat different from my own reaction to the New York subway, although presumably we are both also studying those faces to see if their owners plan to mug us.[13]

Proponents of increased immigration accuse their opponents of racism and nativism. The latter sometimes accuse the former of endorsing national suicide[14]—or, alternatively, of being racist themselves because they neglect the welfare of poor and ethnic minority groups in the United States,[15] preferring instead cheap labor and high corporate profits.

It is difficult to sort out the debate, because conservatives, liberals and progressives can be found on all sides. Conservative proponents of immigration frequently cite the benefit that U.S. businesses obtain from cheap labor and the stimulus that immigration gives to economic growth. They admire the entrepreneurial spirit of immigrants. Some of them oppose border controls as an unwarranted government infringement on individual freedom. Conservative restrictionists are sometimes willing to concede the argument that immigration is good for business; they argue, however, that it is bad for the taxpayers, who bear the burden of providing education, health, welfare and other services for the newcomers. It is also bad, they believe, for the social and ethnic structure of the U.S. population; it leads to conflict between ethnic groups and to the dilution of American culture and values.

Liberal proponents are generally happy with the changing ethnic mix of immigrants. They value diversity—of race, opinion, experience—as enriching the American landscape. They express concern for the well-being and for the human rights of the immigrants. Although they do not necessarily endorse the argument that immigration is good for business, they are careful to refute any suggestion that immigration harms the economic well-being of residents. Liberal opponents are concerned mostly with the impact of immigration on American workers and on low- to moderate-income people; they worry that immigration lowers wage rates and increases unemployment. Although they value ethnic diversity, they believe that the first duty of the country is to improve the living standards of disadvantaged Americans. Liberal opponents also worry that population growth caused by immigration will lead to a deterioration of the country's natural environment.

Everyone in the debate seems to think that his or her opponents are not only unprincipled but also better organized. Julian Simon, for example, introduces his pro-immigration book by noting sadly, "there are no organizations that lobby for more immigration."[16] Richard Lamm (the former governor of Colorado) and Gary Imhoff begin their restrictionist book by lamenting that "efforts to . . . moderate the high levels of legal immigration are stymied in Congress by an unlikely coalition of the far right and the far left, fueled by a coalition of big business and Hispanic pressure groups."[17]

Within the overall debate about immigration are many subdebates, about both facts and values. The sections that follow outline some of the most important subdebates, beginning with the demographic arguments and then moving to the economic consequences of immigration, the social and cultural consequences, the questions relating to priority categories and to the undocumented and finally to the issues of values, human rights and ethics. Although these sections are based on the writings and on the advocacy of many different people, they do not pretend to be a complete, accurate rendering of any particular person's opinion. They are a mélange that, taken together, reveals most of the serious views about American immigration at the end of the twentieth century.[18]

The Demographic Debate

Two demographic issues arise over and over: *Is the current wave of immigration unusually large? Will it transform the ethnic composition of the country?*

Opponents of immigration characterize today's inflow as massive and, if not unprecedented in American history, at least unusual.[19] They point out that it was matched only once before, in the decades just before and after the beginning of the twentieth century, a period in which immigration was virtually unrestricted by the federal government. Today, immigration is controlled; even so, the numbers match those of the earlier era. Opponents of immigration believe that if controls were lifted, the influx into the country would be both unprecedented and overwhelming.

Not so, reply many of the defenders of immigration. America is a country of immigrants; in most periods of its history, its people have been accustomed to welcoming newcomers. The current flow of immigration may seem large to some, but that is only because it follows a most unusual period, from the 1920s through the 1960s, when immigration was artificially low. Those four decades are the anomaly in American history, not today. The absolute numbers of immigrants may be relatively high today, but, they argue, seen as a proportion of the U.S. population, immigration is just at an average level, well below the heights in several previous periods.

The second important demographic debate has to do with whether immigration is changing the character of the American population. Some of the opponents of immigration fear a shift in the ethnicity of the population, away from its predominantly European origins.

Everyone agrees that the sources of today's immigration have shifted radically, away from Europe and toward the third world, particularly toward the countries of East Asia and the Caribbean Basin. The great majority of the newcomers are non-Anglo. Some observers believe that if the current rate of immigration from the third world continues, the United States will be transformed into a country with no majority ethnic group and with greatly increased proportions of people of Asian and Latin American descent.[20]

On the other side of the argument, some argue that this sort of shift is not likely, for at least two reasons. First, the current wave of immigration will ease, long before the ethnic composition of the population is radically changed. Second, the national origins of the immigrants are irrelevant to anything important about the U.S. population. Immigrants change when they come to America, or at least their children and grandchildren do. They abandon their ethnic identities and their languages and they conform to American cultural patterns. They intermarry; their descendants have mixed and unidentifiable ethnic backgrounds. The predominant complexion of the country may darken a degree or two, it is argued, but immigration will produce no long-run, fundamental change in the character of the American people.[21]

On the whole, it is the opponents of immigration who foresee a marked shift in the ethnic composition of the population and the proponents who tend to believe that it will not happen. Still, some proponents of immigration agree that the national origins of the population are shifting fundamentally, and they welcome the shift.

The Economic Debate

Much of the debate has focused on the economic consequences of immigration, both short and long term. Some proponents of immigration argue that the newcomers contribute to the vitality of the American economy, helping to improve the standard of living of everyone, whether immigrant or native. Others do not go so far but argue that immigrants at least cause no economic harm to Americans. Those on the other side of the economic debate claim that immigrants impose significant material burdens on Americans and that they reduce the country's prospects for long-term prosperity.

Is the quality of the immigrant labor force deteriorating? Critics worry that the United States is now attracting immigrants who are relatively unskilled and uneducated, who dilute the quality of the American labor force. One analyst, George Borjas, has developed data to show that immigrants have become progressively less fit for American jobs since 1940.[22] The country's prosperity depends on the productivity of its workers; consequently, the critics argue, the decline in labor quality bodes ill for the entire population.

Although everyone concedes that today's immigrants come from poorer countries, on average, than previous generations of immigrants did, not everyone agrees that they have less ability. Many supporters of immigration argue that the newcomers bring significant skills with them and are well able to contribute to the American labor force. Some say that the decline in immigrant skills was real in the past, but that since 1980, the trend has turned around, and immigrants are closing the skills gap between themselves and natives. Others argue that the skills gap is a myth, that the typical immigrant is as proficient as the typical American worker, perhaps even more skilled.[23] Although immigrants may earn less money than natives when they first arrive, the argument goes, this is purely a transitional problem, not an indicator that they are less skilled. Over time, they learn how to compete in American labor markets, and their performance matches that of natives.[24]

Still others say that the argument is posed improperly, that there is little point in comparing average immigrants with average natives. Both immigrants and natives are diverse. The skill levels of some immigrant streams are low and declining, whereas skills of other immigrant groups are so high as to allow them to compete effectively with the most proficient Americans.[25]

Are immigrants unusually enterprising? Some supporters of immigration argue that newcomers are responsible for much of the economic growth in the country. Immigrants bring with them their talents, energy and entrepreneurship. Those who choose to leave the security of their home communities are the risk takers, the people who are dissatisfied with the way things are and who are willing to venture into the unknown in search of a better life. Although they may not always have high levels of education and skills, they have the get-up-and-go to succeed. They work longer and harder than native workers do. They are more motivated to succeed, and they save more. They are more likely to be entrepreneurial, to take business risks, to start and expand enterprises.

"Immigrants create jobs, new businesses, spend, invest, and raise productivity," reads the position paper of an immigrant rights group in California. "They bring with them important values; they come to work and sacrifice."[26] "Our own view remains that the problem is not too many immigrants, but too few," pens an editorial writer in the *Wall Street Journal.* "In a world in which human capital is increasingly the coin of international 'competitiveness,' the U.S. needs more of the energetic risk-takers willing to come here."[27]

This view is met with skepticism.[28] Of course, it is argued, some immigrants are energetic and entrepreneurial, but many are not. Nothing about being an immigrant necessarily implies exceptional character, say the critics. Some immigrants are refugees forced to leave their home countries, others are relatives of American residents seeking simply to join them and others are the victims of social dislocation in their home communities. They may be fine people, critics argue, but they are not necessarily more forward-looking than Americans.

Is immigration desirable because it helps alleviate labor shortages? Here the debate is not so much over the facts as over the significance of the facts. There is no question but that the American economy is dynamic, growing and changing. As it changes, as some sectors gain and others lose, the demands that employers have for labor are not always matched by the availability of workers. Immigration helps solve this problem. In some cases, immigrants have skills that employers cannot find among the available American workers. In other cases, low-skilled immigrants are willing to work in occupations and for wages that Americans shun. Whatever the circumstances, the availability of immigrant labor often helps firms stay in business and be competitive. Hardly anyone disagrees with the proposition that immigration helps alleviate labor shortages.

The disagreement arises over whether this is ultimately good or bad for the American economy. Many proponents of immigration say that it is good, even essential. Without new workers, they say, the economy would not be able to expand. Whole sectors might not be able to compete, either domestically or internationally. Immigrant workers allow the structure of American industry to adjust to changing markets and changing opportunities.[29] This is the heart of the pro-immigration argument made by conservatives.

The contrary argument, made by some liberals who oppose immigration, is that in the long run the American economy is helped by labor shortages.[30] Faced with a shortage, employers may try to economize by developing more efficient methods of production. They may develop new technology and new machinery. If they cannot find enough workers at the going wage rate, they have the options of raising wages to attract workers or providing on-the-job training to people who do not yet have the requisite skills. All these responses to labor shortages help raise productivity and raise the standard of living of Americans. If a firm cannot respond effectively to a labor shortage and cannot compete, the liberal opponents argue, perhaps it is best for it to go out of business, yielding its place in the economy to firms that are capable of competing.

Seen from this latter perspective, immigration hurts the economy and damages the standard of living of Americans, because it gives employers an easy alternative to improving technology and productivity.

Does immigration reduce American wages?[31] Some opponents claim that immigration lowers the wages of Americans. It must necessarily have this effect, they say, as any student of introductory economics could show in a few seconds. Immigration increases the supply of labor in the country. It allows employers to play one group of workers (the natives) against another group (the immigrants) and thereby lower average wages.

This is completely unproven, either empirically or theoretically, argue supporters of immigration. A long series of statistical investigations has shown that the effect of immigration on American wages is either nil or trivially small. Moreover, there is no a priori reason, supporters say, to think that immigration will lower wages, because although it increases the supply of labor (and this, admittedly, should cause wages to fall), it also increases production and therefore the demand for labor (and this should cause wages to rise). With two contradictory forces at work, immigration will cause neither a rise nor a fall in wages. The worries about declining wages, says this group, are unjustified.

Does immigration lead to a more unequal distribution of income? This part of the debate is related to the preceding argument but goes further. Does immigration not only lower average wages but also lower the incomes of the poorest Americans while raising the incomes of the richest? This argument is predominant among liberals, who worry that the gap in incomes is too great in the United States.

Liberal opponents of immigration make several points. If immigration lowers average wages, they say, it reduces the costs of production and thereby increases firms' profit rates. Income is thereby transferred from workers to owners, and since the former generally have less income than the latter, this increases income inequality in the country. A related but different argument is that low-skilled immigrants reduce the incomes and job prospects of low-skilled Americans, and this increases the gaps between Americans of different skill levels.

These propositions are all denied by proponents of immigration. They claim that immigrants are not predominantly low-skilled and that they do not lower average wages, so they do not widen the wage gap. Some make a different sort of argument. Immigrants often take jobs that are low-skilled, low-paid and unpleasant, jobs that would otherwise have to be filled by Americans, and this releases those Americans to rise to more attractive jobs, effectively reducing the gap in incomes among natives.

Does immigration increase unemployment? Yes, say some critics of immigration. It is obvious, they claim, that the American economy cannot provide enough decent jobs for its resident population. Unemployment is almost always a problem. So too is underemployment—people working part time when they would like full-time work, or holding jobs for which they are overqualified. If the economy is failing to provide enough jobs for Americans, how can it possibly provide additional jobs for the newcomers? If they get jobs, they take them away from Americans.

No, say proponents. Immigrants create jobs. They spend money, which leads to growth in sales and production; this, in turn, leads firms to hire more workers. Sometimes the chain is more direct: immigrant entrepreneurs hire other immigrants. Unemployment is, of course, a serious problem for both Americans and immigrants, but immigration does not cause it or even worsen it, say supporters. The worst unemployment in American history occurred during the 1930s, when immigration had almost ceased.

Do immigrants impose a fiscal burden on Americans? Some of the sharpest debates concern whether immigrants are costly to American residents in terms of taxes and public expenditures. The subject has become a major political issue in some of the states most heavily impacted by immigration, especially California and Florida, which have demanded greatly increased federal compensation for their expenditures.

Those asserting that there is a burden say that governments spend enormous sums of money on immigrants for services such as education, health care, welfare, social security and criminal justice. The taxes paid by immigrants do not compensate for these expenditures. The critics are particularly incensed that undocumented immigrants can qualify for public benefit programs; California's Proposition 187 is a consequence of this anger. Some go so far as to say that immigrants are attracted to the United States because of its benefit programs. Columnist George Will writes:

> Today, immigrants are received into a welfare culture that encourages an entitlement mentality. That mentality weakens the mainspring of individual striving for upward mobility. A generous welfare state such as the United States, and California especially, can be a "magnet" for migrants.[32]

The argument is rebutted on every level. Immigrants do not cost the public coffers more than they pay in taxes, the counterargument goes. Although the governments of some localities may feel a burden, in the United States as a whole, immigrants pay more in than they take out. This happens because, contrary to widely held opinion, they do not qualify disproportionately for public expenditure programs. Although their children are eligible for public education, most cannot qualify for welfare and support programs for five years after entry. The undocumented are infrequent participants in public expenditure programs, because they are afraid to identify themselves and risk deportation. Moreover, the assertion that immigrants come in order to participate in American entitlement programs is pure myth, they say. Immigrants come to work.

Why do immigrants come? The dispute over whether immigrants come to the United States to share in its entitlement programs is just the beginning of the disagreement over the causes of migration. The oldest theory of immigration is called "push-pull": people are pushed out of their country of origin because of poor economic conditions and pulled into their country of destination by its prosperity. This theory is criticized by those who argue that it is not disparities in income levels that create migratory flows but rather social dislocation in the home communities, caused perhaps by modernization or foreign investment. If this latter explanation is correct, perhaps emigrants are pushed out of their countries by growing economies, not economic stagnation. Other explanations focus on individual and family decision making, sometimes for the purpose of minimizing risk. One school of thought argues that the initial causes of many migratory streams soon lose their relevance because they are supplanted by a supportive network of veteran migrants who ease the way for newcomers.

To a large extent, the debate over the causes of immigration is academic,[33] but it spills over into policy and political debates, most obviously to the question of whether immigrants are really motivated to work. It is also relevant to the question of whether the current wave of immigration will continue unabated throughout the twenty-first century. If the identifiable causes of immigration are likely to wane, the immigration wave may subside on its own without policy intervention, but if the causes will remain and even intensify, so will the immigration.

Do immigrants generate enough economic growth to improve the living standards of Americans? No one denies that immigrants contribute to the economy and generate growth in the production of goods and services. They bring their labor power, and they may bring other resources as well: skills, savings and capital. The dispute is over whether they raise production enough to raise the average living standards of Americans. An important determinant of the standard of living of the population is output per person. Consider, for example, a wave of immigration that raises the population by 10 percent. If it raises the country's production of goods and services by, say, 5 percent, it will lower average output and reduce the average standard of living. Americans may be hurt by the immigration, in spite of the growth it generates. If the immigration leads to a 10 percent increase in output, the average standard of living will be unaffected, and if it leads to a 15 percent increase in output, the standard of living will rise.

Is there reason to think that a 10 percent increase in population through immigration will lead to a 15 percent increase in the country's production? Some defenders of immigration argue yes, that the immigrants bring so many resources with them—skills, energy, capital and so on—that this is a plausible consequence. It happened in the past, they believe; waves of immigrants so stimulated the economy that they raised the standard of living of other Americans. Others are doubtful. They are not sure about the past, and in any case, they think that economic conditions in the future will be different from those in the past, and less likely to permit this kind of effect.

Will immigration reduce America's international competitiveness? Some critics argue that continued high immigration will lead the United States down an economic path leading to its inability to compete effectively in international markets. Immigration will increase the amount of labor in the country, especially the amount of low-skilled labor. U.S. firms will have to absorb that labor, and they will do so by specializing in production methods that are labor intensive and for which wage rates are low. This will be a dead end for the United States, because it will lead it into competition with low-income countries, where wages are much lower than American wages. A brighter future for American competitiveness lies down the road of high-productivity, high-technology methods,

methods that economize on the use of labor and for which high wage rates are therefore not much of a handicap. High immigration will push U.S. firms down the path that will do the country the least good in the long run.[34]

Nonsense, say the supporters of immigration. This view of competitiveness is based on the faulty assumptions that immigrants are low-skilled and that they lack energy and enterprise. Neither assumption is true. Even if they were true, the argument about competitiveness relates to the long run, several generations hence, and over the long run, the children and grandchildren of immigrants will have the same skills as other Americans. Today's high-tech economy is driven by the descendants of the Irish, Jewish, Italian and other immigrants of the nineteenth century; tomorrow's will be driven by Mexican and Chinese Americans, they believe.[35]

Will immigration harm the natural environment and deplete natural resources? Some of the strongest criticisms of immigration come from environmentalists. It is not that they have anything against immigrants per se, nor that they think that immigrants are any worse than natives. It is simply that immigration is an important component of population growth in the country, and population growth puts pressure on natural resources and ecosystems that are fragile and deteriorating. Of course, environmentalists are quick to say, ecological problems are global, and world population growth is a greater ecological threat than population growth in any given country. Moreover, within a country such as the United States, a great deal can be done, with any population size, to improve or worsen natural conditions. Population size is not the only factor, but it is an important one, they say. People consume scarce natural resources; they pollute the land, atmosphere and waters; they expand into natural areas and destroy habitats; they drain water systems for their own uses and they destroy species. Unwilling to live within the stringent limits that nature imposes, they (we) are destroying the very basis on which human life exists. Anything that can be done to reduce the pressure of population, nationally or globally, makes the task of achieving ecological balance easier.[36]

The expansionists have little patience with the idea that immigration will have harmful environmental consequences. If this argument were correct, they say, the country's population growth over the last hundred years should have led to severe ecological problems, growing pollution and ever scarcer raw materials. The opposite has happened, they claim. A new appreciation of ecological relationships has led to improved stewardship of the environment. Waterways are cleaner, urban sanitation is incomparably better and smog is retreating. Even the so-called nonrenewable natural resources are more plentiful today than in previous generations.[37]

The Cultural Debate

For many, the economic issues are less important than the social and cultural issues raised by immigration. "I have concluded that economics in general can give no large answer as to what the immigration policy of a nation should be," writes sociologist Nathan Glazer.[38] Columnist George Will adds that, even though immigration probably is of net economic benefit, its harmful effect on the country's culture outweighs this benefit.[39]

What is the cultural problem that they see? Briefly, they argue that today's immigrants are so different, culturally and racially, from the natives that they threaten to transform the country into something less desirable than it is now. The concern about culture is expressed in several debates.

Does America have one culture or many? Some of those who worry about the cultural consequences of immigration believe that a single, identifiable culture predominates in the United States. A "strong motivation of the [restrictionist] movement comes from the sense that there was—is—an American culture that is threatened by too great diversity," writes Glazer.[40] How can this group believe there to be a single American culture, when the U.S. population has been formed over the generations by the immigration of so many different ethnicities? They believe in the melting pot. In this vision, Americans have many ethnic and cultural traditions, but those traditions have been mixed together in an amalgam that is different from any of its components and that has substantially if not completely erased those traditions. Americans are thought to share values, lifestyles, commitments and a language: they have "melted into" an American culture.

This unified vision of American culture is denied by those who hold a plural or multicultural view. The United States is composed of many nationalities, many ethnicities and many cultures, they maintain. The experience of being in America has changed those cultures (Polish Americans, for example, are not the same as Poles) but it has not suppressed them. In their view, the best image for describing the United States is not a melting pot but a mosaic. What is central about American life is not the characteristics of a single, preeminent culture but rather the way in which the different cultures interact: at times to enrich each group, but at other times to create an exploitative structure of dominance and subordination.[41]

Some uniculturalists worry about the current wave of immigration, thinking that today's immigrants are too different from Americans. Uniculturalists fear that the immigrants will not adapt to American customs; as a consequence, the character of American society will be transformed in ways that are unfamiliar and uncomfortable to today's residents. They also contend that Americans should not have to put up with the transformation: Americans have never expressed such basic dissatisfaction with who they are and how their lives are structured that they called for a wholly new country.

The multiculturalists reply that immigration may well change customs in the United States, but that this is the normal pattern of cultural evolution in American history. Each wave of immigrants has been different, and each has made its own contribution. There is no reason to think that this tradition will change, nor should it change, they believe, since the interaction of different cultures is the defining characteristic of American life.

Has the melting pot stopped melting? This is a debate among the melting pot adherents; for the multiculturalists, it is beside the point. For those who believe in a dominant American culture, the debate is whether that culture is strong enough to accept the new immigrants from the third world and shape their attitudes, practices and beliefs so that within several generations they will become part of the American mainstream. Those who believe that the melting pot is still working tend to be unconcerned about the country's changing ethnicity. "If today's immigrants assimilate to American ways as readily as their predecessors at the turn of the century—as seems to be happening—there won't be a minority majority issue anyway," writes historian Stephan Thernstrom. "Whatever their origins, they will have joined the American majority, which is determined not by bloodlines but by commitment to the principles for which this nation stands."[42] Those who, like Thernstrom, believe that the melting pot is still strong tend to be unconcerned about current immigration.

Many of those who believed that the melting pot worked in the past are skeptical, however, about its power to assimilate present and future waves of immigrants from the third world. The melting pot has worked well only with European immigrants, they believe. It never brought African Americans into the American mainstream consensus, and it will fail as well with Latinos and Asians. They are simply too different, this group believes. Their cultural differences will always be marked by their race. Better to reduce immigration and keep their numbers low, it is argued, since they will never be part of mainstream American culture.

Can the United States increase its cultural diversity without increasing conflict? This question is inherent in the multicultural view of American society. Most people who understand the United States as being composed of a variety of cultural groups see two opposed consequences of that variety. On the one hand, the different groups interact with one another constructively; while retaining their own uniqueness, they enrich the experience of each other group. On the other hand, the different cultural groups are unequal in status and power, so a pattern of dominance, subjection and conflict results.

Both patterns are clear in the relationship of African Americans to the rest of the United States. Brought to the country in chains, they have been subject to oppression, racism and economic disadvantage— and although the terms of their subjection have changed, the basic fact of it has not. From time to time they have responded in protest and anger, and sometimes in violence. At the same time, they have participated in and added to American culture as no other group has, in such realms as music, sports, linguistic innovations, literature and many others.

The question naturally arises, therefore: will increased immigration from the third world enrich the lives of other Americans or lead them into greater friction and conflict? Some whose views are far from unicultural, and who see the principal theme of American history and culture as being relations between the races, nevertheless are worried about the current immigration. They fear that it will lead the new groups into the same sorts of subordinate positions that African Americans have had to endure. They also fear that the arrival of other groups will disadvantage African Americans in their economic and social struggles.[43]

Others take the opposite view. Although the United States is diverse, they believe, it is not diverse enough: as long as Anglos are numerically predominant, they will have the power to make other groups socially inferior. The promise of immigration is that it will build up the numbers of the other ethnic groups so that they can face each other from positions of greater equality. When Americans have no choice but to recognize themselves as a society of many cultures, and not as a predominantly Anglo country with a smattering of minorities, they will be more likely to treat one another well and learn from one another.

Debating the Limits of Immigration Policy

Until the latter part of the nineteenth century, immigration into the United States was virtually unrestricted. In the 1920s, the golden door was closed—not completely, but most of the way. Since that time, immigration has been closely regulated by the federal government, with limits on overall numbers and complex priority categories governing who is legally admissible. Since the laws advantage some and disadvantage others, they are all controversial. Controversy also exists over how effective the laws are, and can be, in influencing streams of immigration.

How should immigrant applicants be prioritized? Under current law, the largest number of immigrant slots is made available for relatives of American residents. Visas are also available to people on the basis of their ability to contribute to the U.S. economy and their refugee status. A few places are available to people who do not fit into one of the priorities. Within each category, several subcategories exist, and the regulations governing admissibility under each are complex. The evolution of these categories is a result of compromise among conflicting interest groups; almost no one is completely happy with them.

Some, particularly members of immigrant groups themselves, argue that although family reunification accounts for the largest number of slots, those slots are still in short supply. It is of the utmost importance for them to be reunited with their kin, and the waiting periods they are subject to can be heartbreaking. Their belief is that nothing is as important as the integrity of the family, and they are joined in this belief by many Americans.

Some argue, however, that the immigration laws give too much weight to family reunification. This is nepotism, they believe, or at best a response to a specific interest of a few Americans, and not to the national interest.[44] It would be better, they think, to admit people primarily on the basis of their job market skills and their education.[45] Others agree that potential economic contribution should count for more in determining admissibility, but they believe that because Americans can fill the high-skilled positions, what is really needed is low-paid manual labor to do the jobs that Americans would prefer to avoid. Still others think that neither family unification nor economic contribution should be the leading criterion. Instead, Americans should try to do the most good in the world with their immigrant slots; this principle argues in favor of increasing the number of refugees, people who cannot return to their home countries.[46]

Could the education and skills of immigrants be upgraded? As was just stated, some of the participants in the debate believe that the United States is being hurt by the low skills of the immigrants, and that the laws should be changed to emphasize skills and education as criteria for admission. They point to Australia and Canada, which give more weight to those characteristics than the United States does.[47]

The rejoinder is that not much can be done about the skills and education of immigrants.[48] The least-prepared immigrants are the illegal entrants and the refugees, but changes in the admissibility criteria would not pertain to them. The remaining legal immigrants, who could, in theory, be subjected to more rigorous standards, have relatively high educational attainments already.

This is a considerable overstatement, comes the reply. To take just one example, the country sending the largest number of legal immigrants to the United States is Mexico, and Mexicans have, on average, about the lowest educational levels of any immigrants. Granted, many Mexican immigrants are undocumented, but a serious attempt to reform the immigration categories could make a difference.

Whatever the answer, this dispute makes it clear that limits exist to the authority of governments and laws in regulating immigration. The limits are of even more concern in areas other than the skills of the immigrants.

Has the United States lost control of its borders? The most explosive part of the debate has to do with immigrants who are in the country illegally, either because they entered without inspection or because they entered legally in a nonimmigrant status and then overstayed the time limits of their visas. That so many people regard the undocumented as *the* immigration problem is surprising; they are greatly outnumbered by legal immigrants, so even if the inflow of the undocumented were to cease altogether, most of the other issues related to immigration would still be unresolved.

Nevertheless, a great many Americans are angry about the presence of the undocumented in their midst. To cite just one small example, a supermarket in suburban San Francisco printed 40,000 shopping bags with an inspiring story of how a nine-year-old Salvadoran boy had risked great peril to journey to the United States and join his mother, facing deserts, treacherous rivers, smugglers and hunger. The supermarket was forced to destroy the bags when faced with the outrage of its customers, who objected to the fact that the boy had entered the country illegally.[49] Some resent what they regard as the unfair behavior of illegal immigrants in jumping ahead of law-abiding people who often have to wait years in order to enter, and even then are frequently unsuccessful. The unauthorized immigrants have thumbed their collective noses at the American legal and administrative system, they believe, and they have placed the effectiveness of that system in question.

Even many who generally welcome immigrants are opposed to the arrival of the undocumented. They believe that illegal immigration must be stopped; otherwise, the country will not be able to welcome legal immigrants.[50]

Some American residents are not distressed with the presence of the undocumented. They see little relevance in the legal status of immigrants. The undocumented are just as worthy as their fully documented colleagues, they believe. Many Americans—including employers, colleagues, friends and relatives of the undocumented—are particularly committed to them and to their presence in the country.

In any case, the worries about losing control of the border are greatly overstated, say some. The number of undocumented immigrants in the United States is much less than was once thought. Many people attempt to enter the country illegally, and many succeed, but many of those people return after a short stay; the number of illegal entries is far greater than the growth of the undocumented population in the country. The Border Patrol cannot seal off the country completely, but it does a fairly effective job, keeping immigration far below the level it would attain were the borders simply open, this group believes. The United States has not lost control of its borders.[51] Furthermore, say some, the authorities should not try to crack down further on the undocumented, since that would entail a kind of police presence in Americans' lives that a free society cannot tolerate.

These reassurances are unpersuasive to those who are most worried about the continued growth of the undocumented population. They fear that the United States has lost the ability to cut immigration. If the authorized categories were reduced in size, what would prevent the illegal flow from simply increasing in response? The debate about the effectiveness of border controls therefore spills over into almost all the other debates. Those who are concerned about immigration for any reason, be it economic, cultural, environmental or anything else, want to take policy action to reduce the flow or to change its character. If the United States has lost control of its borders, however, none of these policies can be effective.

Not everyone who believes that the United States has lost control of its borders regrets the fact. Some think that a mixing of the world's populations, especially in the Western Hemisphere, is both inevitable and desirable, and that it is fortunate that the laws pertaining to that mixing are becoming increasingly irrelevant.

The Debate about Ethics

Americans are skilled at looking out for their own interests, but most do not like to be thought of as selfish. They would prefer to do the right thing, to behave ethically. Perhaps they, like other people, too easily confuse their own interests with what is right. Still, the concern to do what is morally defensible is not just a screen for unscrupulous behavior; it is a genuine and honorable goal. When Americans think about the ethics of immigration, however, they run into some difficult problems.

Who is guilty of racism, nativism and immigrant bashing? The debate is fraught with accusations about stereotypical and oppressive thinking. The history of American race relations is anything but admirable; discourse about social issues has long been tinged with racism and accusations of racism. Participants in the immigration debate frequently claim to see racism in their opponents' arguments, whatever side they are on. To the usual categories of racism is added a category unique to the discussion of immigration: nativism or discrimination against foreigners.

Most of the accusations of racism come from the multiculturalists, who often see the unicultural, melting pot view as a veil for white supremacy. People in favor of particular immigrant flows, for example, Jewish or Haitian refugees, often accuse those who oppose those flows of having racial motivations. The accusations sometimes come from opponents of immigration, who say that the proponents are willing to flood the country with newcomers who will destroy prospects for the progress of American minority groups, particularly African Americans.

Hardly anyone these days is willing to accept the mantle of racist voluntarily; this is one respect in which today's discourse differs from that of earlier eras. The rejoinder to most accusations of racism or nativism is that they are not true and, further, that they are cheap and easy ways of diverting the discussion from the real issues surrounding immigration.

A related accusation has to do with what is called immigrant bashing. Proponents of immigration sometimes claim that the critics make scapegoats of immigrants, blaming them for many of the problems in American society for which they actually bear no responsibility at all, problems such as recession, unemployment, fiscal stringency and racial tensions. Immigrants—especially undocumented immigrants—are blamed not because they are really responsible but because they are the most vulnerable group available. The rejoinder to this accusation comes in two parts: first, that immigration is indeed responsible for many social problems in the country, and second, that for the most part, the critics are blaming the phenomenon of immigration without blaming individual immigrants for their behavior.

What rights should undocumented immigrants have? Neither of the two extreme answers to this question is plausible, and where to come down in the middle is an almost impossible dilemma. One extreme position is that since the undocumented have no right to be in the United States, they should not expect to be protected by any of the rights that American citizens and legal residents have. The opposite extreme view is that since they are human beings of equal worth with everyone else, they should be treated exactly the same as Americans. The first position fails because it would allow the undocumented to be enslaved, abused, killed or treated in any way that any American would like. The second position fails, as long as Americans want to maintain any border controls at all, because it amounts to saying that the border controls are null and void. Without immigration restrictions, of course, there would be no undocumented residents. The realistic debate therefore comes down to a question of just what rights undocumented immigrants should have.

A substantial number of people in the United States are of the opinion that they should have fewer rights than they do now. They argue that the undocumented should be rigidly excluded from the benefits of any program of public expenditure, both because this will reduce the attractiveness of the United States to them and because American taxpayers should not have to spend a dime on people who do not belong in the country. They think that the undocumented should not have the right to a public education or to public health care and that the Constitution should be amended to deprive their American-born children of the right of citizenship.

The contrary view is that the undocumented are here to stay, even if most Americans would prefer otherwise. Many Americans benefit from their presence and encourage it, whatever the laws may say. That being the case, say the defenders of the rights of the undocumented, the country should have the decency to accord them, if not equal rights, at least substantial rights, so that they can pursue a decent life. The proposals to deprive them of participation in the few public programs for which they now qualify should be resisted, not only because it would be unfair to them but also because it would hurt other Americans to live among a class of people kept unhealthy and uneducated by public policy. The proposal for a constitutional amendment is particularly to be resisted, this group argues, since it would establish in perpetuity two different classes of American residents with unequal rights. One way in which the rights of the undocumented need enhancement, it is argued, is by allowing them to make complaints to public bodies about illegal, abusive treatment, without thereby becoming vulnerable to deportation. Some argue that the world as a whole needs a bill of rights for migratory workers, be they documented or undocumented.

Would an ethical immigration policy differ from one that is in the national interest?[52] For many people, the question never arises, since they presume that in a democracy the best course of action is one that is in the national interest. What should be avoided is policy in the service of special interests, when those special interests are at variance with the general interest. The national interest may be hard to identify when different groups of people in the country have conflicting interests, but still, that is the goal.

The contrary view is that the national interest is not necessarily a guide to good policy because, by definition, it excludes the interests of foreigners. As fellow human beings, we should accord them at least some standing, perhaps equal standing.

Are American border controls morally justified? Almost every party to the debate agrees that some sort of restrictions on immigration are in the national interest. Some argue for a reduction in the number of immigrants and some for an increase, but only a few believe that the United States should return to its nineteenth-century policy of virtually open borders.

An articulate minority argues, however, that whatever policy the national interest might lead to, morality calls for the abolition of border controls or at least for their relaxation to such an extent that they cease to matter very much. Border controls are unjustified because they discriminate against the needy, the potential immigrants, and they do so only for the purpose of protecting the privileges of people who are already among the world's most privileged, the Americans. It cannot be ethical, it is argued, to enact policies whose principal purpose is to exacerbate the world's inequalities.

Unpacking the Debate

The debate on immigration has been joined, but it is in danger of producing more heat than light. The disputes are capable of generating enormous passion. It is important, therefore, to step back from the fray if only a little and to see, if one can, what the relevant facts are. A great deal is known about immigration; the next chapters survey the research.

The research on immigration helps frame the debate, but it cannot resolve all the disagreements, for two reasons. First, although much is known, much is still unknown. Scholars disagree about their conclusions. To take just one example, some econometricians find no effect of immigration on the wages of American workers, whereas others find a sharp negative effect. More fundamentally, however, the heart of the immigration debate is not about facts at all but about values. What sort of country do we want the United States to be, and how do we see immigrants and their descendants fitting in to that country?

The chapters that follow marshal the most important facts, and they attempt to structure those facts in support of an argument about immigration that is based on values and ethics.

Notes

1. Garrett Hardin, "Zero Net Immigration as the Goal," *Population and Environment* 14 (1992):197–200.
2. "The Simpson Curtain," *Wall Street Journal* (February 1, 1990), A8.
3. See, for example, the citations in Vernon M. Briggs Jr. and Stephen Moore, *Still an Open Door? U.S. Immigration Policy and the American Economy* (Washington, D.C.: American University Press, 1994), 18–19.
4. Fred Arnold, "International Migration: Who Goes Where?" *Finance and Development* 27 (1990):46–47. For a more complete presentation of the data, see Fred Arnold, *Revised Estimates and Projections of International Migration, 1980–2000* (Washington, D.C.: World Bank, Population and Human Resources Department, 1989).
5. Robert Pear, "Change of Policy on U.S. Immigrants Is Urged by Panel," *New York Times* (June 5, 1995), A1; and Robert Pear, "Clinton Embraces a Proposal to Cut Immigration by a Third," *New York Times* (June 8, 1995), A9.
6. Both polls are reported in Rodolfo O. de la Garza, Angelo Falcon, F. Chris Garcia and John A. Garcia, "Attitudes toward U.S. Immigration Policy, the Case of Mexicans, Puerto Ricans and Cubans," *Migration World* 21 (1993):13–16.
7. Tom Morganthau, "America: Still a Melting Pot?" *Newsweek* (August 9, 1993), 16–23.
8. For a concise discussion of Proposition 187, see Philip Martin, "Proposition 187 in California," *International Migration Review* 29 (Spring 1995):255–63.

9. Steve Johnson, "Half Would Deny Illegal Immigrants Schools, Citizenship," *San Jose Mercury News* (June 10, 1994), 1A, 24A.
10. Alexander Hamilton, James Madison and John Jay, *The Federalist Papers*, ed. Clinton Rossiter (New York: New American Library, 1961), no. 2.
11. Benjamin Franklin, *Observations Concerning the Increase of Mankind, Peopling of Countries, &c.* (Boston: S Kneeland, 1775). The quotations from Jay and Franklin are used in Roger Daniels, *Coming to America, a History of Immigration and Ethnicity in American Life* (New York: Harper-Collins, 1990), 108–10.
12. Julian Simon, *The Economic Consequences of Immigration* (Oxford: Basil Blackwell, 1989), xxix.
13. Peter Brimelow, *Alien Nation, Common Sense about America's Immigration Disaster* (New York: Random House, 1995), 110.
14. Laurence Auster, *The Path to National Suicide, an Essay on Immigration and Multiculturalism* (Monterey, Va.: American Immigration Control Foundation, 1990).
15. See, for example, Briggs and Moore, *Still an Open Door?* 55.
16. Simon, *The Economic Consequences of Immigration*, xxvi.
17. Richard D. Lamm and Gary Imhoff, *The Immigration Time Bomb, The Fragmenting of America* (New York: New American Library, 1985), 1–2.
18. Throughout this chapter and the rest of the book, readers will find many citations of the principal participants in the debate. Among the strong general attacks on current immigration are Leon F. Bouvier, *Peaceful Invasions, Immigration and Changing America* (Lanham, Md.: University Press of America, 1992); Brimelow, *Alien Nation*; Jack Miles, "Blacks vs. Browns," *Atlantic Monthly* (October 1992), 41–68; Palmer Stacey and Wayne Lutton, *The Immigration Time Bomb* (Monterey, Va.: American Immigration Control Foundation, 1988); and Dan Stein, ed., *Immigration 2000: The Century of the New American Sweatshop* (Washington, D.C.: Federation for American Immigration Reform, 1992). Among the defenders of immigration are Simon, *The Economic Consequences of Immigration*, and Michael Fix and Jeffrey S. Passel, *Immigration and Immigrants, Setting the Record Straight* (Washington, D.C.: Urban Institute Press, 1994). The editorial page of the *Wall Street Journal* takes a strong stance in favor of immigration. Daniels, *Coming to America*, is primarily a history but contains good general arguments for immigration. In separate essays in *Still an Open Door?* Briggs and Moore take opposing views.
19. For examples of opposing views on this question, see Brimelow, *Alien Nation*, and Ben J. Wattenberg and Karl Zinmeister, "The Case for More Immigration," *Commentary* 89 (April 1990):19–25.
20. This prediction is supported by projections made by the Census Bureau. See U.S. Bureau of the Census, Current Population Reports, P25-1092, *Population Projections of the United States, by Age, Sex, Race, and Hispanic Origin: 1992 to 2050* (Washington, D.C.: U.S. Government Printing Office, 1992).
21. Stephan Thernstrom, "The Minority Majority Will Never Come," *Wall Street Journal* (July 26, 1990), A16.

22. George J. Borjas, *Friends or Strangers, the Impact of Immigrants on the U.S. Economy* (New York: Basic Books, 1990).
23. For this argument, see, among others, Dorian Friedman, Mary C. Lord, Dan McGraw and Kukula Glastris, "To Make a Nation," *U.S. News and World Report* (October 4, 1993), 47–54, and Alejandro Portes and Ruben G. Rumbaut, *Immigrant America, a Portrait* (Berkeley, Calif.: University of California Press, 1990), chs. 1, 3.
24. Harriet Orcutt Duleep and Mark C. Regets, "The Elusive Concept of Immigrant Quality," Policy Discussion Paper (Washington, D.C.: Urban Institute Press, 1994).
25. Fix and Passel, *Immigration and Immigrants.*
26. Ad Hoc Committee for Immigrant Rights of the Monterey Bay Region, "Immigration and Immigrants: The Issues" (Santa Cruz, Calif., 1993).
27. "The Simpson Curtain," A8.
28. See, for example, Donald Huddle, "Give Us Your Tired Masses," in Stein, *Immigration 2000,* 53–57.
29. Michael J. Piore, "Illegal Immigration to the U.S.: Some Observations and Policy Suggestions," in *Illegal Aliens, an Assessment of the Issues* (Washington, D.C.: National Council for Employment Policy, 1976); and Wattenberg and Zinmeister, "The Case for More Immigration."
30. See, for example, Bouvier, *Peaceful Invasions,* ch. 5, and Richard Estrada, "Myth of Labor Shortage Is Harmful," in Stein, *Immigration 2000,* 129–30.
31. For the extensive literature on debates about immigration's effect on wages, distribution of income, unemployment, and fiscal burdens, see the citations in Chapter 6.
32. George F. Will, "Assimilation Is Not a Dirty Word," *Los Angeles Times* (July 29, 1993), B7.
33. The academic literature is reviewed in Chapter 4.
34. Bouvier, *Peaceful Invasions,* ch. 5.
35. This view is central to Simon's argument in *The Economic Consequences of Immigration.*
36. For examples of this sort of argument, see, among many others, the *Newsletter* of Californians for Population Stabilization, published quarterly in Sacramento.
37. Simon, *The Economic Consequences of Immigration,* ch. 9.
38. Nathan Glazer, "The Closing Door," *New Republic* (December 27, 1993), 15–20.
39. Will, "Assimilation Is Not a Dirty Word."
40. Glazer, "The Closing Door."
41. Ronald Takaki, *A Different Mirror, a History of Multicultural America* (New York: Little, Brown, 1993).
42. Thernstrom, "The Minority Majority Will Never Come," A16.
43. Miles, "Blacks vs. Browns."
44. "Immigrants Have Worlds to Offer," *Business Week* (July 13, 1992), 154.
45. Peter D. Salins, "Take a Ticket," *New Republic* (December 27, 1993), 13–15.
46. Peter Singer and Renata Singer, "The Ethics of Refugee Policy," in *Open Borders? Closed Societies? The Ethical and Political Issues,* ed. Mark Gibney (Westport, Conn.: Greenwood Press, 1988), 111–30.

47. Borjas, *Friends or Strangers*, ch. 12.

48. See, for example, Fix and Passel, *Immigration and Immigrants*, ch.3.

49. Associated Press, "Immigrant Furor Kills School Promo," *Santa Cruz Sentinel* (July 27, 1994), A8.

50. See, for example, Lawrence H. Fuchs, "The Search for a Sound Immigration Policy: A Personal View," in *Clamor at the Gates, the New American Immigration*, ed. Nathan Glazer (San Francisco: Institute for Contemporary Studies, 1985), 17–48.

51. Fix and Passell, *Immigration and Immigrants*.

52. On this question and the one following, see the papers in Gibney, *Open Borders? Closed Societies?*

2

The Background

America, as the saying goes, is a nation of immigrants. So are other countries, perhaps all other countries, if one delves back far enough into the prehistory of human wanderings. American immigration is recent, however, and Americans feel their connection to the immigrant experience as few other people do.

Most Americans, when queried, can say what their ethnic ancestry is. For some, the connection to the immigrant experience is central to their sense of themselves—perhaps because they belong to a disadvantaged group suffering discrimination on account of their origins, perhaps because of a lively sense of ethnic solidarity kept alive by their community or perhaps because they are children of immigrants or immigrants themselves. Even if they do not bear the immigrant identity so completely, almost all have a sense that their existence as Americans is the consequence of immigration in the past. The only ones for whom this is not true are the Native Americans, and their experience of immigration was that it almost totally destroyed their people, so they are not indifferent to it.

The bosom of America is open to receive not only the Opulent and respectable Stranger, but the oppressed and persecuted of all Nations and Religions; whom we shall welcome to a participation of all our rights and previleges [*sic*], if by decency and propriety of conduct they appear to merit the enjoyment.
—George Washington[1]

Once I thought to write a history of the immigrants in America. Then I discovered that the immigrants *were* American history.
—Oscar Handlin[2]

Underlying many of the debates about immigration outlined in Chapter 1 is a difference of opinion about American history. One view is that the United States has centuries of experience absorbing immigrants, that it has always done so successfully and that current immigration is similar in most respects to earlier immigration, perhaps even easier for the country to absorb. In this view, today's immigration is unlikely to be seriously disruptive and will probably contribute positively to the American economy and to American culture, as previous immigration did. The other view is that today's immigration is different from yesterday's, larger, less manageable and more likely to be disruptive. To shed light on this disagreement, we need to understand something about the shifting patterns of immigration in American history.

This chapter discusses the history of American immigration. It begins the investigation of the first two questions: (1) Is today's immigration unusually large? and (2) Is today's immigration transforming America's ethnicity?

Four Immigration Waves

Over 60 million immigrants have come to the United States, and of these, two-thirds were European. In the colonial period (1607 to 1789), fewer than 1 million people arrived to take up permanent settlement, about 600,000 Europeans and about half that number of African slaves.[3] These two groups were, by later perspectives, small in number; their total was exceeded by the annual immigration nine separate times during the twentieth century.[4] Nevertheless, they gave the United States its initial ethnic character and its principal ethnic conflict.

Historians of immigration customarily describe the movement of people into the country in terms of a series of "waves." The waves are distinguished in two ways, by the numbers of immigrants and by their ethnic origins.[5] Roughly, they are as follows:

First Wave: 1607 to the 1820s. The first wave began with the first attempt at English colonization in Virginia and lasted through the early years of the new republic, to the 1820s. The white immigrants were predominantly English, but significant groups of Scots, Irish, Dutch, Germans, Swedes and French also arrived. The importation of African slaves began about 1700; the slave trade was made illegal by Congress in 1807 but continued through the Civil War.

Second Wave: 1840s through the 1870s. About 15 million immigrants entered the country during this period. The English no longer predominated; Ireland and Germany became the leading source countries. With the annexation of the Southwest, several hundred thousand Spanish speakers became Americans. Chinese laborers came to California.

Third Wave: 1880s to the 1920s. This is the period of heaviest immigration into the United States, about 25 million in total. The "traditional" sources—England, Ireland and Germany—were now supplemented by southern and eastern Europe. The United States took in Italians, Poles, Greeks, Russians, Jews and Austro-Hungarians. Opposition to immigration built up during this period. The Chinese Exclusion Act, the first legislation to restrict immigration, was passed in 1882. In the 1920s, a series of laws cut immigration back significantly and biased it in favor of northwestern European sources.

Fourth Wave: 1965 to the Present. The flow of immigration in the modern period is approaching the figures of the third wave. This time, the sources are completely different. Europe accounts for only about 13 percent of the recent immigrants. The largest number come from Mexico. Other Central and South American and Caribbean countries send significant numbers, as do several Asian countries. Immigration into the United States is now overwhelmingly from the third world.

If the word *wave* connotes fluctuations that are regular, it is not the best word to describe the history of immigration into the United States. The first wave was more like a steady trickle, at least from the viewpoint of later years. The second wave merged into the third wave without much change in overall numbers; what marks the transition is the shift in national origins. A gap exists between the third and fourth waves; the middle years of the twentieth century were a period of low immigration. The fourth wave, the one we are currently experiencing, may abate at some time in the future, but so far it shows no signs of doing so. Still, if the word *wave* is not felicitous, at least this classification helps in sorting out the ways in which the national origins of the immigrants have changed over time.

Figure 2.1 shows the annual number of immigrants into the United States from 1820 to 1993 (solid line), as well as the ratio of annual immigration to United States population (broken line).[6] Official statistics do not exist for the years before 1820. Figure 2.1 begins after the first wave. It shows the number of immigrants rising throughout the nineteenth century, irregularly but inexorably, reaching a peak at the beginning of the twentieth century. After the peak, immigration fell to low levels in the 1930s, almost to zero. Beginning after the Second World War, the numbers began to climb again, this time regularly. The steep

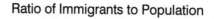

Ratio of Immigrants to Population

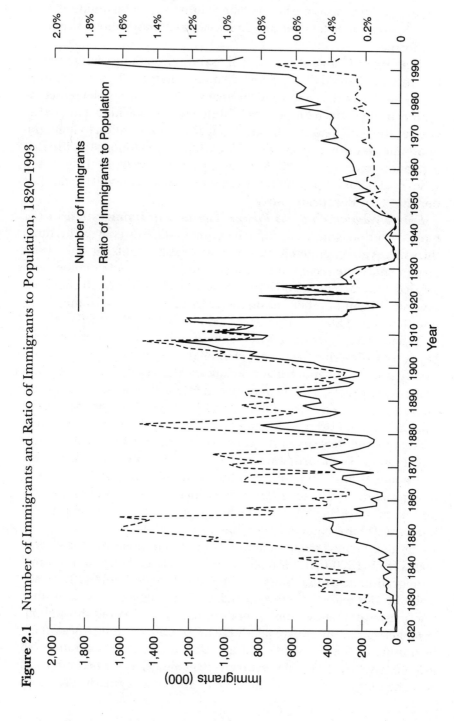

Figure 2.1 Number of Immigrants and Ratio of Immigrants to Population, 1820–1993

jump from 1989 through 1991 was caused by the 1986 amnesty law for undocumented immigrants (see point 3 below). A person studying the solid line in Figure 2.1 would come to the conclusion that the United States is once again a country of high immigration, with numbers at least as great as and perhaps greater than those that occurred at the beginning of the century.

The official statistics, on which Figure 2.1 is based, can be misleading for at least five reasons:

1. Undercounts of early immigration. The Immigration and Naturalization Service (INS) figures for immigration before the 1920s are doubtless undercounts. Since the United States did not exclude immigrants (with relatively few exceptions) before that decade, it had no administrative motive to count the immigrants carefully. Immigrants arriving by sea were counted, but one suspects not always with diligence. People arriving overland from Canada and Mexico were not counted systematically before 1908.[7]

2. Undercounts of recent immigration. The INS has missed millions of immigrants in recent decades, for a different reason. Once stringent legal restrictions on immigration were established in the 1920s, people began to immigrate illegally. Research has shown that the flow of illegal immigration has increased significantly in the last three decades. With one major exception (see point 3 below), undocumented immigrants are not counted by the INS and are not shown in Figure 2.1.

3. IRCA legalizations. The Immigration Reform and Control Act of 1986 (IRCA) allowed people who had been in the country illegally since before 1982 (and some others in the agricultural sector) to legalize their status. Almost 3 million people did so. The INS counts these people as immigrants in the year they regularized their status, not the year they took up residence in the United States. Therefore, the huge jump on the right-hand side of the graph should be distributed over the previous decade if it is to reflect accurately the actual flow of people into the country. Note, however, that even with the IRCA legalizations, there are still many undocumented immigrants in the country. Therefore, the second point still holds: the official statistics represent an undercount of recent immigration.

4. Lack of emigration statistics. The official data show gross immigration, with no subtraction for emigration from the United States. The government keeps no statistics on emigration. Demographers have estimated that emigration has been substantial (although not as large as immigration) and also uneven. Figure 2.1 should not be interpreted as representing net immigration.

5. Immigration-to-population ratio. Finally, although the numbers have increased greatly in recent years and have approached the level of the peak at the beginning of the twentieth century, the relative importance of immigration, in comparison to the population of the country, is less than it was a century ago. In 1990, the U.S. population was over three times greater than it was in 1900 (250 million as opposed to 76 million). At its greatest, recent annual immigration has reached the level of about one-half of 1 percent of the resident population. In comparison, earlier waves reached levels of over 1 percent annually, several times. This point is illustrated by the broken line in Figure 2.1, which shows the ratio of annual immigration to population since 1820.

The peaks and valleys of both lines occur during the same periods in Figure 2.1, but the heights of the peaks differ considerably. The broken line shows that the highest ratio of immigration to population occurred neither in the current wave nor at the beginning of the twentieth century but much earlier, in the period 1849–54. The broken line shows that, relative to the population, the current wave of immigration is much less significant than the nineteenth- and early twentieth-century waves.

The other misleading factors in Figure 2.1 are not as easily corrected. Nevertheless, demographers have attempted to amend the official statistics for undercounts, illegal immigration and emigration. Table 2.1 contains recent estimates of immigration and emigration in intercensal decades since 1900, plus the foreign-born resident population at the end of each decade.[8] In the table, immigration includes illegal as well as legal immigration. The "net" columns depict immigration minus emigration.

The estimates in Table 2.1 change our understanding of immigration considerably. First, the inclusion of illegal immigration—which is substantial in recent decades but barely existed at the beginning of

Table 2.1 Net Immigration by Decade in the United States, 1900–1990

Decade	Number (in Thousands)			Percentage of Population at Decade Beginning			Foreign-Born Population at Decade End (%)
	Immigrants	Emigrants	Net	Immigrants	Emigrants	Net	
1900–10	8,024	3,104	4,920	10.5	4.1	6.5	14.6
1910–20	5,906	3,376	2,530	6.3	3.6	2.7	12.7
1920–30	4,185	1,395	2,790	3.8	1.3	2.5	11.3
1930–40	750	882	–132	0.6	0.7	–0.1	8.4
1940–50	1,849	59	1,790	1.4	0.0	1.3	6.9
1950–60	3,011	660	2,352	1.9	0.4	1.5	5.7
1960–70	3,738	1,054	2,684	2.1	0.6	1.5	5.1
1970–80	7,726	860	6,866	3.8	0.4	3.3	6.6
1980–90	9,972	1,772	8,200	4.4	0.8	3.6	8.5

Some figures may not total correctly because of rounding.

Source: Jeffrey S. Passel and Barry Edmonston, "Immigration and Race: Recent Trends in Immigration to the United States," in *Immigration and Ethnicity, the Integration of America's Newest Arrivals,* ed. Barry Edmonston and Jeffrey S. Passel (Washington, D.C.: Urban Institute Press, 1994), 31–71, tables 2.1 and 2.2.

the century—increases the relative importance of recent immigration. When the undocumented entrants are included, gross immigration in the period 1981–90 is almost 25 percent greater than it was in the first decade of the century.

Second, the number of people emigrating has been uneven over the century. High at the beginning, emigration fell sharply in the middle of the century, then rose to a moderate level in the most recent period. When emigration is subtracted from gross immigration to give an estimate of net immigration, the recent numbers are much higher than the earlier ones.

The table also provides a revised picture of immigration as a proportion of the U.S. population. Emigration was very important at the beginning of the century, with more than 4 percent of the population emigrating during the first decade. In the last two-thirds of the century, it has never exceeded 1 percent in any one decade. Recent net immigration is smaller in relationship to the population than early immigration was, but the difference is not as substantial as the dotted line in Figure 2.1 would indicate.

The last column in Table 2.1 shows that after falling to a minimum in midcentury, the proportion of the population that is foreign born has begun to rise again in latter years. The proportion of foreign born builds slowly, since it includes surviving immigrants of many years earlier.

In sum, current immigration is very large, by historical standards. Depending on how one views the data, the present, fourth wave is either larger than the great third wave or somewhat less. More people are arriving in the United States at the end of the century than arrived at the beginning, and fewer people are leaving. The proportion of net immigration to population is lower at the end of the twentieth century than it was at the beginning, however, and the proportion of the foreign born has not reached previous heights. Even if today's immigration is seen as somewhat less, it should be remembered that the third wave was huge, with an enormous impact on American society. At both the beginning and end of the twentieth century, immigration rose to new heights, following very low levels of immigration several generations before.

Moreover, it should be understood that the current wave of immigration is occurring in the presence of legal, quantitative restrictions on the inflow of people, whereas immigration at the beginning of the century took place under a regime of virtually open borders. This has at least two implications. First, it is all but certain that if restrictions were abolished at the present time, the immigrant flow would increase enormously. The pressure for immigration is much greater today than it was a century ago. Second, the large immigration of the third wave led to a reaction among the American people, who imposed severe restrictions on immigration in the 1920s. If history is a guide, therefore, one would not be surprised to find Americans greatly reducing the level of authorized immigration in the future.

The earlier immigrant waves were predominantly male. In the latest wave, however, women have made up about half of legal entrants.[9] The flow of undocumented immigrants is still, however, heavily male. The majority of women come as part of a family unit: with a husband and perhaps children, or in some cases intending to join a man who is already in the country. A higher proportion of immigrant women than native women is married. Not all are married, however. An increasing number of single women are entering the country, and the 1990 census showed that almost one-quarter of the immigrant women in the country had never been married.[10]

Immigration as a Component of Population Growth

How has immigration influenced the growth of the American population? This apparently simple question turns out to be difficult, if not impossible, to answer. The difficulty lies in the fact that we do not know what would have happened to the population had immigration been different from what it was. To take an example, Native Americans are currently less than 1 percent of the U.S. population. Does this imply that immigration since 1600 is responsible for over 99 percent of U.S. population growth? No, because without immigration, the Native population would surely be much larger than it is now. The Natives were almost completely exterminated by the immigrants and their descendants. Perhaps the population would be just the same today, had no immigration occurred—no one can tell.

One way of constraining the question is to assume that the birth and death rates of the resident population were unaffected by immigration. Although spectacularly wrong in the case of Native Americans, this assumption can lead to revealing results. Campbell Gibson of the U.S. Census Bureau has made some interesting calculations, using this assumption.[11] He estimated the proportion of the 1990 population that resulted from immigration between 1790 and 1990. The starting year

1790 was chosen because it is the date of the first census of the new United States of America, and also because little immigration is thought to have occurred between then and 1820, so it represents a convenient break point between immigration waves.

At first glance, one would think that the great majority of the 1990 population would be accounted for by post-1790 immigration. Almost all Americans are descended from immigrants, and of the roughly 49 million net immigrants (that is, immigrants minus emigrants) who arrived before 1990, only about 1 million arrived before 1790. It is not the case, however, that descendants of post-1790 immigrants completely dominate the modern population. Gibson shows that, given some reasonable assumptions, of the 1990 American population of 249 million, 122 million (or 49 percent) are attributable to the population resident in the country in 1790, and 127 million (51 percent) are attributable to net immigration since that date. The 1 million immigrants before independence, the first wave, produced almost as many people in the modern United States as the 48 million since that date.

The lesson is that although immigration affects the size of the population, so does the natural increase of the residents. The excess of births over deaths leads to population growth, and over time, the effects can be enormous.

There are many other ways of showing the impact of immigration on population growth. One is to compare immigrants and births in the United States. In the 1930s, immigrants totaled only 2 percent of births. In the 1950s, the ratio was 6 percent, and in the 1980s 16 percent.[12] One can also calculate the contribution that net immigration makes to population growth in each decade, as shown in Table 2.2.

The last column of Table 2.2 shows that the contribution of net immigration to each decade's population growth fell from the beginning of the century to midcentury, then rose again toward the end. Both the third and the fourth waves contributed substantially to the country's population growth. Since 1970, net immigration has accounted for about a third of the country's population growth, a higher proportion than was achieved at any time earlier in the century.

One might ask how net immigration could be a higher proportion of population growth now than at the beginning of the century, in view of the fact that the ratio of net immigration to population is lower today than earlier (see Table 2.1). The answer is shown in the "% Change" column of Table 2.2. The rate of population growth in the country has slowed during the twentieth century. The slowdown has not been uniform, because of the baby boom in midcentury, but looking over

Table 2.2 Contribution of Net Immigration to U.S. Population Growth by Decade, 1900–1990

Year	Population (in Thousands)	Change from Previous Decade (in Thousands)	% Change from Previous Decade	Net Immigration (in Thousands)	Net Immigration as % of Population Change
1900	76,195	—	—	—	—
1910	93,879	17,684	23.2	4,920	27.8
1920	110,747	16,868	18.0	2,530	15.0
1930	127,585	16,838	15.2	2,790	16.6
1940	136,928	9,343	9.3	−132	—
1950	155,156	18,228	13.3	1,790	9.8
1960	182,055	26,899	17.3	2,352	8.7
1970	205,567	23,512	12.9	2,684	11.4
1980	226,625	21,058	10.2	6,866	32.6
1990	248,712	22,087	9.7	8,200	37.1

Source: Jeffrey S. Passel and Barry Edmonston, "Immigration and Race: Recent Trends in Immigration to the United States," in *Immigration and Ethnicity, the Integration of America's Newest Arrivals,* ed. Barry Edmonston and Jeffey S. Passel (Washington, D.C.: Urban Institute Press, 1994), table 2.1.

the century as a whole, birth rates fell considerably faster than death rates. Therefore, the rate of natural increase—the growth rate of the population that would be generated simply by the births and deaths of the resident population—is much lower today than a century ago. Hence net immigration is a higher proportion of population growth in recent decades, even though it is a lower proportion of the population itself.

In summary, although immigration has not contributed as much to the past population growth of the United States as one might expect, the current immigrant wave constitutes a higher proportion of growth than ever before. One might object that this is not a very meaningful statement. Suppose, for example, that the natural increase of the resident population fell to zero; then the immigration of just one person would constitute 100 percent of the population growth, even though the impact of the entry of that one person on the population would be trivial. We are more worried today about population growth than previous generations were, however. Before the era of environmental consciousness, almost all Americans thought that population growth was a sign of health. Now many are concerned about overcrowding, pollution, the disappearance of the wilderness and the consumption of nonrenewable natural resources, and many believe that population growth contributes to all these problems. In that light, the fact that today's immigration constitutes a high portion of the country's population growth is a relevant consideration.

The discussion thus far has begun to give some clarity to the question of whether today's immigration is unusually large. In absolute numbers, and in its contribution to population growth, it is larger than any previous wave, but as a proportion of the population it is not exceptional. History can give only part of the answer, however; Chapter 5 provides a more forward-looking perspective.

The Changing Ethnicity of Immigration

Part of the current concern about immigration is the changing ethnic mixture, the fact that most newcomers are now from the third world. Some of the opposition to immigration is racist—and some is perhaps not racist but based on a worry that the immigrants are so different culturally from the natives that they will seriously disrupt the social life of the country.[13] In view of this worry, it is useful to consider the changing national origins of immigrants. Every new wave of immigration has brought new ethnic groups, and each time this fact has evoked concern and resistance among the natives.

Tables 2.3 and 2.4 show the national origins of immigrants during different periods. Table 2.3 contains the numbers of immigrants and Table 2.4 the proportion of each national origin. The different waves can be distinguished in the columns. The first column shows the relatively low immigration before 1840, the 1840–81 column represents the second wave, 1881–1930 the third wave, 1931–60 the relatively low immigration in the middle of the twentieth century, and 1961–93 the fourth wave up to 1993. The last column shows total immigration since 1820.

Table 2.3 contains evidence of the extraordinary drama of American social history. Not only is the United States a nation of immigrants, it is also a nation of immigrants from almost everywhere in the world. They are not in representative proportions—people of European origin are overrepresented in comparison to their share of the world's population—but Americans come from everywhere. This is a fact worth contemplating and celebrating in a period in which ethnic nationalism is provoking so many civil and international conflicts in other countries.

Table 2.3 Legal Immigrants (in Thousands) into the United States, 1820–1993

Origin	1820–40	1841–80	1881–1930	1931–60	1961–93	1820–1993
America	45	708	3,488	1,512	9,419	15,172
Canada	16	639	2,243	658	806	4,361
Caribbean	16	47	368	188	2,416	3,036
Central America	—	1	42	72	931	1,047
Mexico	11	14	730	383	4,039	5,177
South America	1	7	104	121	1,206	1,440
Africa	—	1	23	23	370	418
Asia	—	231	828	207	5,786	7,051
China	—	229	148	47	951	1,375
India	—	—	9	4	558	572
Japan	—	—	275	50	162	487
Korea	—	—	—	6	697	704
Philippines	—	—	—	25	1,198	1,222
Vietnam	—	—	—	—	536	536
Europe	602	8,387	23,132	2,294	3,151	37,567
Austria-Hungary	—	80	4,051	143	78	4,354
Germany	160	2,892	2,855	818	391	7,117
Ireland	262	2,567	1,740	79	106	4,755
Italy	3	79	4,570	311	457	5,419
Norway-Sweden	1	355	1,657	74	65	2,152
Poland	—	16	381	35	243	675
Soviet Union	—	43	3,299	3	228	3,572
United Kingdom	103	1,845	2,286	373	569	5,178
Oceania	—	11	52	30	131	224
Not Specified	103	101	50	13	1	268
Europe/Canada/ Oceania	618	9,037	25,426	2,983	4,088	42,152
All Other Specified	29	301	2,097	1,083	14,770	18,280
Total	751	9,438	27,573	4,079	18,859	60,699

Some figures may not total correctly because of rounding.

Source: Calculated from U.S. Immigration and Naturalization Service, *1993 Statistical Yearbook* (Washington, D.C.: U.S. Government Printing Office, 1994), table 2.

Table 2.4 Legal Immigrants (Fraction of Total*) into the United
States, 1820–1993

Origin	1820–40	1841–80	1881–1930	1931–60	1961–93	1820–1993
America	.070	.076	.127	.372	.499	.251
Canada	.025	.068	.008	.162	.043	.072
Caribbean	.025	.005	.013	.046	.128	.050
Central America	—	—	.002	.018	.049	.017
Mexico	.018	.001	.027	.094	.214	.086
South America	.002	.001	.004	.030	.064	.024
Africa	—	—	.001	.006	.020	.007
Asia	—	.025	.030	.051	.307	.117
China	—	.025	.005	.012	.050	.023
India	—	—	—	.001	.030	.009
Japan	—	—	.010	.012	.009	.008
Korea	—	—	—	.002	.037	.012
Philippines	—	—	—	.006	.064	.020
Vietnam	—	—	—	—	.028	.009
Europe	.930	.898	.840	.564	.167	.622
Austria-Hungary	—	.009	.147	.035	.004	.072
Germany	.247	.310	.104	.201	.021	.118
Ireland	.404	.275	.063	.019	.006	.079
Italy	.004	.008	.166	.076	.024	.090
Norway-Sweden	.002	.038	.060	.018	.003	.036
Poland	—	.002	.014	.009	.013	.011
Soviet Union	.001	.005	.120	.001	.012	.059
United Kingdom	.159	.198	.083	.092	.030	.086
Oceania	—	.001	.002	.007	.007	.004
Europe/Canada/ Oceania	.955	.968	.924	.734	.217	.698
All Other	.045	.032	.076	.266	.783	.302
Total	1.0	1.0	1.0	1.0	1.0	1.0

* The denominator of each fraction is total immigration for the period, minus
"not specified" (see Table 2.3).

Source: Calculated from U.S. Immigration and Naturalization Service, *1993 Statistical Yearbook* (Washington, D.C.: U.S. Government Printing Office, 1994), table 2.

Table 2.3 begins after the two centuries in which the American colonies were peopled primarily by English and African newcomers. About a million people arrived in the colonies in the seventeenth and eighteenth centuries; their natural increase produced a population (excluding Natives) of just under 4 million people at the time of independence. Smatterings of Germans, French, Swedish and other continental Europeans arrived during the colonial period, but by 1790, immigrants from England and the British Isles accounted for six-sevenths of the white population.[14]

In the first thirty years of the newly independent country, immigration remained modest. As Figure 2.1 shows, immigration began to pick up after 1820. In the succeeding two decades, three-quarters of a million people arrived—not a lot by later standards, but a significant addition at the time. The first column of Tables 2.3 and 2.4 shows that the national origins of the immigrants were beginning to shift. By far the largest number still came from Europe, but now the leading sources were Ireland and Germany, not England. These new groups presented new problems of cultural assimilation. The majority of Irish and Germans were Catholic, and the Germans were non-English speaking.

This shift was accelerated in the second immigration wave from the 1840s to the 1880s. The same three areas of origin predominated—with Germans jumping to first place—but the numbers increased greatly: about 10 million people arrived. In comparison to earlier periods, the circumstances of these immigrants' departure from Europe were different; the America in which they arrived was different as well.

Economic change was sweeping Europe, as industrial capitalism expanded out from England. Death rates fell and population growth accelerated. In the German principalities, the old feudal order was uprooted, peasants were evicted from their holdings, factories displaced craft workshops and city slums grew. Commercialization of agriculture displaced huge numbers of rural people just as their numbers were growing, and many of them failed to find urban niches.[15] Anti-Semitism drove Jews from their communities. A steady and growing stream of people wound its way to the northern port cities, willing to accept whatever fate had to offer in America. In Ireland the industrial revolution was delayed, but the disaster that substituted for it was the great potato famine of the 1840s. Potatoes were the staple of the Irish, but in several years in mid-decade, almost the entire crop was destroyed. Healthy potatoes that would normally have been kept for seed were eaten, so the crop could not recover for years. The 1841 population of 8.2 million people fell to 6.6 million in 1851. Over a million people died in the famine and accompanying epidemics; more than that emigrated. Eventually the famine was spent, but the emigration continued—as did the decline in the Irish population.[16]

The consequence was that many of the Germans and Irish who arrived in the second wave were economically battered and weak. They were victims of a changing world over which they had no control, a world that had chewed them up and spit them out on a strange shore. The skills they had, if any, were appropriate to Old World agriculture; their experience had little application in the new land.

In any case, most did not transplant themselves to the American agricultural sector. The western frontier of the United States was still expanding, but not as fast as the northeastern cities, with their new industrial machinery and factories, and not as fast as the canals and railroads. To a large extent, the Irish and German immigrants got jobs in the cities and on construction gangs. They got the toughest jobs, the worst jobs, the most dangerous jobs, the lowest paying jobs. They took the jobs that resident Americans were thankful to hand over to them, jobs that the new industrial system created but that seemed designed to break a man.

A parallel exists between those mid-nineteenth-century immigrants and the latest immigrants into the United States from the third world. Large numbers of both groups left their native lands because of social dislocation, they came to a country whose customs were foreign and they were equipped for only the lowest level of jobs. In retrospect, one can see that an advantage the earlier group had was that it arrived at a time when the United States had an almost insatiable demand for unskilled labor. The new factories, the railroads, the canals and the new buildings all needed, most of all, men with strong backs. Today, in the information age, the value of a strong back is questionable.

The second wave included immigrants from other countries. The Scandinavians began their trek to the United States, as did a few southern and eastern Europeans. A substantial number crossed the border overland from Canada (probably considerably more than were enumerated). Of these, many were really European immigrants whose ships had simply docked at Halifax or Montreal. Others were legitimate Canadian residents, whose participation in the westward movement of the period took no special notice of national boundaries. The small number of immigrants from Mexico were outnumbered by the Mexicans who became Americans, without moving, because of annexations in the Southwest. Several hundred thousand Chinese—almost all men—were brought into California as laborers to build the railroads.

Although a relatively small group, the Chinese were the first non-whites to arrive since the African slaves; they provoked much more opposition and hysteria than did the larger number of European immigrants.

The third great wave of immigration, which peaked in the first decade of the twentith century (the 1881–1930 column of Tables 2.3 and 2.4) still had an overwhelming majority of European immigrants, but it was a different Europe. The British, Irish and Germans continued to come, in numbers roughly equivalent to their numbers in the middle of the century. The overall flow of immigration increased, however, so the relative importance of these three groups declined. They were joined by immigrants from other parts of Europe: Scandinavians, Italians, Hungarians, Jews, Poles, Armenians, Serbs, Romanians, Greeks, Arabs from what is now Turkey and many others. Immigration from the American continent grew greatly, particularly among French Canadians and Mexicans. Chinese immigration fell, but Japanese immigration increased.

The expansion of emigration from southern and eastern Europe occurred as economic development and industrial capitalism grew in those areas. The new economic system brought with it both dislocations and new opportunities. As was the case earlier in Britain and the German states, capitalism brought commercial relations to the agricultural sector and, consequently, the displacement of feudal peasants who had worked the land for generations. Their subsistence crops were replaced by grazing animals, their manual labor was replaced by rudimentary farm machinery and they were evicted from the land. Many went to the nearby cities, but some migrated further afield, to the United States and other countries. Emigration to America was possible for them, whereas it had not been possible for previous generations, because of the improvement and cheapening of transportation brought about by the industrial revolution. Part of the mythology of immigration is the squalor and danger of the journey—and this is an accurate picture, according to modern norms. Still, for the first time, mass transportation was available for people seeking to leave the steppes of Russia and the Balkan mountains, and millions took advantage of it.

Although the American population was still predominantly rural at the turn of the century, and although most of the new immigrants came from rural backgrounds, they moved almost exclusively into the country's major cities. For the most part, they lived together in ethnically homogeneous neighborhoods. They established their own churches, synagogues and community centers. Although many learned English, they kept their native languages and passed them on to their children. New York became one of the great polyglot immigrant cities

of the world. Just as the earlier Irish and Germans had, the new southern and eastern Europeans started at the bottom economically, in construction, the trades and manufacturing. This was the era in which big
businesses and huge manufacturing plants began to dominate the
American economy; the immigrants provided much of the unskilled
and semiskilled labor that these new institutions required.

The new immigrants provoked controversy and hostility. Eventually
the opposition became so great that Congress passed a series of laws
in the 1920s restricting both the number and the national origins of
the immigrants. An 1882 poem by Thomas Bailey Aldrich catches the
spirit of hostility:

> Wide open and unguarded stand our gates,
> And through them passes a wild motley throng,
> Men from the Volga and Tartar steppes,
> Featureless figures from the Hoang-Ho,
> Malayan, Scythian, Teuton, Kelt and Slav,
> Flying the Old World's poverty and scorn;
> These bringing with them unknown gods and rites,
> Those tiger passions here to stretch their claws,
> In street and alley what strange tongues are these,
> Accents of menace in our ear,
> Voices that once the Tower of Babel knew.[17]

The third wave eventually produced a new doctrine of American
nationality, the melting pot. Where once John Jay had celebrated the
(white) American population as being ethnically pure, the new idea
was that America was made up of a homogenized mixture of many
ethnicities. The term *melting pot* came from the title of an otherwise
undistinguished play written by Israel Zangwill in 1909. Its theme was
that representatives of warring, European ethnic groups would lay aside
their enmity once they reached the shores of the New World; they
would join together, intermarry and produce the new, harmonious
American nationality. It is an idea that gained great force as the uni-
fying theme of American society in the twentieth century.

The immigration acts of the 1920s cut the flow of new arrivals back,
although they did not eliminate them. The acts did not place limits
on immigration from the Western Hemisphere, so the door was open
in this period to Mexican immigration. The numbers were small, but
the proportion was prescient; almost 10 percent of the immigrants in
this three-decade period came from just south of the U.S. border.

The most remarkable feature of the current immigration wave is the change in national origins. From 1961 through 1993, only 17 percent of the immigrants came from Europe. Fifty percent came from the Americas, particularly Mexico and the Caribbean Basin, and 30 percent from Asia.

As the national origins of the immigrants have changed in the current wave, so too has their racial composition. "Race" is not the same as "national origin," and the tables show the latter, not the former. A fairly good idea of the shift can be discerned nonetheless. Most Anglo (or non-Latino white) immigrants have come from Europe, Canada, Australia and New Zealand; most non-Anglos have come from the rest of the world. The rows near the bottom of Tables 2.3 and 2.4 divide the immigrants into those two groups. They show a dramatic change in the most recent wave, when almost four out of every five immigrants came from the non-Anglo source countries of the third world.

This discussion has just begun consideration of whether immigration is fundamentally changing the ethnic structure of the United States. Certainly today's immigrants have a different ethnic composition from that of earlier waves. An understanding of what this means for the future of the American population awaits Chapter 5.

The Legal Evolution

Most of the debate on immigration has a policy focus. People question the wisdom of the laws regulating the numbers, national origins and qualifications of immigrants, the prevention of illegal immigration and the entitlements of immigrants. If one is to make sense out of the debate, therefore, it is important to understand the development of immigration law in the United States.

Until the late nineteenth century, immigration into the United States was affected only marginally by the country's laws. This began to change at the end of the nineteenth century and changed completely in the twentieth, when legislation effectively reduced the number of immigrants who would otherwise have entered and influenced the mixture of national origins, education and skills among the immigrants. For decades now, laws affecting immigration have been passed by the federal government almost annually.[18] The volume of immigration law has become enormous; textbooks are written on the subject,[19] and scholars devote their careers to it. Immigration has become a major topic of public policy.

In the period before independence, various of the thirteen colonies attempted, from time to time, to restrict or influence immigration into their territories. They wanted to discourage the entry of criminals (sometimes transported at the order of English courts) and paupers. In some cases, colonies tried to prevent the entry of certain religious groups, such as Quakers or Catholics. By and large, however, the colonies lacked both the legal authority and the administrative structures to have much influence over immigration.

Control over borders is taken today to be an inherent attribute of national sovereignty. This is a recent idea. When the United States became an independent republic, it was not clear that the federal government had authority over immigration at all, since the subject was not mentioned in the Constitution. From time to time in the first hundred years of the Republic, individual states attempted to restrict immigration. These attempts were sporadic and usually unsuccessful. In 1875, almost a hundred years after the country's independence, the U.S. Supreme Court finally ruled that the federal government had exclusive jurisdiction over immigration, because of its constitutional authority to regulate foreign commerce.

If the federal government's authority over immigration was in doubt, its jurisdiction in the area of naturalization or citizenship was not. After the Constitution was enacted in 1789, one of the first acts passed by the new Congress was the Naturalization Law of 1790. To be eligible for citizenship under this act, a person had to be both free and white. This provision was perhaps not remarkable for its time; what is remarkable is that it stayed largely untouched on the books for over a century and a half, until the Immigration and Nationality Act of 1952 stated that a person's right to become a citizen "shall not be denied or abridged because of race." Two contending themes therefore mark American legal policy toward foreigners from the beginning of the Republic: an open welcome on the one hand, and racial exclusion on the other.[20]

The most important immigration legislation in the first hundred years of the United States was the 1808 law forbidding the importation of slaves. The Constitution specifically prevented such a law before that date; as soon as the constitutional injunction had expired, the slave trade was outlawed.

The fact that immigration into the United States was virtually unrestricted by law until the end of the nineteenth century does not imply that it was unopposed. Many groups in the country were distressed by the continuing high rate of immigration and especially by the changing national sources of the immigrants. As the mostly Protestant English gave way to the mostly Catholic Irish and Germans, nativists campaigned to restrict the inflow. They failed, in part because of the huge demands for labor in the quickly developing country, and in part because the Irish and German immigrants rapidly established themselves as groups with political influence.

By the latter part of the nineteenth century, however, the forces in the country that were opposed to immigration became strong enough to have at least some influence over federal legislation. In 1870, a naturalization act whose main purpose was to allow for the citizenship of the former slaves specifically excluded Chinese from citizenship. In 1875, Congress passed the first law restricting immigration. It was not intended to have a major impact on immigration—it excluded only criminals, prostitutes and Chinese who had been coerced into entering—but it was the first in a long series of much more restrictive acts.

In retrospect, as legal scholar Peter Schuck has argued, one can see the marked change in judicial philosophy relating to immigration that was set in motion toward the end of the nineteenth century.[21] During the Republic's first century, American law held that all (white male) people had equal rights to the benefits of American civilization. Some distinctions were made between citizens and noncitizens: only citizens had the right to vote, and only a native-born citizen could become president, for example. For white people, however, legal access to American citizenship was virtually unrestricted. Potential immigrants might not be able to afford the passage to the United States, but once they were here, the law (if not necessarily the residents) welcomed them; naturalization was theirs for the asking. The law did not intrude on people's rights to travel, to change their residence or to decide their own destiny. An important consequence was that whites who arrived on American territory were automatically subject to the protection of the American Constitution and laws.

In the second century, this philosophy changed. American citizens asserted the right to decide who should join their company. By making this assertion, they transformed non-Americans, including whites, from people who had equal rights in the eyes of the law to people who had seriously inferior rights, or perhaps no rights at all. When dealing with immigrants, Congress "regularly makes rules that would be unacceptable if applied to citizens," as one judge put it.[22] Whether foreigners had a right to enter the United States and to become naturalized citizens was a matter to be judged solely by Americans, without regard for the interests of the foreigners. What was once a universal concept of rights and protection under the law was therefore transformed into the idea that only Americans, plus those whom the American government specifically—and, if it wishes, arbitrarily—chooses, have equal rights.

Federal legislation to restrict and control immigration began in earnest in 1882 with two laws, the Chinese Exclusion Act and the Immigration Act. If the shift from English to Irish and German immigrants had been difficult for many natives to bear, the arrival of large numbers of Chinese was intolerable to them. Chinese laborers began to enter at the time of the California gold rush in 1849. They continued to come over the next several decades, moving into railroad building as well as mining, with some becoming agricultural workers and farmers as well. The 1880 census showed over 100,000 Chinese in the country, almost three-quarters of them in California.[23] They were regarded by most Americans as alien, unwilling to adapt to American ways and unwanted. These sentiments led to the adoption of the Chinese Exclusion Act, which totally barred Chinese immigration to the United States for a ten-year period and strengthened the ban against their becoming American citizens. The act was later made permanent and was only repealed in 1943, as a consequence of the alliance between the United States and China in the Second World War.

The Chinese Exclusion Act was the first major piece of federal legislation influencing the volume and character of immigration into the country. Its only purpose was racial exclusion. It was not passed out of concern about overpopulation or labor surplus in the West. Its sole intent was to prevent a new non-white population group from establishing a significant foothold in the country.

The Immigration Act of 1882 was an important milestone, although it did not change the flow of immigration very much; rather, it asserted comprehensive federal responsibility for immigration for the first time. It set up a system of state boards, under the Department of the Treasury, to monitor immigration. It widened the grounds for exclusion, barring "convicts," "prostitutes," "lunatics," "idiots" and those "likely to become a public charge."[24] The last category was particularly important; Congress for the first time asserted the principle that immigrants should not become a fiscal burden on the natives. Also for the first time, the act imposed a head tax of fifty cents on all immigrants (the amount was raised in subsequent years). The tax served two purposes: to discourage the entry of people who had no means at all, and to generate revenue to pay for at least some of the costs of administering the immigration system. The acts of 1882 established precedents for future legislation that would impose closer controls over the entry of foreigners into the United States.

Many immigration acts were passed over the next forty years, gradually increasing the grounds for exclusion and asserting greater federal administrative control over immigration. An act in 1891 established the Bureau of Immigration, the precursor to the present Immigration and Naturalization Service. A 1907 "gentlemen's agreement" with Japan restricted Japanese immigration (it was followed by the Japanese Exclusion Act of 1924 that completely barred Japanese immigration). The Mann Act of 1910 prohibited the immigration of women for immoral purposes. A 1917 act expanded the Chinese Exclusion Act by barring immigration from a broad area of Asia, the so-called Asia-Pacific triangle. These and other restrictions kept some people out, but they completely failed to stem the overall flow of immigration. As was shown earlier, the last two decades of the nineteenth century and the first two of the twentieth were the period of heaviest immigration into the United States. The political pressure to restrict immigration mounted.

The legislation enacted before and during the First World War was only the faint beginning of restrictive legislation, and in retrospect, its importance lies more in the direction that it pointed than in its actual effects. Immigration fell during the war to a low level, but this was the result of the shortage of civilian transportation, not U.S. immigration legislation. It rose again after the war, reaching 800,000 in 1921.[25]

The stage was set for the passage of the two most severe immigration acts in U.S. history, the Quota Law of 1921 and the Immigration Act of 1924. These two acts had the effect of not only significantly reducing the overall amount of immigration but also skewing it strongly toward the traditional source areas of Britain, Ireland and northwestern Europe.

The 1921 act was the first quantitative immigration act. It reduced immigration in a straightforward manner by legislating maximum numbers, or quotas. Annual immigration from a country was limited to 3 percent of the number of foreign-born persons of that nationality who lived in the United States in 1910. Although recent immigration had been heavily from southern and eastern Europe, the foreign-born population of 1910 was dominated by northern and western European nationalities. The law had the effect, therefore, of both reducing overall immigration and shifting it away from the areas that were in disfavor. The total quota was 357,000, but in some years, the northern and western Europeans did not use their full portion of it. The law exempted Western Hemisphere natives from the quota, and it also allowed Eastern

Hemisphere natives to enter, regardless of the quota, if they had resided in the Western Hemisphere for one year (later changed to five years).

Although the 1921 quota law was restrictive, it was not restrictive enough for most Americans, so it was replaced by the tougher Immigration Act of 1924. This act reduced the annual quota from 3 percent of the number of foreign born to 2 percent for a three-year period (later extended to five years). In addition, it used as its base the 1890 rather than the 1910 census. The consequence was that the overall quota was cut by more than half, to 165,000, and the slots for southern and eastern Europeans almost disappeared. In 1929, the restrictions became even tighter. As of that year, the quota was reduced to 150,000 (plus certain close family members), and a new "national origins" formula used as its base the ethnic origins of the entire American population, not just the foreign born. The annual quota for any group was in the same proportion to 150,000 as the number of U.S. inhabitants of that ethnic background was to the whole population in the 1920 census. People of southern and eastern European descent were a very small portion of the overall American population, so the immigration quotas for people from those regions almost disappeared.

The immigration acts of the 1920s established no specific quotas for residents of the Western Hemisphere. Quotas for the Western Hemisphere did not seem necessary because that area had produced so little immigration up to that time. In any case, Canadian immigrants were not seen by Americans as a problem. Mexican and other Latin American immigrants might have been, but few people from south of the border wanted to enter. Of those who did, some were effectively barred by the provision that excluded people who were likely to become public charges.

In the 1920s, therefore, the United States changed abruptly from an open immigration country to one in which access was tightly restricted. The annual inflow fell from about 1 million in the prewar years to between 200,000 and 300,000 by the end of the 1920s. In those years, the quotas were usually filled, and any additional immigrants were those coming from the Western Hemisphere plus close family members of Americans, who were not covered by the quotas.

By restricting immigration, Congress automatically created a new category: illegal immigrants. The authorities began to have to deal with such problems as marriage fraud and clandestine border crossings, problems that have plagued the administration of the immigration laws since that time. In 1924, Congress established the U.S. Border Patrol, charged with apprehending illegal immigrants. For over sixty years, the only sanction the Border Patrol had available to it was deportation. In 1986, Congress added sanctions against employers of undocumented immigrants.

During the period 1930–45, when immigration fell to low levels, the quotas were almost irrelevant. The national origins legislation became effective again after 1945, limiting immigration to under 300,000 a year up to 1965.

The next major revision of legislation occurred in 1952, with the passage of the Immigration and Nationality, or Walter-McCarran, Act. Although the act fundamentally changed the rules for naturalization by removing the racist provisions of the 1790 act, it did not change immigration policy a great deal. It did, however, consolidate the legislation from previous decades into one comprehensive statute. Over President Truman's veto, the act retained the national origins quota system and the overall limit of 150,000 people a year from the Eastern Hemisphere. For the first time, it gave a quota preference to people with skills and job experience needed by the American labor market, and it set up a series of preference categories both for relatives of U.S. residents and for worker skills. This act remains the basic legislation governing immigration into the United States today; most of the subsequent legislation has been formulated as amendments to it.

Truman opposed the 1952 act and established a commission to review its provisions. The commission recommended in 1953 that the national origins provisions be replaced with a system based on family reunification and on labor market needs. Twelve years later, the commission's recommendations were accepted.

The 1965 amendments to the 1952 act constituted the most important changes in immigration policy since the 1920s. They were seen at the time as important principally because they removed the racism that was inherent in the immigration system. They were not, however, expected to change the number of immigrants, their national origins or their labor market skills in any substantial way. As matters turned out, the 1965 amendments had a major impact on immigration in all these respects; they led to a large increase in numbers, a shift in countries of origin toward the third world and a deterioration in the education and skill levels of at least some of the new immigrant streams.

One important way in which the 1965 legislation differed from that of the 1920s was that in the earlier period, Congress understood what its goals were and crafted laws that achieved those goals. In 1965, in contrast, public opinion was concerned hardly at all with immigration. The great issue that engaged the attention of Americans in the early

1960s was the conflict over civil rights and racial oppression. In 1964, Congress passed the Civil Rights Act and, in 1965, the Voting Rights Act, both of which were seen as the culmination of the most important moral struggle in the country since the Civil War. The immigration act, originally proposed by President Kennedy, was drafted as part of the civil rights legislation. Most people did not even know about its passage, but to the extent that they did, they saw it as a civil rights act, intended to expunge racism from American immigration policy.

The legislation abolished the national origins quota system that had been in effect for over forty years. It replaced that system with overall hemispheric limits. The limit for the Eastern Hemisphere was raised from 150,000 to 170,000 and, for the first time, a limit of 120,000 was placed on Western Hemisphere immigration. For the Eastern Hemisphere, but not for the Western, a seven-preference system gave first priority to family members of American citizens and permanent resident aliens. The preference system recognized the claims of people with job skills needed in the American labor market but gave them lower priority than the 1952 act had done. Within the preference categories, immigration was to proceed on a first come, first served basis, with the provision only that annual immigration from a single country not exceed 20,000 people. Over and above the global limit of 290,000 immigrants and the per-country limit of 20,000, immediate relatives (spouses, minor children and parents) of American citizens were allowed to immigrate without restriction.

The drafters of the 1965 laws, as well as the legislators and the contemporary commentators, expected the new provisions for family reunification to be used only sparingly, certainly not in such a way as to shift the ethnic origins of immigration.[26] Since the majority of families in the United States had European or Canadian—that is, white—origins (and the principal minority, blacks, had almost no remaining family connections to Africa), observers anticipated little change in the character of immigration. In fact, however, following passage of the act, non-Latino white immigration fell to very low levels, and Latino (especially Mexican) and Asian immigration rose to unprecedented amounts. At the same time, the overall amount of immigration rose substantially in the 1970s and 1980s.

This is not to say that the 1965 law was the sole cause of the new wave of immigration into the United States. There have been many causes, including shifting income patterns, economic dislocation, warfare and cuts in transportation costs. Chapter 4 considers the determinants of immigration in greater detail. The 1965 act allowed these changes to occur, however. By lifting the national origins quotas, it permitted the entry of immigrants from new, Asian sources. By placing such a high priority on family reunification, it effectively downgraded the importance of labor market skills. By allowing the immigration of close family members to occur outside the numerical limits, it provided a mechanism for the overall numbers to exceed the stated limits.

The effect of the 1965 law on immigration from Mexico and the rest of Latin America is a bit of a puzzle. Before 1965, no numerical quota restricted immigration from the Western Hemisphere. In that year, a quota of 120,000 immigrants a year was imposed, with a 20,000 maximum for any one country. It is hard to claim, therefore, that the 1965 act opened the floodgates to Latino immigration.

For two decades prior to 1965, however, Mexican workers had come to the United States primarily under the terms of the "Bracero" program, which provided for temporary entry of field workers in the southwestern states. The end of the Bracero program in 1964 did not mean the end of the demand for low-wage Mexican field workers; the demand appears to have grown. So immigration from Mexico grew apace. Some was legal, under the terms of the new 1965 act, and a growing portion was illegal.

The United States began the twentieth century with an almost completely open immigration policy. It slammed the gates shut in the 1920s and then, without its legislators really intending to, partially opened them again in 1965. These shifts in policy are part of the explanation for the numerical fluctuations in immigration discussed at the beginning of the chapter, the reduction in midcentury and the resumed large inflow toward the end. They are not the only cause of the fluctuations—large-scale immigration into the United States was impossible during the two world wars and the Great Depression, regardless of the legal framework—but they are an important cause. Experience shows that legislation can have a major effect on immigration; therefore, the debate over immigration is appropriately focused on government policy. Chapter 3 continues the discussion of legislation, dealing with the laws that currently govern immigration.

Notes

1. Quoted in Lawrence H. Fuchs, *The American Kaleidoscope: Race, Ethnicity, and the Civic Culture* (Hanover, N.H.: Wesleyan University Press, 1990), 1.
2. Oscar Handlin, *The Uprooted, the Epic Story of the Great Migrations that Made the American People* (Boston: Little, Brown, 1951), 3.

3. Roger Daniels, *Coming to America, a History of Immigration and Ethnicity in American Life* (New York: HarperCollins, 1990), 23. This is the best single-volume history of American immigration.
4. U.S. Immigration and Naturalization Service (INS), *1993 Statistical Yearbook of the Immigration and Naturalization Service* (Washington, D.C.: U.S. Government Printing Office, 1994), table 1.
5. See, for example, Leon F. Bouvier, *Peaceful Invasions, Immigration and Changing America* (Lanham, Md.: University Press of America, 1992), and Thomas Muller and Thomas J. Espenshade, *The Fourth Wave, California's Newest Immigrants* (Washington, D.C.: Urban Institute Press, 1985).
6. INS, *1993 Statistical Yearbook.*
7. INS, *1993 Statistical Yearbook.*
8. One way in which this table differs from the official data is that it counts movement from Puerto Rico to the mainland as immigration.
9. INS, *1993 Statistical Yearbook,* table 12.
10. Hans Johnson, "A Socioeconomic and Demographic Overview of Women Immigrants in California," testimony presented to the California Select Committee on Statewide Immigration Impact, Sacramento, June 19, 1994.
11. Campbell Gibson, "The Contribution of Immigration to the Growth and Ethnic Diversity of the American Population," *Proceedings of the American Philosophical Society* 136 (1992):157–75.
12. George J. Borjas, "National Origin and the Skills of Immigrants in the Postwar Period," in *Immigration and the Work Force, Economic Consequences for the United States and Source Areas,* ed. George J. Borjas and Richard B. Freeman (Chicago: University of Chicago Press, 1992), 17–47.
13. A good example of opposition to immigration primarily because of its ethnic composition is Peter Brimelow, *Alien Nation, Common Sense about America's Immigration Disaster* (New York: Random House, 1995).
14. Daniels, *Coming to America,* 66.
15. Timothy J. Hatton and Jeffrey G. Williamson have assembled statistical tests to show that emigration from northern and western Europe in the last part of the nineteenth century was related positively to the pace of industrialization, to the wage gap between sending and receiving countries, to the growth rate of the labor force and to the existence of migration networks. See "What Drove the Mass Migrations from Europe in the Late Nineteenth Century?" *Population and Development Review* 20 (1994):533–59.
16. The history of nineteenth-century Irish and German immigration is summarized in Daniels, *Coming to America,* ch. 6.
17. Thomas Bailey Aldrich, "The Unguarded Gates," *Atlantic Monthly,* 1882; cited in Daniels, *Coming to America,* 275–76.
18. A good summary of the history of immigration law is contained in David Weissbrodt, *Immigration Law and Procedure in a Nutshell* (St. Paul: West Publishing, 1992). The definitive scholarly treatment of the history of immigration law from 1798 to 1965 is E. P. Hutchinson, *Legislative History of American Immigration Policy 1798-1965* (Philadelphia: University

of Pennsylvania Press, 1981). An overview of federal legislation pertaining to immigration is contained in INS, *1993 Statistical Yearbook,* appendix 1. For a brief review of the highlights of the history of immigration law, see Barry Edmonston and Jeffrey S. Passel, "Ethnic Demography: U.S. Immigration and Ethnic Variations," in *Immigration and Ethnicity, the Integration of America's Newest Arrivals,* ed. Barry Edmonston and Jeffrey S. Passel (Washington, D.C.: Urban Institute Press, 1994), 1–30.

19. Recent texts include Thomas A. Aleinikoff and David A. Martin, *Immigration, Process and Policy,* 2d ed. (St. Paul: West Publishing, 1991); Richard A. Boswell, *Immigration and Nationality Law, Cases and Materials,* 2d ed. (Durham, N.C.: Carolina Academic Press, 1992); Stephen Legomsky, *Immigration Law and Policy* (Westbury, N.Y.: Foundation Press, 1990).

20. See Ronald Takaki, "Reflections on Racial Patterns in America," *Ethnicity and Public Policy* 1 (1982):1–23. Takaki uses the naturalization law and related legislation to develop his argument that the principal historical thrust of American public policy has been exclusionist and racist.

21. See Peter H. Schuck, "The Transformation of Immigration Law," *Columbia Law Review* 84 (1984):1–90.

22. *Mathews v. Diaz,* 426 U.S. 67, 80 (1976), quoted in Schuck, "The Transformation of Immigration Law."

23. Daniels, *Coming to America,* 240.

24. Weissbrodt, *Immigration Law,* 7.

25. INS, *1993 Statistical Yearbook,* table 1.

26. See, for example, Daniels, *Coming to America,* 338: "Much of what [the 1965 law] has accomplished was unforeseen by its authors, and had the Congress fully understood its consequences, it almost certainly would not have passed."

3

Today's Immigrants

This chapter discusses current immigration: the legal framework and the characteristics of the immigrants. It presents information needed to make a judgment about several of the questions from Chapter 1.

In 1990, the census counted 19.7 million foreign-born people in the United States, a 34 percent increase over 1980. They represented over 8 percent of the total population. About one-third were naturalized citizens, almost one-half were legal permanent residents, almost one-sixth were undocumented and the remainder had some other legal, nonimmigrant status.[3] The great majority had entered the country since the 1965 amendments to the Immigration and Nationality Act.

Three Groups of Immigrants

One way of dividing today's immigrants, based on a suggestion by Michael Fix and Jeffrey Passel of the Urban Institute, is into the categories of conventional, humanitarian and unauthorized.[4] Each of these groups can be further subdivided.

I love immigrants. Legal, illegal— they're not to be despised.
   —Mario M. Cuomo, Governor of New York, 1994[1]

As surely as the winds and rains of Hurricane Andrew assaulted South Florida in a crisis that forever changed it, there is another storm, illegal immigration, that is battering our shores today.
   —Lawton Chiles, Governor of Florida, 1994[2]

The largest number of conventional immigrants are admitted for the purpose of family reunification. Immediate family members of U.S. citizens—spouses, parents and minor children—are admitted without restriction. Other family categories have numerical restrictions and are prioritized as follows: (1) unmarried adult children of U.S. citizens, (2) immediate family members of legal permanent residents, (3) married children of U.S. citizens and (4) siblings of adult U.S. citizens. Slots that are not used in a priority category revert to the next highest category.

A second type of conventional immigration is related to employment. Applicants are admitted in priority categories depending on the labor market needs in the American economy. Again, in the case of employment preferences, numerical ceilings are placed on each category, with the unused slots reverting to the next category. The priority categories are (1) those with extraordinary ability, (2) professionals, (3) skilled workers, (4) a variety of "special" immigrant groups and (5) investors.

A third conventional type relates to what is called "diversity"; it is intended to provide for immigration from countries whose people would otherwise have little or no access.

The humanitarian group is made up largely of refugees and asylees, people who are unable to return to their home countries because of a justifiable fear of persecution. The distinction between the two is that refugees are outside the United States and asylees are in the United States or at a port of entry at the time of their application for admission.

Two groups of unauthorized immigrants exist that are not, of course, recognized by law: people who crossed the border without inspection, and people who crossed the border legally but in a nonimmigrant status and then overstayed their visas.

Table 3.1 shows the numbers who immigrated legally in the conventional and humanitarian categories in fiscal year 1993.[5] For obvious reasons, no official statistics are available for unauthorized entries.[6]

The numbers for total immigration and for most of the categories that are shown in Table 3.1 have been growing fairly steadily since the 1960s. The biggest jump in the 1990s has been in the employment preference and diversity categories, in both cases the result of changes in the immigration law in 1990. Otherwise, the proportional distribution of immigrants shown in Table 3.1 is fairly typical of recent immigration. By far the largest number of immigrants, almost two-thirds, enter under provisions for family reunification.

Table 3.1 Immigration by Category, Fiscal Year 1993

Category	Immigrants	Percent
Total	880,014	100.0
Conventional	725,721	82.5
Family	537,179	61.0
Immediate relatives of U.S. citizens	255,059	29.0
Family preferences	226,776	25.8
IRCA legalization relatives	55,344	6.3
Employment preferences	147,012	16.7
Diversity immigrants	33,480	3.8
Other conventional	8,050	0.9
Humanitarian	154,293	17.5

Source: Calculated from U.S. Immigration and Naturalization Service, *1993 Statistical Yearbook* (Washington, D.C.: U.S. Government Printing Office, 1994), table 4.

The category not included in Table 3.1 is undocumented immigrants. Demographers have put considerable effort into estimating how many are in the United States, how many enter the country each year and how fast the number living in the country is growing.[7] A study by Robert Warren of the Immigration and Naturalization Service estimates that in October 1992 there were about 3.4 million unauthorized immigrants in the United States. The number was higher in 1986, probably almost 5 million, but an amnesty in that year led to the legalization of about 3 million people. According to Warren, the number of undocumented residents appears to be growing moderately but regularly, at a rate of almost 300,000 people a year.[8]

The Legal Framework

Three separate federal laws deal with the three immigrant categories. They build upon the historical immigration legislation that was outlined in Chapter 2. Humanitarian entries take place under the terms of the Refugee Act of 1980. The problem of undocumented immigrants is addressed by IRCA, the Immigration Reform and Control Act of 1986. Conventional immigrants are regulated by the Immigration Act of 1990, which amended the 1952 and 1965 legislation.

The 1980 Refugee Act

Refugees and asylees were dealt with separately for the first time in the Refugee Act of 1980. Previously, in the 1952 and 1965 acts, refugees had been one of the preference categories. In 1980, the global quota was reduced from 290,000 to 270,000, exclusive of refugees, and refugees were dealt with separately under this new act. The act broadened the definition of a refugee, to conform with a 1967 United Nations protocol on the subject. Under the act, a refugee or asylee is a "person who is unable or unwilling to return to his country of nationality or habitual residence because of persecution or a well-founded fear of persecution on account of race, religion, nationality, membership in a particular social group or political opinion."

The Refugee Act was a component of the Carter administration's attempt to put human rights at the forefront of American foreign policy. This was a new direction in foreign policy, and it did not outlast the one-term Carter presidency. It left behind some lasting achievements, however, one of which is the Refugee Act.

Americans concerned about refugee policy were not proud of their country's stance before that time. One of the worst periods in the collective memory of American immigration policy was the Second World War. In 1939, Congress defeated a bill to accept 20,000 children fleeing Nazi Germany—children who already had willing American sponsors—because the number would have exceeded the German quota. Later in the war, the United States turned back a shipload of Jewish refugees; they eventually returned to Germany and perished in the Holocaust. Following the war, and following the accommodation of displaced persons who had been victimized by the war, refugee policy was used consistently as an ideological, anticommunist tool of the cold war. The intent of the 1980 act was to reform the country's sorry and in some ways shameful refugee policy by making it consistent with neutral, nonideological, internationally recognized humanitarian goals.

Even if the act had been sympathetically administered, it would not have been completely adequate to the task, since refugees exist for many reasons other than those recognized by the statute. People forced to flee their countries because of natural disasters or because of life-threatening poverty, for example, are not eligible for refugee status, even when they are demonstrably outside their countries and unable to return. The distinction between an "economic refugee" (who is not admissible as a refugee) and a "political refugee" (who is admissible) is frequently one that makes no sense to people escaping their countries. How, for example, did one classify a Haitian in the 1980s fleeing a country that was at the same time desperately poor and violently repressive?

In any case, the act was soon being implemented not by Carter but by the Reagan and Bush administrations. The Republican administrations regarded Carter's elevation of human rights to a guiding principle of foreign policy as hopelessly naive and dangerous to American interests. They were not in sympathy with the basic purpose of the Refugee Act; they continued, as is shown later in this chapter, to skew refugee policy in the direction of anticommunism.

The number of refugees is set each year by the president in consultation with Congress, and provisions are made for unanticipated emergencies. The first unanticipated emergency occurred almost immediately after the bill was enacted. The Mariel boatlift sent more than 100,000 Cuban refugees to Miami in the spring and summer of 1980, a number far greater than anything anticipated by the legislation. Eventually the Carter administration removed the Mariel boatlift from the purview of the Refugee Act and initiated special legislation for it. For the first years under the act, the number of applications for refugee status was under 100,000, but since 1988, the number has exceeded 100,000. The number of refugee applications approved has exceeded 100,000 since 1991.[9]

Under the act, refugees are eligible for special adjustment assistance. In addition, they have full access to the welfare system and all the features of the social safety net in the United States. In this respect, they are treated more generously than other legal immigrants; the latter are effectively excluded from eligibility for most social services for five years after arrival.

The 1986 Immigration Reform and Control Act

As the number of authorized immigrants grew, so did the number of undocumented immigrants. The question of how to deal with illegal immigration was one of the principal topics addressed by the Select Committee on Immigration and Refugee Policy, which was appointed by President Carter and chaired by Rev. Theodore M. Hesbergh, then the president of the University of Notre Dame. The committee made its final report in 1981. The recommendations of the committee led to legislative proposals that were repeatedly defeated or dropped in Congress. In 1986, however, Congress adopted some of the committee's proposals in the form of the Immigration Control and Reform Act, or IRCA. IRCA did almost nothing to change the overall framework of immigration policy in the United States, but it established the basis for dealing with illegal immigrants.

IRCA was a compromise between the champions of the rights of undocumented immigrants and the rights of ethnic minority groups on the one hand, and those concerned that the country had "lost control of its borders" and was being inundated with unauthorized people on the other hand. The first group won an extensive amnesty program and provisions for nondiscrimination in employment; the second group won increased resources for the Border Patrol and sanctions on employers who hired illegal entrants.

The amnesty provisions applied to undocumented people who had been in the country continuously (except for brief trips) between 1982 and 1986. In the agricultural sector, agribusiness interests won a more generous amnesty provision: it applied to special agricultural workers (SAWs) who had been in the United States a minimum of only 90 days between May 1, 1985, and May 1, 1986. Eventually, nearly 3 million people regularized their status under IRCA.

Having provided amnesty for a good portion of the illegal immigrants in the country, IRCA attempted to stem the continued flow. Prior to the passage of IRCA, the only tool the Border Patrol had was deportation of offenders. IRCA added to this by providing for sanctions, including fines and imprisonment, for employers who hire undocumented immigrants either knowingly or without using the employment verification process specified in the act. Employer sanctions were the most controversial feature of the act. They were opposed not only by employer representatives, who argued that employers should not be expected to perform the police task of determining legal status, but also by people who feared that, in complying with the act, employers would discriminate against members of minority groups, regardless of their legal status.

The experience of employer sanctions under IRCA has not been encouraging.[10] Surveys by the Government Accounting Office (GAO) have shown that many employers are unaware, or not fully aware, of their obligations under IRCA. The GAO surveys have also shown that discrimination in employment is associated with IRCA, even though the act attempted to ban discrimination. As some opponents of IRCA had feared, some employers decline to hire Latinos—even though they may be citizens or legal immigrants—simply on the grounds that they *may* be undocumented.

The inadequacy of employer sanctions has led to a renewed call for a universal employment identity card. The question was debated vigorously prior to the passage of IRCA and was rejected by Congress on the grounds that it smacked of totalitarian control. The question has been put back on the agenda for discussion in the 1990s because of the failure of IRCA's employer sanctions.

The other principal provision of IRCA was to increase the resources of the Border Patrol, in order to improve its ability to prevent illegal crossings. There is no evidence that this has had any effect in reducing illegal immigration, except perhaps for a year following passage of the law.[11]

This raises the question of whether the Border Patrol has any effect on illegal immigration at all, and whether the United States has lost complete control of its borders. As demographer Thomas Espenshade shows, the activities of the Border Patrol could, theoretically, have an effect on illegal immigration at any or all of three points: when an illegal trip is being contemplated but is not yet undertaken, when a potential immigrant is in transit and after an undocumented immigrant has settled in the United States. From his empirical research, Espenshade found that changes in Border Patrol activity have had almost no impact on attempted trips. At least at the U.S.-Mexico border, studies have shown that virtually everyone who wants to make it across can do so—if not on the first attempt, then on subsequent attempts. And the arrests of undocumented residents beyond the border are so few as to make the annual probability of arrest and deportation only about 1 percent.[12] It is difficult to show empirically, therefore, that the Border Patrol has any effect at all on undocumented immigration. It has even been suggested that IRCA increased the number of undocumented residents by encouraging people to stay in the country for longer periods of time, in order to compensate for the increased risks of being caught at the border.[13]

This does not mean, however, that the United States has virtually open borders. It appears that the great majority of people who wish to enter the United States are law abiding and are unwilling to enter illegally. The best evidence for this is the long waiting list for legal entry. For example, married sons and daughters of U.S. citizens whose applications for entry from Mexico were approved in October 1985 were not admitted until March 1994. Some legal applicants from the Philippines who were approved in 1977 had still not been admitted as of 1994.[14] Long queues exist for approved applicants from many other countries. One can conclude from this that the immigration laws matter, and that if they were abolished, the flow of immigration into the United States would be much larger.

Nevertheless, the fact that Border Patrol activity seems to have so little impact should give pause to those who think that illegal immigration can be significantly reduced by stronger enforcement. IRCA did not resolve the problem of illegal immigration. In all likelihood, the problem will never be solved to the satisfaction of most Americans, as long as the United States remains a relatively wealthy country and continues to try to restrict immigration.

The 1990 Immigration Act

IRCA focused on the problem of illegal immigration and left largely untouched the myriad issues relating to legal immigration. The latter were addressed in a comprehensive manner by the Immigration Act of 1990. This act increased the numbers eligible for immigration, changed the priority categories, reduced the political and ideological grounds for deportation and made other changes in virtually all areas of immigration law.

The Immigration Act expanded the numerical limits by about 35 percent. Such an expansion could not have happened a few years later, when the national debate was dominated by anti-immigration sentiment. In 1990, however, the United States was coming to the end of an unprecedented decade of economic expansion; the predominant view was that the country had the capacity to absorb more immigrants. In such an atmosphere, the different interest groups arguing for increased access of one group or another found themselves up against little effectively organized opposition.

The act established an annual worldwide limit of 700,000, falling slightly to 675,000 in 1995. This figure does not include a variety of other groups, including 125,000 refugees, so the overall limit exceeds 800,000. The act increased the allocation for both family-related and employment-based immigration and added a new category for "diversity."

The act reserved more than half of the immigration slots, 465,000, for family members of American citizens and residents. In 1995, the figure rose to 480,000.

The act responded to concerns about the declining skill level of the American labor force and the imperatives of global competition by expanding the number of employment-related visas to 140,000 a year. Although this was less than many critics wished, it represented a considerable increase. The act reduced the number of visas for un-skilled workers and increased the number for highly skilled. A new category established in 1990 is the "employment creation" preference, which allows entrance to people willing to invest at least $1 million and employ at least ten U.S. residents (in low-income areas, the fig-ure can be reduced to $500,000). As things have turned out, this cat-egory is undersubscribed. In most of the employment categories, a job offer is required, plus labor certification showing that qualified U.S. workers are not available.

The strangest category in the 1990 act is the "diversity" visa. Veter-ans of the multicultural wars in the United States might think that they know what *diversity* means: non-white, third world, other than the main-stream culture. In the Immigration Act, however, diversity means the opposite. The act provides for the entry of citizens from "adversely affected" countries. These include many of the predominantly white countries of northern and western Europe that once provided most of the American immigrants; those immigrant flows are now so far in the past that the remaining kinship ties are too distant to allow for family reunification under U.S. law. Thanks mostly to Senator Kennedy's interest in the subject, fully 40 percent of the diversity visas were allo-cated to Ireland for the period 1992 through 1994. Diversity visas are almost the only way for nonrefugee immigrants to enter the United States legally without a family or an employer sponsor.

In sum, the most recent revisions to immigration law are relatively expansive, increasing the number of immigrants, liberalizing the pri-ority categories and reducing the grounds for exclusion. The 1990 act continues the liberalizing trend begun in 1965.

The Goals of Immigration Policy

Whether all this legislation adds up to a coherent, defensible immi-gration policy is debatable. At least some proponents of the current system claim that all is well, that the purposes of American immigra-tion policy are clear and that the legislation is well designed to achieve those purposes. Fix and Passel assert that there are five principal goals, well understood by Congress when the various laws were passed:[15]

1. Social: family reunification

2. Economic: improving U.S. incomes

3. Cultural: increasing diversity

4. Moral: human rights

5. Security: reducing illegal immigration

This view is not persuasive. One can deduce goals such as these from a review of the legislation, but that is not the same as showing that the goals represent a consensus of the American political process, that they are what Americans want or even that they are mutually consistent. A conservative critic of immigration policy, Otis L. Graham, writes, "Existing U.S. immigration policy goals, insofar as we may make them out, are indefensible."[16]

Graham's use of the word *indefensible* is perhaps extreme, but at least one can say that the goals of current immigration policy are unclear. The central problem with the present legislation can be traced back to the 1965 amendments, in which the framers abolished the national origin quotas of the 1920s without a clear understanding of what sort of immigration patterns would replace that system. The vast changes in immigration since 1965—the increase in numbers and the shift to third world countries of origin—were facilitated by the legislation but were not its intended consequences.

The 1980 Refugee Act and the 1986 IRCA represent straightforward attempts by the United States to establish clear policies in the areas of refugees and undocumented immigrants, respectively. But they have failed to achieve their objectives completely; refugee policy remains controversial, and IRCA did not stem the flow of illegal immigration. Nevertheless, one can at least say that the policy goals in those two areas were defined and that the legislation was a reasonable if not altogether adequate attempt to meet the goals.

In the area of conventional immigration, however, which represents the largest part of the flow, what we see is the outcome of a process of political conflict and negotiation, not a coherent policy. Various interest groups in the country favor family reunification, the inflow of skilled and unskilled labor and renewed immigration from predominantly white countries. The 1990 act represents a compromise among these various groups, but one that leaves almost no one satisfied. To return to Fix and Passel's five goals, the first three are in some respects contradictory. Family reunification, the first goal, leads to the admission of people without regard to their impact on American productivity and standard of living, the second goal. Admissions under the second goal are many fewer than admissions under the first, so they cannot compensate completely. Moreover, even in terms of the second goal, the conflict in purpose between American employers (who want low wages) and American workers (who want high wages) has not been resolved. The very reason for the third goal, cultural diversity, is to counteract the cultural effects of the first two goals, and although they increase the diversity of the immigrant flow, these provisions actually reduce the ethnic diversity of the American population. Moreover, no consensus prevails in the country that the current overall amount of immigration is optimal. The different acts and provisions do not add up to a coherent policy. The federal Commission on Immigration Reform recommended a new and more restrictive set of policies in 1995, but it is not clear whether these recommendations will influence policy and whether a more coherent system will ensue.

The review of immigration legislation in this chapter and Chapter 2 leads to the conclusion that the law reflected a national consensus about policy goals in the 1920s, when the restrictive quotas based on national origins were instituted. Today's legislation does not reflect such a consensus. This does not mean that the 1920s legislation was good for the country or better than the current laws, for it was racist and restrictive. Nevertheless, it represented the will of the country, whereas today's laws do not. Perhaps this is inevitable. Perhaps it would be impossible today to devise an immigration policy that represents the will of the country, since that will is so fractured. Chapter 9 turns to the question of the basis on which American immigration legislation should be formulated.

Where Today's Immigrants Come From

Since 1965, the most dramatic change in immigration has been the shift in national origins. The great majority of current immigrants come not from Europe but from the third world, in particular from the Caribbean Basin and from South and Southeast Asia. The country sending the most people to the United States is Mexico.

The United States shares a 2,000-mile border with Mexico. In the nineteenth century, the United States annexed almost half of Mexican territory, and the Mexican population with it. Mexico has sent people across its shifting northern border at least since the time that statistics were first gathered. The latest period, however, has seen a huge increase in Mexican immigration (see Tables 2.3 and 2.4). From 1961 through 1993, over 4 million Mexicans arrived legally, or 21 percent of the total documented immigration into the country. When the undocumented arrivals are factored in, the Mexican share of immigration in the fourth wave is well above one-quarter.

Most Mexicans come into California or the southwestern states, particularly Texas—both of which were formerly part of Mexico. Over most of American history, a majority of Mexican immigrants provided agricultural labor. In this respect, the Mexican immigrants differed from the Europeans, whose backgrounds were often rural but who immigrated to American cities. An acute labor shortage in the fields of the Southwest during World War II led to the American and the Mexican governments' negotiating the Bracero program. Under this program, Mexicans entered the country temporarily in order to provide seasonal agricultural labor. They were guaranteed certain standards of wages and working conditions (although, in practice, the guarantees often failed), and they returned to Mexico after the work was finished. The program was dropped between 1947 and 1951 and then resumed again until 1964. In peak years, it brought almost half a million workers to the United States.

The Bracero program ended, but the demand for Mexican workers did not. Immigration, both legal and illegal, grew from the 1960s until the present. The border became porous, with people moving back and forth across it. In earlier periods, Mexican migrants were concentrated in certain specific sending communities, but over time, the appeal of emigration has broadened. The 1980s and 1990s have seen a significant flow into the United States of non-Spanish-speaking Indians from Mexico, the largest group being Mixtecs from the southern state of Oaxaca.[17] Chapter 4 considers the causes of the acceleration in emigration from Mexico.

In the United States, Latinos have become the second-largest ethnic minority group—and Mexican Americans constitute the largest number of Latinos. Mexican Americans remain concentrated in California and the Southwest, where they have a major effect on the culture. Native Mexican Americans, or Chicanos, along with Mexican immigrants, provide the largest share of agricultural labor in the region. The struggles of the United Farm Workers, under the charismatic leadership of the late Cesar Chavez, to organize them and improve their living conditions caught the imagination and sympathy of much of the country. Still, Mexican immigrants, and the Mexican American population generally, are no longer predominantly agricultural. Like other immigrant ethnic groups, they have moved to the cities. Los Angeles has become a principal center of Mexican population—

especially East Los Angeles and, increasingly, the formerly predominantly African American area of South Central Los Angeles.

Immigrants are entering the United States in larger numbers than ever before from Central America and the Caribbean islands. From the Dominican Republic, El Salvador, Guatemala, Haiti, the Bahamas, Nicaragua and Cuba, the streams have been growing. Puerto Ricans are American citizens, not immigrants, but their movement to the mainland has paralleled that of other groups from the Caribbean Basin.

Cuban immigration is a special case, a consequence of the cold war rivalries in the Western Hemisphere. Until 1995, the great majority of Cuban immigrants were classified as refugees. The U.S. government encouraged refugees from Fidel Castro's regime, then was caught flat-footed when Castro permitted over 100,000 people to leave in 1980. As part of its long-standing policy of opposition to Castro, the U.S. government provided subsidies and established programs to help the Cuban immigrants—most of whom stayed in Florida—get established in their new country.

The largest group of Asian immigrants in the latest wave comes from the Philippines. Filipino arrivals date back many decades, at least to the beginning of the twentieth century. After the Spanish-American War, however, when the United States annexed the Philippines, they were considered American nationals and hence were not counted as immigrants. With Filipino independence in 1946, the newcomers became immigrants. Early Filipino arrivals worked in agriculture in the West; more recent immigrants have tended to be better educated and able to qualify for professional or semiprofessional jobs.

Korean immigration began in the aftermath of the Korean War and expanded greatly after 1965. Occupationally, the Koreans have concentrated in the merchant and professional ranks. The visible success of their stores in some cities has brought them into conflict with African Americans, most notably in New York and Los Angeles.

Indians are the one Asian group not to settle disproportionately in California. Scattered throughout the country, they have been successful entrepreneurs, merchants, academics and motel operators.

Vietnamese immigration stems from the long and destructive Vietnam War. Until 1994, all Vietnamese immigrants were regarded as refugees. Some, including many South Vietnamese government officials and military officers, fled the country at the time of the fall (or liberation, depending on one's point of view) of the south in 1975. Many others are the survivors of harrowing journeys in the succeeding years. Many of the refugees came without financial resources or skills appropriate to the U.S. labor market; this is even more true of associated groups, including Cambodians, Laotians and Hmong. With the regularization of diplomatic relations, the United States no longer regards most immigrants from Vietnam as refugees.

The principal countries of origin are quite different for the three categories of immigrants. Tables 3.2, 3.3 and 3.4 show the top ten countries of birth for conventional, humanitarian and illegal immigrants, respectively. The tables are not quite comparable with one another. Tables 3.2 and 3.3 show the number of legally admitted immigrants (exclusive of IRCA regularizations) in fiscal year 1993. In the case of illegal immigrants (Table 3.4), demographers cannot estimate the annual flow from each country and have to be satisfied with the total number of residents in the country as of a certain date, in this case, October 1992. Moreover, the estimates of undocumented immigration are necessarily less certain than those of legal entries. Still, the three tables together give a good picture of the origins of recent immigrants.

The overlap in the three tables is small. Seventeen countries appear on only one of the three lists, and five appear on two; only one, the Philippines, appears on all three. With a few exceptions, countries "specialize" in the types of immigrants they send to the United States.

The principal exception is Mexico, which ranks first in both conventional and illegal immigrants (and many legal immigrants from Mexico have had one or more previous periods of U.S. residence as undocumented immigrants). Still, of the total immigration during the 1980s from Mexico, El Salvador and Guatemala (the top three in Table 3.4), only 30 percent was legal, and 70 percent was undocumented, according to the most informed demographic analysis.[18]

The sources of conventional immigration are spread broadly, with a concentration in the Caribbean region (Mexico, the Dominican Republic and El Salvador) and Asia (the Philippines, China, India and Korea). Although Mexico is the largest single source, it does not dominate. In 1993, the top ten countries sent just 58 percent of the total conventional immigrants.

The other categories are more concentrated. The top ten countries of origin for undocumented residents provided 70 percent of that population, and in the case of humanitarian entries, 87 percent.

A perusal of Table 3.3 shows the basic problem with the administration of American refugee policy. In spite of the goals of the 1980 act, it proved all but impossible to administer the act in a neutral way rather than as a tool of American foreign policy. Three of the top ten

Table 3.2 Top Ten Countries of Birth of Conventional Immigrants, Fiscal Year 1993

Rank	Country	Number of Immigrants	Percent of Total
1	Mexico	109,003	15.0
2	Philippines	61,516	8.5
3	China (Mainland)	56,704	7.8
4	Dominican Republic	44,905	6.2
5	India	38,316	5.3
6	Poland	26,597	3.7
7	El Salvador	24,702	3.4
8	Canada	23,722	3.3
9	United Kingdom	20,273	2.8
10	Korea	17,245	2.4
	Top 10	422,983	58.3
	Total	725,721	100.0

Source: Calculated from U.S. Immigration and Naturalization Service, *1993 Statistical Yearbook* (Washington, D.C.: U.S. Government Printing Office, 1994), table 9.

source countries—Vietnam, Laos and Thailand—are Southeast Asian countries that were buffeted severely by American involvement in the Vietnam War. For them, the immigration is best seen as a consequence of American warfare. Four of the countries are, or recently were, communist regimes—the Soviet Union, Cuba, Romania and Nicaragua (as well as Vietnam). Ethiopia has at times had a Marxist government. It was convenient for the United States to classify people wanting to leave those countries as refugees, as part of its cold war strategy. Iran also has been an enemy country, although not a communist one. Of the top ten suppliers of humanitarian immigrants, only the Philippines is relatively uncontaminated by the recent history of American cold and shooting wars.

Although Table 3.3 refers only to 1993, the same basic pattern in humanitarian immigration has held for a long time. During the 1980s, the two largest groups of refugees were from Indochina and Cuba. One should not conclude, however, that only these countries generated people whom a reasonably neutral observer would classify as genuine refugees. To take just the Caribbean Basin, the governments of El Salvador, Guatemala and Haiti all waged war in the 1980s against segments

Table 3.3 Top Ten Countries of Birth of Humanitarian Immigrants,
Fiscal Year 1993

Rank	Country	Number of Immigrants	Percent of Total
1	Soviet Union	54,994	35.6
2	Vietnam	31,046	20.1
3	Thailand	22,966	14.9
4	Cuba	11,287	7.3
5	Romania	2,892	1.9
6	Nicaragua	2,829	1.8
7	Laos	2,257	1.5
8	Iran	2,038	1.3
9	Ethiopia	1,745	1.1
10	Philippines	1,630	1.1
	Top 10	133,684	86.6
	Total	154,293	100.0

Source: Calculated from U.S. Immigration and Naturalization Service, *1993 Statistical Yearbook* (Washington, D.C.: U.S. Government Printing Office, 1994), table 9.

of their own population and thereby produced refugees. Because of American friendship with those regimes, however, the United States refused to recognize such people as refugees under the terms of the 1980 act. It is ironic, to understate the point, that Cuba, where no war took place, created refugees in the eyes of the American authorities, but El Salvador, Guatemala and Haiti, where warfare, repression by government forces or both were vicious, did not.

To be fair, administration of the Refugee Act is inherently difficult. To classify a substantial number of people leaving a country as refugees is tantamount to accusing its government of serious violations of human rights, and that is something the American government has been loath to do in the case of allies and trading partners. The only American government that tried seriously to elevate human rights to a position of prominence in foreign policy, the Carter administration, ran immediately into insuperable contradictions. Nevertheless, it is clear from Table 3.3—and from the complete record of humanitarian admissions since 1980—that the Refugee Act was not successful in insulating refugee policy from the national security and ideological goals of American foreign policy.

Table 3.4 Top Ten Countries of Birth of Undocumented Immigrants, as of October 1992

Rank	Country	Residents (in Thousands)	Percent of Total
1	Mexico	1,321	39.1
2	El Salvador	327	9.7
3	Guatemala	129	3.8
4	Canada	97	2.9
5	Poland	91	2.7
6	Philippines	90	2.7
7	Haiti	88	2.6
8	Bahamas	71	2.1
9	Nicaragua	68	2.0
10	Italy	67	2.0
	Top 10	2,349	69.5
	Total	3,379	100.0

Source: Robert Warren, "Estimates of Unauthorized Immigrant Population Residing in the United States, by Country of Origin and State of Residence: October 1992" (Washington, D.C.: Statistics Division, Immigration and Naturalization Service, 1994), table 2.

Where Do They Go?

Immigrants do not settle randomly in the United States; they go to specific locations. Often people from a particular locality abroad move to a single neighborhood or town in the United States.

Most immigrants move to large cities. The 1990 census shows fully 93 percent of the foreign-born population living in metropolitan areas, in contrast to 73 percent of the native population. In 1990, half the immigrants who entered the country in the 1980s resided in just eight cities: in descending order, Los Angeles, New York, Miami, Anaheim, Chicago, Washington, Houston and San Francisco. Although for the country as a whole, just 8 percent of the population was foreign born in 1990, in Miami the figure was 46 percent, in Los Angeles 33 percent and in Jersey City (which ranks third in the country in foreign-born proportion) 29 percent.

The concentration by state is also marked. Just over three-quarters of the 1980s' immigrants settled in six states: California (38 percent), New York (14 percent), Texas (8 percent), Florida (8 percent), New Jersey (4 percent) and Illinois (4 percent).[19]

One might predict that once immigrants become well established in the country and better integrated, they would disperse geographically. Ann Bartel has shown that, at least in the 1970s, this did not occur. Between 1975 and 1980, immigrants who lived outside the cities of most intense concentration moved into those cities in greater numbers than immigrant residents of the cities moved out.[20]

The degree of residential concentration varies by educational attainment. Immigrants with more years of schooling are less concentrated and tend to move more widely within the United States. Ethnicity is also a factor: Latino immigrants are the most concentrated in particular cities, whereas Asian and European immigrants are less so. Mexican immigrants tend to concentrate in California, especially in the Los Angeles and San Diego areas; Cubans concentrate in Miami, and Dominicans in New York. The top cities of choice for Asians are Los Angeles, New York and San Francisco.[21]

Undocumented immigrants appear to be more concentrated than the other categories, although, of course, information about them may be subject to considerable error. According to Warren's estimates for 1992, 85 percent of the undocumented lived in the top six states, with California hosting fully 43 percent.[22] Illegal immigrants probably concentrate in the same states and cities where legal immigrants of the same nationality settle.[23]

The geographical concentration of immigration helps explain why the political response to the issue has been so varied across the country. In many regions, immigration is not an important political issue. In California and Florida, however, the public is seriously concerned about immigration, and politicians at the local and state levels have made immigration control a central campaign issue.

Interestingly, the political response to immigration in New York has been much less alarmist than in California or Florida, even though that city is a major receiver of immigrants. Even the problem of undocumented immigrants has failed to generate much interest, let alone outrage, in New York. "Some of the hardest-working and most productive people in this city are undocumented aliens," Mayor Giuliani was quoted as saying. "If you come here and you work hard and you happen to be in an undocumented status, you're one of the people who we want in this city."[24] The response in New York can perhaps be explained by the facts that it has a much longer history of receiving immigrants than other American cities, that it has a larger population base to begin with and that many different ethnic groups tend to move to New York, in contrast with other cities, where there is a greater concentration of one or two groups. Also in New York, immigrants may be replacing people who are moving away or dying.

Personal Characteristics of Today's Immigrants

Much of the debate over immigration has to do with the "quality" of the newcomers. Critics worry that the skills, education and labor market abilities of the immigrants are low and that immigration therefore leads to a deterioration in the economic performance of the country. Economist George Borjas has strongly argued this position.[25] People on the other side of the debate, such as Julian Simon and Stephen Moore, claim that most immigrants have appropriate skills for the U.S. labor market, that they make up quickly whatever skills they are lacking and that they compensate for any deficiency in skills with their energy, enthusiasm and commitment.[26] The next sections look at the question from three perspectives: the education of the immigrants, their ability to speak English and their earnings.

The overall conclusion of these sections is that the skill levels of the immigrants are, on average, below those of American residents. Furthermore, at least in some respects, the gap between immigrants and natives has been growing over time. This average trend conceals as much as or more than it reveals, however. When the immigrant flows are broken down by area of origin, diverse patterns emerge. On the whole, non-Latino white and Asian immigrants have relatively high skill levels that are improving over time. Immigrants from Latin America have the lowest achievement levels, and, at least in some respects, those levels have been dropping over time. To the extent that the gap in skills between immigrants on average and natives on average has been growing, it is a reflection of the increased proportion of Latin American immigration.

As we saw earlier in Table 3.4, by far the largest number of undocumented residents in the United States is from Latin America. Another way of stating the basic finding, therefore, is that the skills of undocumented workers tend to be much lower than the skills of authorized immigrants.

The significance of this finding for the debate over immigration is that many voices are calling for a revision of admissions criteria, to give greater weight to education and skills when choosing immigrants. Changes in the admissions criteria would affect only conventional immigrants, however, not refugees or the undocumented—yet it is the latter two groups that are largely responsible for the deterioration in latter two groups that are largely responsible for the deterioration in skill levels.[27] It will therefore be difficult to upgrade the skills of immigrants by adjusting the priority categories (see the discussion of how applicants should be prioritized in Chapter 1).

Education

The education of immigrants into the United States varies considerably, both over time and by national origin. In the half century between 1940 and 1990, the educational attainment of immigrants fell steadily behind that of natives. According to census data, from 1940 through 1960, immigrants were on average better educated than residents— or at least they had attended school for a longer period. In 1970, the positions were reversed, and the gap grew in the 1980 and 1990 censuses.[28] Moreover, according to economist Barry Chiswick, there is some evidence that foreign schooling is not as effective as American schooling in producing labor market success in the United States. Whether because schools in the immigrants' home countries teach skills that are less applicable to the American labor market, or simply because of bias, an extra year's schooling abroad appears to do an immigrant less good in terms of wages and employment than an extra year's schooling does an American resident.[29]

The average educational attainment of immigrants is a deceiving statistic, however. When comparing recent immigrants with U.S. natives along a scale of educational attainment, one discovers a U shape. Although a higher proportion of immigrants than natives have low educational achievement, a higher proportion of immigrants have high educational achievement as well. In 1990, at the bottom of the educational scale, 23 percent of U.S. native adults had not completed high school; for immigrants of the previous ten years, the figure was 41 percent. At the top of the scale—those with a college degree or more—the figure for natives was 20 percent and for recent immigrants 24 percent.[30] It is in the middle of the scale, therefore, that natives exceed immigrants: 57 percent of natives but only 35 percent of recent immigrants had a high school diploma but less than a college degree. Averaging all the groups, it turns out that immigrants on the whole are less well prepared than natives—but the immigrants still include a large proportion of well-educated people.

Immigrants from different countries have quite different educational levels; some countries specialize in sending low-skilled workers and others in sending highly educated ones. Latin American immigrants, and especially Mexicans, have the lowest level of schooling, and Asians have the highest.[31]

Borjas makes the interesting comparison, for example, between Mexican and Filipino immigrants counted in the 1980 census. Among the Mexicans, 64 percent had eight years or less of education; among the Filipinos, the figure was only 18 percent. Looking at immigrants with sixteen years of education or more, the Mexican figure was 3 percent and the Filipino 37 percent. The difference is startling. What is fascinating about this difference is not just how large it is but the fact that it does not reflect a similar difference between the overall Mexican and Filipino populations in their home countries. The average educational attainment in Mexico and the Philippines is about the same.[32] One cannot assume, therefore, that the national differences in educational levels of immigrants are a necessary consequence of different levels of social development throughout the world. The difference may have something to do with the relative opportunities of various groups at home, as Chapter 4 shows.

The relatively high educational level of Asian immigrants has remained roughly constant over several decades.[33] In the case of Latin American immigrants, however, educational attainment is low and has declined. The least schooling is found among Mexican immigrants. Mexican entrants in 1987 and 1988 had just 5.7 years of schooling for males and 6.4 years for females.[34]

Women immigrants are generally less educated than men from the same countries. The differences are particularly great in the case of Southeast Asia: many fewer women than men from Vietnam, Cambodia and Laos are high school graduates. Again, the Philippines is an exception; according to the 1990 census, it is the only country for which the proportion of women immigrants with college diplomas exceeds the proportion of men.[35]

The national differences in immigrant educational attainment are correlated strongly with the different categories of immigration: conventional, humanitarian and illegal. The census does not list people by type of immigration, only by country of birth. Nevertheless, as was shown by Tables 3.2 through 3.4, countries specialize in the type of immigrants they send. Fix and Passell used this fact to construct the interesting figures in Table 3.5. The first row shows the educational attainment of immigrants from the three principal senders of undocumented aliens—Mexico, El Salvador and Guatemala; as noted earlier, during the 1980s, 70 percent of the immigrants from these three countries were unauthorized, and only 30 percent were legal. The

Table 3.5 Educational Attainment by Immigration Type, 1990 Census

Type	Percentage with Less than a High School Diploma	Percentage with a College Degree or Higher
Illegal: Mexico, El Salvador, Guatemala	75.4	4.6
Humanitarian: top 11 refugee sources*	46.1	16.2
Conventional: all other countries	26.5	33.3
Natives	23.0	20.3

* Afghanistan, Albania, Cuba, Ethiopia, Iraq, Laos, Philippines, Poland, Romania, Soviet Union, Vietnam.

Source: Michael Fix and Jeffrey S. Passel, *Immigration and Immigrants, Setting the Record Straight* (Washington, D.C.: Urban Institute Press, 1994), fig. 11.

the other two categories. The third row shows all other countries, from which the majority of immigrants were conventional. Although some overlap of categories exists, the huge differences between the three groups are sufficient to establish the point: conventional immigrants are relatively well educated, with a much higher proportion of college graduates than natives. Refugees, and to a larger extent undocumented immigrants, have comparatively low levels of education.

English-Language Proficiency

English is the common language of the United States, and immigrants who do not speak it are at a disadvantage in terms of employment and earnings. That this is so may not be obvious, in view of the growth of Spanish-speaking enclaves. Many areas exist in California, Florida, Texas and some other states where Spanish is the predominant language and people interact from morning to night, both socially and at work, in that language. English-language proficiency might not seem important in those environments. Nevertheless, research has shown that it is. People who are confined to a Spanish-speaking enclave because of their inability in English are restricted in their job searches and generally have to resign themselves to lower paying positions than they could obtain if they were able to look more broadly. According to a study by McManus, Gould and Welch in 1983, the learning of English represented a lifetime gain of $79,000 to a Latino immigrant.[36]

Non-English-speaking immigrants are found in every national group, except, of course, in those whose native language is English. They predominate, however, among Latin American groups. Jasso and Rosenzweig showed that Latinos represent less than a third of current immigrants but over three-quarters of the immigrants who cannot speak English.[37] A 1989 survey reported by Gillian Stevens found that among people who had entered the country since 1987, 42 percent of those from countries where Spanish is the dominant language could not speak English, as opposed to 14 percent from countries where neither English nor Spanish is dominant.[38]

In addition to the Latinos, some non-Latino immigrants never learn English. Fewer enclaves exist for other language groups, but they are not absent. The Chinatowns in several large cities are examples. The manager of a credit union serving Asian immigrants revealed that some Vietnamese immigrants who move to downtown San Francisco find that assimilation into their new surroundings is best achieved by learning Chinese, not English.[39]

A smaller proportion of female than male immigrants can speak English well. According to research by Hans Johnson, the gender differences are especially strong for immigrants from Cambodia, China, India, Iran, Taiwan and Vietnam.[40]

A multitude of foreign languages are heard today in areas of the country that have been impacted heavily by immigration. In 1990, three-quarters of Miami's population, one-half of Los Angeles's and one-third of Houston's spoke a language other than English at home.[41] The public schools in those and other cities are populated increasingly by children for whom English is a second language—and the number of first languages in a school is sometimes very high.

One of the principal complaints against immigrants is what is perceived as their refusal to learn English. American culture is in danger of fragmenting, it is argued, and losing its common language. In view of this worry, it is useful to put the current state of the country's linguistic diversity into a historical context. Jasso and Rosenzweig compared non-English-speaking immigrants in 1980 with their counterparts in 1900. In the earlier period, the largest group of non-English speakers were German speakers. In the 1900 census, 12 percent of the immigrant men and 15 percent of the immigrant women could not speak English; these figures compare with 6 percent for men and 9 percent for women in the 1980 census. That is, non-English speaking is about half as prevalent in the latest wave of immigration as it was at the height of the third wave.[42] Chapter 2 showed that immigrants in the earlier period represented a higher proportion of the total population. From today's perspective, we can see that the third wave of immigration did not dislodge or even threaten English as the principal U.S. language. Today, few Americans of German ancestry speak German, and that is a cultural loss, not a gain for the country. It is unlikely that the smaller proportion of non-English speakers today will constitute more of a threat to the predominance of English.

Immigrants are learning English at the rate that immigrants have always learned English, if not faster. The number who do not speak English is relatively small. The pattern of English-language acquisition among non-English-speaking immigrants is clear, as Portes and Rumbaut have shown. The immigrants themselves may learn some English, but they retain their native language as primary. Their children speak the native language at home but learn English at school. Their grandchildren are primarily English speakers, struggling to retain an acquaintance with what is by now a foreign language.[43]

Employment and Earnings

One way of learning how well prepared today's immigrants are to work and compete in the American labor market is to see how well they do. Do they get good jobs? How do their wages compare with the wages of natives? Under some circumstances, a comparison of wages earned by different workers may reveal their relative productivity, or their contribution to output. Unfortunately, wages are often a misleading indicator of productivity, and this can be the case for several different reasons. For example, if employers discriminate against immigrants (or, as some have alleged, in favor of immigrants), a comparison of immigrants' earnings with the earnings of natives is not a good indicator of their relative skills. To take another example, if entry to some occupations is artificially restricted, and immigrants are forced by circumstances into other relatively overpopulated occupations, the wage differences will reflect more about the relative supplies of workers than about their skills and productivity. Nevertheless, the information that has been analyzed by economists about the occupations and earnings of immigrants is interesting, and in spite of these analytical problems, it may indicate something important about the changing skills of immigrants.

The evidence on occupations is that immigrants tend to cluster in, or be restricted to, occupations that have less prestige and lower earnings than those of natives. The 1990 census showed a relative concentration of immigrants in the operators/laborers/fabricators group and the service workers group. Correspondingly, they are less likely than natives to have jobs as clericals, professionals and managers.[44] The occupational data indicate, therefore, that immigrants tend to be less skilled than natives, or at least less successful.

The occupational differences between immigrants and natives are greater for women than for men: a higher concentration in the low-prestige occupations and a lower concentration in the high-prestige occupations. For undocumented women, the choices are especially limiting; one survey found almost all these women in domestic service, baby-sitting, hotel cleaning, office janitorial work or restaurant service. These are jobs with not only low pay and status but also no security and almost no chance for advancement.[45]

Labor economists disagree on the question of whether the quality of immigrant labor has declined over the last several decades.[46] Borjas has been in the forefront of those claiming to identify a decline. Analyzing data from the censuses of 1940 through 1980 relating to people who had entered the country in the previous five years, he showed that (1) the labor force participation rate of recent immigrants fell faster than that of natives, (2) the average hours of work of recent immigrants fell further behind those of natives, (3) the unemployment rate of recent immigrants rose above that of natives and (4) the average real wage rate of recent immigrants fell further behind the wage rate of natives. The last finding is the most important. In 1940, immigrants who had arrived in the United States in the period 1935–39 actually had higher wage rates than native workers. The situation was reversed in 1960, and the gap grew in 1970, 1980 and 1990.[47] This finding has been the basis for much of the worry about the economic impact of immigrants. Where once immigrants improved the quality of the American labor force, now it is feared that they dilute it and that the dilution is becoming greater over time.

The contrary argument, made by a number of economists, including Barry Chiswick as well as Harriet Duleep and Mark Regets, is that although Borjas's data are accurate, they do not imply a decline in the quality of immigrant labor. The argument is made that immigrants initially have lower earnings than natives not because they have less ability but because they are learning the appropriate skills, and learning English, so that they can be successful in the long run. Over time, their earnings rise faster than the earnings of natives; the lower their initial earnings, the faster their eventual rate of growth in earnings. To the extent that this is an accurate picture, the low earnings of immigrants when they first arrive is simply a short-run adjustment problem and not an indicator that the quality of the labor force is being diluted.[48]

Some recent studies on the subject come down in the middle. Robert LaLonde and Robert Topel estimated that between 1970 and 1980, the earnings of new immigrants did not catch up with the earnings of average American workers, but they did catch up with the earnings of residents in the same ethnic group.[49] Still later studies indicate that LaLonde and Topel may have overestimated the pace of assimilation.[50] Our understanding of the subject is in flux.

As a whole, the research literature, although evolving, indicates what we probably could have guessed in the absence of all the econometrics: immigrants assimilate into the labor market somewhat, but not completely. Interestingly, the age at which people immigrate seems to matter. People who immigrate as children, and whose first entry into the labor market is in the United States, may have the same earnings success as natives, whereas those who immigrate as adults never quite catch up. Moreover, LaLonde and Topel's finding about ethnicity is important. Mexican immigrants may come close to catching up to the earnings of native-born Mexican Americans, but Mexican Americans have lower earnings than all Americans. One should not lose sight of the fact that serious ethnic inequalities persist in the United States; the immigration streams are part of this picture, not an exception to it.

The last word has not been said in the dispute, and further research may resolve it one way or another. Most of the analyses have been based on data collected in 1980 and earlier years. New data show several surprising changes in the decade of the 1980s. Over that ten-year period, the average earnings of long-term immigrants stopped improving, the average earnings of recent immigrants stopped deteriorating and the experience of the different national-origin groups differed strongly. The experience of the 1980s shows that, whatever may be happening to the average earnings and the average skills of immigrants, the more important phenomenon is the increasing bifurcation of the immigrant labor force.

The experience of the 1980s is summarized in Table 3.6, taken from a study by Elaine Sorensen and Maria Enchautegui. It shows that although the earnings of recent immigrants are still below the earnings of natives, the gap is narrowing. The 1980s was a bad decade for American labor, whether immigrant or native; the gap between high- and low-paid workers increased,[51] and the average real hourly earnings of workers fell. Foreign-born workers did worse than native workers. In the midst of all this deterioration, however, recent immigrants managed to hold their own and reduce the gap with native workers.

The top section of Table 3.6 shows that real hourly earnings for all men fell by 5.3 percent over the decade, more for the foreign born (8.0 percent) than for natives (4.7 percent). The decline in earnings of immigrants over the decade was exclusively among long-term residents, however; the earnings of recent immigrants held virtually constant. A consequence is that the gap in earnings between recent immigrants and natives fell.

Whether this is clear evidence that the gap in skill levels between immigrants and natives is reversing is a little hard to say, since the 1980s, with its declining real earnings, was such a peculiar decade. One would want to see the gap fall during a more normal period of rising earnings before saying conclusively that the problem has disappeared. At the very least, however, the most recent evidence casts some doubt on the view that the quality of immigrant labor is inexorably declining, relative to that of native labor.

The lower sections of Table 3.6 show that the averages do not tell the principal story. The fact that the real earnings of recent immigrants stayed constant over the decade appears to be a statistical coincidence, the result of completely different trends among the different ethnic groups. The earnings of Latino immigrants fell over the decade, whereas the earnings of all other groups of immigrants rose, even though the earnings of natives in their corresponding ethnic groups fell.

Take, for example, the case of white males. Native earnings fell by 3.5 percent, but the earnings of the foreign born rose by 4.5 percent, with a higher rate of increase for the more recent arrivals. Foreign-born white men had higher earnings than native white men, and the gap increased over the decade. The story is similar, but even more pronounced, for blacks. The earnings of natives fell by 8.1 percent, but the earnings of immigrants rose by 11.1 percent. As a consequence, in 1979, native blacks earned more than immigrant blacks, but in 1989, the positions were reversed.

The situation with Asians is a little different. As with whites and blacks, the earnings of natives fell while the earnings of immigrants rose. In this case, however, the latter increase is due entirely to the remarkable increase in the earnings of recent immigrants, of 22.1 percent.

When we turn to people of Latino heritage, however, the performance of earnings in the 1980s is completely different. The earnings of each group—natives, recent immigrants and long-term immigrants—fell by roughly the same proportion. At the beginning of the decade, the

Table 3.6 Real Hourly Pay of Men in 1979 and 1989, in 1989 Dollars

Group	1979	1989	Percent Change
All	$11.20	$10.61	-5.3
Natives	11.26	10.73	-4.7
All foreign born	10.23	9.41	-8.0
0–5 years in U.S.	7.77	7.75	-0.2
6+ years in U.S.	11.15	9.84	-12.5
Natives by Race and Ethnicity			
White	11.58	11.18	-3.5
Black	9.12	8.38	-8.1
Latino	9.76	8.92	-8.6
Other race	10.53	10.05	-4.6
Foreign Born by Race and Ethnicity			
White foreign born	12.42	12.98	+4.5
0–5 years in U.S.	10.18	10.93	+7.4
6+ years in U.S.	12.79	13.48	+5.4
Latino foreign born	8.19	7.61	-7.0
0–5 years in U.S.	6.50	5.89	-9.4
6+ years in U.S.	8.84	8.07	-8.7
Asian foreign born	10.32	10.87	+5.3
0-5 years in U.S.	8.29	10.12	+22.1
6+ years in U.S.	12.04	11.11	-7.7
Black foreign born	8.36	9.29	+11.1

Source: Elaine Sorensen and Maria Enchautegui, "Immigrant Male Earnings in the 1980s: Divergent Patterns by Race and Ethnicity," in *Immigration and Ethnicity, the Integration of America's Newest Arrivals,* ed. Barry Edmonston and Jeffrey S. Passel (Washington, D.C.: Urban Institute Press, 1994), table 5.3. Data derived from the Current Population Survey, 1979 and 1989.

earnings of recent Latino immigrants were lower than those of recent white or Asian immigrants. At the end of the decade, the disparity was accentuated; among recent immigrants, the earnings of Latinos were barely half of the earnings in the other two groups.

These differences by ethnic group are dramatic. Latin American immigrants are less able to compete successfully for jobs with decent earnings, whereas immigrants from other areas of the world, particularly Asia, are increasingly successful.

The statistics show that there are two streams of immigrant workers. One is predominantly Asian, legal, well educated and able to compete on a fairly equal basis with Americans in the labor market. The other is predominantly Latin American, mostly Mexican, many of them undocumented, with low educational and skill levels and typically qualified for only the lowest-paying jobs in the country. Many exceptions to these generalizations exist, but the gap between the two streams is growing, not converging.

One of the consequences of this bifurcation is that poverty among immigrants has grown over time. During the 1980s, when household poverty rates rose for natives, they rose much faster for immigrants. The incidence of poverty is higher among immigrants than among natives and, as Fix and Passel have shown, it is particularly high among recent immigrants.[52]

In addition to the income differences based on national origins, there are those based on gender. The women of each nationality earn significantly less than the men do, and the differences in income are greater than the differences in their education. Looking only at immigrants living in California, as reported in the 1990 census, Hans Johnson found that men over the age of fifteen earned on average $19,000 a year, yet women earned less than $10,000. Women's incomes ranged from 41 percent of men's for immigrants from Japan, to 81 percent for immigrants from the Philippines.[53]

Notes

1. Quoted in Deborah Sontag, "Politicians Treating Illegal Immigration Softly in New York," *New York Times* (June 10, 1994), A1–A12.
2. Quoted in Deborah Sontag, "3 Governors Take Pleas on Aliens to the Senate," *New York Times* (June 23, 1994), A10.
3. The figures in this paragraph come from Michael Fix and Jeffrey S. Passel, *Immigration and Immigrants, Setting the Record Straight* (Washington, D.C.: Urban Institute Press, 1994), and in turn are based mostly on the 1990 census.
4. Fix and Passel, *Immigration and Immigrants.* For the first category, Fix and Passel use the term *legal* instead of *conventional,* which I find confusing, since the humanitarian admissions are also legal. There are many other ways of categorizing immigrants. For example, Alejandro Portes and Ruben G. Rumbaut, in *Immigrant America, a Portrait* (Berkeley, Calif.: University of California Press, 1990), focus not on the legal status but on the purpose for immigration. They refer to labor migrants, professional immigrants, entrepreneurial immigrants and refugees and asylees.

5. For the federal government, fiscal year 1993 is the twelve-month period preceding October 1, 1993.
6. Table 3.1 does not include the 124,278 people whom the government lists as immigrants in 1993 but who actually entered the country illegally in earlier years and regularized their status in 1993 under the terms of the 1986 amnesty law.
7. See, among others, Frank D. Bean, Barry Edmonston and Jeffrey S. Passel, eds., *Undocumented Migration to the United States, IRCA and the Experience of the 1980s* (Washington, D.C.: Urban Institute Press, 1990), and Robert Warren, "Estimates of the Unauthorized Immigrant Population Residing in the United States, Country of Origin and State of Residence: October 1992" (Washington, D.C.: Statistics Division, Immigration and Naturalization Service, 1994).
8. Warren, "Estimates of the Unauthorized Immigrant Population."
9. U.S. Immigration and Naturalization Service, *1993 Statistical Yearbook*, (Washington, D.C.: U.S. Government Printing Office, 1994), table 23.
10. B. Lindsay Lowell and Zhongren Jing, "Unauthorized Workers and Immigration Reform: What Can We Ascertain from Employers?" *International Migration Review* 28 (Fall 1994):427–48; Rosanna Perotti, "IRCA's Antidiscrimination Provisions: What Went Wrong?" *International Migration Review* 26 (Fall 1992):732–53; David Weissbrodt, *Immigration Law and Procedure in a Nutshell* (St. Paul: West Publishing, 1992).
11. Thomas J. Espenshade, "Does the Threat of Border Apprehension Deter Undocumented US Immigration?" *Population and Development Review* 20 (1994):871–92; Karen A. Woodrow, "A Consideration of the Effect of Immigration Reform on the Number of Undocumented Residents in the United States," *Population Research and Policy Review* 11 (1992):117–44.
12. Espenshade, "Does the Threat of Border Apprehension Deter Undocumented US Immigration?"
13. Sherrie A. Kossoudji, "Playing Cat and Mouse at the U.S.-Mexican Border, *Demography* 29 (1992):159–80.
14. Espenshade, "Does the Threat of Border Apprehension Deter Undocumented US Immigration?"
15. Fix and Passel, *Immigration and Immigrants*, 13.
16. Otis L. Graham Jr., *Rethinking the Purposes of Immigration Policy* (Washington, D.C.: Center for Immigration Studies, 1991), 7.
17. Carol Zabin, Michael Kearney, Anna Garcia, David Runsten and Carole Nagengast, *Mixtec Migrants in California Agriculture* (Davis, Calif.: California Institute for Rural Studies, 1993).
18. Fix and Passel, *Immigration and Immigrants*, 34.
19. Data in the last two paragraphs from Fix and Passel, *Immigration and Immigrants*, 29.
20. Ann P. Bartel, "Where Do the New U.S. Immigrants Live?" *Journal of Labor Economics* 7 (1989):371–91.
21. Bartel, "Where Do the New U.S. Immigrants Live?" See also Frank D. Bean, Jorge Chapa, Ruth R. Berg and Kathryn A. Sowards, "Educational and Sociodemographic Incorporation among Hispanic Immigrants to

the United States," in *Immigration and Ethnicity, the Integration of America's Newest Arrivals*, ed. Barry Edmonston and Jeffrey S. Passel (Washington, D.C.: Urban Institute Press, 1994), 73–100.

22. Warren, "Estimates of the Unauthorized Immigrant Population."

23. Kristin E. Neuman and Marta Tienda, "The Settlement and Secondary Migration Patterns of Legalized Immigrants: Insights from Administrative Records," in Edmonston and Passel, *Immigration and Ethnicity*, 187–226.

24. Sontag, "Politicians Treating Illegal Immigration Softly in New York."

25. See, in particular, George Borjas, *Friends or Strangers, the Impact of Immigrants on the U.S. Economy* (New York: Basic Books, 1990), and "National Origin and the Skills of Immigrants in the Postwar Period," in *Immigration and the Work Force, Economic Consequences for the United States and Source Areas*, ed. George J. Borjas and Richard B. Freeman (Chicago: University of Chicago Press, 1992), 17–47.

26. Julian Simon, *The Economic Consequences of Immigration* (Oxford: Basil Blackwell, 1989), chs. 3, 4, and Vernon M. Briggs Jr. and Stephen Moore, *Still an Open Door? U.S. Immigration Policy and the American Economy* (Washington, D.C.: American University Press, 1994), 113–22.

27. This argument is made by Fix and Passel, *Immigration and Immigrants*.

28. See George J. Borjas, "The Economic Benefits from Immigration," *Journal of Economic Perspectives* 9 (Spring 1995):3–22; Borjas, *Friends or Strangers*; Fix and Passel, *Immigration and Immigrants*, 32–34; and Elaine Sorensen and Maria E. Enchautegui, "Immigrant Male Earnings in the 1980s: Divergent Patterns by Race and Ethnicity," in Edmonston and Passel, *Immigration and Ethnicity*, 139–61.

29. Barry R. Chiswick, "The Effect of Americanization on the Earnings of Foreign-Born Men," *Journal of Political Economy* 86 (1978):897–921.

30. Fix and Passel, *Immigration and Immigrants*, fig. 11.

31. Bean et al., "Educational and Sociodemographic Incorporation."

32. See Borjas, *Friends or Strangers*, 52–53.

33. Sharon M. Lee and Barry Edmonston, "The Socioeconomic Status and Integration of Asian Immigrants," in Edmonston and Passel, *Immigration and Ethnicity*, 101–38.

34. Bean et al., "Educational and Sociodemographic Incorporation," tables 3.3 and 3.4.

35. Hans Johnson, "A Socioeconomic and Demographic Overview of Women Immigrants in California," testimony presented to the California Select Committee on Statewide Immigration Impact (Sacramento, June 19, 1994).

36. Walter S. McManus, William Gould and Finis Welch, "Earnings of Hispanic Men: The Role of English Language Proficiency," *Journal of Labor Economics* 1 (1983):101–30. For more recent evidence that an inability to speak English hurts earnings potential, see Sorensen and Enchautegui, "Immigrant Male Earnings in the 1980s."

37. Guillermina Jasso and Mark R. Rosenzweig, *The New Chosen People: Immigrants in the United States* (New York: Russell Sage Foundation, 1990), table 8.3.

38. Gillian Stevens, "Immigration, Emigration, Language Acquisition, and the English Language Proficiency of Immigrants in the United States," in Edmonston and Passel, *Immigration and Ethnicity*, 163–85, table 6.2.
39. Interview with Lily Lo, manager of Northeast Community Federal Credit Union in San Francisco, a community development credit union serving Asian immigrants, May 15, 1991.
40. Johnson, "A Socioeconomic and Demographic Overview."
41. Fix and Passel, *Immigration and Immigrants*, 29, 30.
42. Jasso and Rosenzweig, *The New Chosen People*, ch. 8.
43. Portes and Rumbaut, *Immigrant America*, ch. 6.
44. Fix and Passel, *Immigration and Immigrants*, 36.
45. Michael Smith and Bernadette Tarallo, *California's Changing Faces, New Immigrant Survival Strategies and State Policy* (Berkeley: California Policy Seminar, 1993).
46. The literature on this question is reviewed, and a new contribution made, in Harriet Orcutt Duleep and Mark C. Regets, "The Elusive Concept of Immigrant Quality," Policy Discussion paper (Washington, D.C.: Urban Institute Press, 1994).
47. Borjas, *Friends or Strangers*, ch. 3, and Borjas, "The Economic Benefits from Immigration."
48. For examples of this sort of argument, see Chiswick, "The Effect of Americanization"; Barry R. Chiswick, "Is the New Immigration Less Skilled than the Old?" *Journal of Labor Economics* 4 (1986):168–92; Duleep and Regets, "The Elusive Concept of Immigrant Quality."
49. Robert J. LaLonde and Robert H. Topel, "The Assimilation of Immigrants in the U.S. Labor Market," in Borjas and Freeman, *Immigration and the Work Force*, 67–92.
50. Borjas and Freeman, *Immigration and the Work Force*, 9.
51. Calculations by Jasso and Rosenzweig demonstrate that the increasing inequality in incomes among immigrants did not begin in the 1980s, but continued a trend of growing inequality in the 1970s. *The New Chosen People*, 258.
52. Fix and Passel, *Immigration and Immigrants*, fig. 14.
53. Johnson, "A Socioeconomic and Demographic Overview."

4

Why They Come

Why do immigrants come to the United States? In a way, the answer is obvious. They come to improve their prospects, to get better jobs, to earn more income, to raise their standard of living, to provide more promising opportunities for their children.

The simple answer is doubtless correct. The attractiveness of the United States to immigrants is at least partly its prosperity; as long as the United States remains one of the richest countries, it will surely attract immigrants. The simple answer is not the complete answer, however. If the relative prosperity of the United States were the only cause of immigration, the flow always would have been greatest from the poorest countries. It has not been. When England was the world's richest country, for example, it provided most of the immigrants to the United States. When other European countries began to grow economically and catch up to England in the nineteenth century, they displaced England as the principal source of immigrants to the United States. The question of why immigrants come is more complicated than it first appears.

It is important to the debate on immigration to understand what has caused

A lot of times I've sat down and wondered, am I doing the right thing? I think, jeez, these are just poor people trying to feed their families.

—Agent Joe Ralph, Border Patrol[1]

Alone I would not have come. It was 90 percent for my children.

—Tung Choy, a Hong Kong immigrant who shines shoes at the Four Seasons Hotel, New York[2]

the recent acceleration. Most of the arguments about immigration end up with some sort of policy recommendation: to reduce immigration, to increase it, to change the countries of origin or the skill levels, to block unauthorized entries more completely, to rethink refugee policy and so forth. Policies to change the immigrant flow are in danger of being ineffective, however, if they are developed in ignorance of the forces that lead people to come in the first place.

A Multitude of Patterns

Almost the first thing one notices about immigration is how varied and multifaceted it is. The very meaning of immigration differs among different groups of people. Immigration is perhaps typically thought of as a once-and-for-all decision. People decide to pack up their bags, say goodbye to their neighbors, move to the United States and make a permanent commitment to their new country. In some cases, though, this is not what happens at all. Some people immigrate without cutting their ties to their home countries, intending to stay for only a brief time. After immigrating, they move back home, perhaps in their old age, but perhaps much earlier; some move back and forth frequently. They sometimes maintain personal connections, property and even jobs in both places.

Different groups of immigrants have had different sorts of commitments when they first arrived. Italians, for example, whose immigration began in earnest toward the end of the nineteenth century, often moved back and forth across the ocean, sometimes as often as annually. Many Italians entered the United States as young people, spent their working lives there, then returned to Italy in retirement. In contrast, Jews have usually made a permanent commitment to the United States upon arrival. The victims of persecution throughout Europe, they have had little to return to in their countries of origin.

Perhaps the least permanent immigrants into the United States have been the Mexicans, the largest group of entrants in the latest wave. To be sure, some people of Mexican origin have been in the United States for generations, and some recent Mexican immigrants have no doubt that they are in the United States to stay. Many others cross the border frequently, however. They maintain an active presence on both sides of the border, to such an extent that many areas in both countries are now best viewed as transnational communities.

People move to the United States for a variety of reasons. Part of the fascination of learning about the subject is to begin to understand the variety, not to try to reduce it to a single cause. Jorge Durand and Douglas Massey illustrated this particularly clearly in the case of Mexican immigration to the United States.[3] In a review of studies of thirty-seven Mexican communities, they found enormous differences. Some migrants came from relatively stable communities, others from disrupted communities. Some intended to leave Mexico for good, others for only a brief time. Some migrants were from the poorest stratum of their communities; others were relatively prosperous. Some owned land at home, some did not and some used their U.S. earnings to purchase land. In some cases, the commercialization of local agriculture opened new options to poor people and therefore reduced immigration to the United States; in other cases, commercialization led to unemployment, deprivation, and more emigration. Some communities sent almost exclusively adult men to the United States, whereas others sent balanced groups of women and children along with the men. In some Mexican communities, a majority of the people had migrated to the United States at some point in their lives, and in other communities only a small minority. Among the thirty-seven communities, almost every possible pattern was found. Durand and Massey concluded that the social structures of individual communities differ greatly, that it is the interaction of community structure with individual and family preferences that leads to the decision to migrate and that therefore a large number of different patterns and causes naturally emerge.

Students of migration have approached the subject from many perspectives. Some use economic models, some sociological. Some studies focus on social change at a large-scale level, some on individual decision making. Some are historical, others are ethnographic and still others are abstract and even mathematical. Naturally this variation leads to vigorous scholarly debate among the practitioners. One of the interesting features of the research, however, is how compatible most of the approaches are with one another. Almost all have something useful to add to our understanding, and almost all can be verified empirically.[4]

This chapter reviews the current thinking about the causes of migration. It begins with the simple "push-pull" approach, which concentrates on income differences between sending and receiving countries. It turns then to the idea of social dislocation, rather than low income, as the principal cause of emigration. The two following sections deal with the demand for labor in the United States as a cause of immigration. The next two sections consider the decision-making processes of immigrants, first on an individual and then on a family level. Finally, the importance of immigrant networks is explored.

Push and Pull

The first serious scholarly attempt to understand the causes of migration was by E. G. Ravenstein, who published a paper entitled "The Laws of Migration" in 1889.[5] Although some of his laws seem dated to a modern observer, others are still relevant and have influenced much of the thinking among today's investigators. People migrate, said Ravenstein, because of "the desire inherent in most men to 'better' themselves in material respects." They tend to leave areas characterized by surplus population, unemployment and poverty, and they are attracted to areas with expanding employment and good wages.

Later students of migration summed up Ravenstein's insight—while violating the grace of his prose—by referring to these forces as "push" and "pull" factors. Some migrants were thought to be influenced primarily by push factors, others by the pull of their new country. For decades, "push-pull" was the principal idea that people used to explain migration. It is still a useful notion, although it has been supplanted by more modern formulations.

In an influential paper, economists John R. Harris and Michael P. Todaro proposed a simpler and more elegant way of showing the causes of migration.[6] They combined the push and pull factors by looking at the gap in economic conditions between the sending and the receiving areas. Their model was developed for rural-to-urban migration within a single country, but it can easily be applied to international migration as well. Harris and Todaro assert that migration will continue from a sending to a target area as long as expected earnings in the latter exceed earnings in the former.

The hypothesis is a little trickier than it first appears. A potential migrant is thought to compare his or her *actual* earnings in the home country with *expected* earnings in the new country. The point is that the person knows what earnings are in the sending area (because he or she is actually receiving them) but can only speculate about what earnings may be in the country of destination. Actual wage rates in the target country are fairly easily determined; what is not known is whether the migrant will land a job paying that wage rate. The expected wage is equal to the actual wage in the country of destination, multiplied by the probability of getting a job; since the probability of employment is always less than one, the expected wage is less than the actual wage. The higher the unemployment rate in the country of destination, the lower the probability that the potential migrant will find a job—and hence the lower the expected wage rate is. The Harris-Todaro model therefore predicts that immigration will be greater (a) the lower the wage in the country of origin, (b) the higher the wage in the country of destination and (c) the lower the unemployment rate in the country of destination.

The model works this way. If there is a gap between the wage in the sending country and the expected wage in the target country, immigration will proceed. When the immigrants arrive, some will get jobs at the relatively high wage of the target country and others will be disappointed. Two consequences will ensue in the target country. First, downward pressure will be exerted on the wage rate. With more people competing for jobs, employers will find it possible to hire at lower wage rates. As the wage rate in the target country falls, the country becomes less desirable for potential migrants, and immigration slows. Second, the unemployment rate will rise in the target country, because some newcomers will be unsuccessful in finding jobs. The increase in the unemployment rate lowers the probability of finding a job, and this in turn lowers the expected wage in the target country, independently of any change in the actual wage. As unemployment rises, immigration again tapers off. Eventually, in an equilibrium state, immigration will have lowered the actual wage and increased the unemployment rate so as to reduce the probability of an immigrant's getting a job to such an extent that the expected wage in the target country is equal to the actual wage in the sending country. At this point, immigration ceases.

There is more to the story. Suppose economic growth is proceeding in the target country. Then the tendency of immigration to lower wages and increase unemployment will be countered by economic growth, which tends to raise wages and lower unemployment. If this happens, immigration may continue.

As another possibility, suppose that workers in the target country succeed in achieving an increase in wages. If the probability of getting a job is not affected, the expected wage will rise and immigration will increase. This, in turn, will cause the unemployment rate to rise until the expected wage falls back to its original level. In other words, the same expected wage (and the same level of immigration) can occur with a moderate wage rate and a high probability of getting a job or, alternatively, with a high wage rate and a low probability of getting a job (because of high unemployment).

In sum, the Harris-Todaro model points to differences in wages and, more generally, expected incomes as the chief cause of immigration. Surely differences in incomes are important. Table 4.1 contains information about the fifteen countries that sent the most immigrants to the United States in 1993, in descending order of the number of migrants. For most of the countries, the World Bank has estimated gross domestic product (GDP) per capita. This is a measure of the value of the total output of goods and services over a year, divided by the population. The output of every country is divided unequally among its population—still, the average figure of GDP per capita gives at least an indication of differences in standards of living and average wages among different countries.

The table shows that for each of the principal sending countries, average income was lower than that in the United States. In all but two of the sending countries, income was substantially lower. Therefore, even if the U.S. figure has to be discounted—because the probability of getting a job was less than one—in thirteen of the fifteen cases, a large gap remained between average earnings at home and potential earnings in the United States, and the Harris-Todaro model would predict a flow of immigration.

Immigrants cannot count on earning a wage at the average level of U.S. residents, particularly if they arrive with little education and low skills, as most coming from Latin America do. Nevertheless, the gap between the income figures of most sending countries and those of the United States is sufficient to make it virtually certain that potential earnings are higher in the United States. Overall, the comparative international figures are at least consistent with the hypothesis that the hope for a higher income is what drives migration to the United States. A number of careful empirical studies have shown that international differences in wage rates are tied to immigration.[7]

Table 4.1 reveals that this cannot be the whole story, however. The world's poorest countries do not send the most immigrants, and some prosperous countries send a considerable number. Note, for example, that the lowest ranking countries in the table are India and China, but they are not the world's poorest countries. According to the World Bank, they rank eighteenth and twenty-eighth, respectively. Below them on the scale of world income are many of the African countries, which send relatively few immigrants. The source of the largest number of immigrants is Mexico, which is a poor country in comparison to the United States but not in comparison to many other countries, including most of the rest of Latin America. Canada's average income is almost indistinguishable

Table 4.1 1992 GDP per Capita in Principal Immigrant Sending Countries

Country	Rank*	GDP per Capita (U.S. Dollars)
Mexico	99	3,470
China (Mainland)	28	470
Philippines	46	770
Vietnam	—	[100–675]
Russia	84	2,510
Dominican Republic	58	1,050
India	18	310
Poland	76	1,910
El Salvador	62	1,170
United Kingdom	117	17,790
Korea	106	6,790
Canada	120	20,710
Jamaica	68	1,340
Iran	81	1,648
Taiwan	—	—
United States	127	23,240

* Out of the 132 listed by the World Bank; the higher the rank, the more prosperous the country.

From *World Development Report 1994* by the World Bank, table I, pp. 162–63. Copyright 1994 by The International Bank for Reconstruction and Development/The World Bank. Reprinted by permission of Oxford University Press, Inc.

from that of the United States, and Britain's is only a fraction lower, yet both are on the list of the top fifteen immigrant senders.

Social Dislocation

Although the gap in relative incomes influences immigration, so too must other factors. Economists, demographers and other social scientists have come up with an extensive series of explanations.[8] They range from international trade, investment and warfare on the one hand to the circumstances affecting individual and family decision making on the other.

Research has shown that one of the most important factors leading to emigration is social dislocation. When people have a secure niche in their community, when they are expected to and are able to fill a role that their parents and their grandparents before them filled, they are unlikely to want to move. When their community is altered, when the familiar social roles are taken from them, when their place in the world is uncertain, they may want to or may have to move.

Chapter 2 showed how important this process was in explaining the different waves of European migration to America. When southeastern Europe was backward, stagnant and feudal, it sent out few emigrants, but when capitalism destroyed the feudal system, millions of people were wrenched from their land and from their occupations, and some of them sought to make new lives across the ocean. It was the anti-Semitism and the pogroms of the nineteenth and twentieth centuries that forced the Jews to migrate, and the potato famines that forced out the Irish.

The migration that results from social dislocation does not fit well in the framework of the Harris-Todaro model. Perhaps we can understand the potato famine as lowering the Irish standard of living and therefore increasing the motivation to look elsewhere for employment. But the capitalist penetration of central Europe actually brought with it an overall increase in incomes and an increase in the standard of living. According to the Harris-Todaro model, this should have reduced migration. Capitalism destroyed communities and traditional ways of life, however, and it thereby instigated migration.

Social, economic, political and military changes have enveloped parts of the third world in the latter part of the twentieth century much faster than was the case in nineteenth-century Europe. Vast numbers of people have been jarred out of communities and relationships to which they had been accustomed. It is among these people whose life circumstances have been altered by social change that one is most likely to find emigrants.

In a series of books and papers, Saskia Sassen of Columbia University has shown the ways in which capitalist international relations between economically advanced countries and the third world have intensified, leading to the transformation of traditional ways of life and the generation of migration flows.[9] Migration to the United States has been particularly strong from countries that have absorbed a disproportionate amount of American foreign investment, she argues.

Korea, for example, is a prosperous third world country, with a relatively high amount of American investment and an exceptionally fast rate of economic growth. From 1970 to 1992, the Korean economic growth rate was 9.5 percent a year, compared with the world rate of just over 3 percent.[10] Looked at through the lens of the Harris-Todaro model, Korea is generating the jobs and the income that should keep its people at home, yet it is one of the principal source countries of U.S. immigration. The same is true of Taiwan and, to a lesser extent, of the Philippines. Although Mexico's performance in economic growth has been less impressive than that of some of the East Asian countries, it too has used foreign investment to transform large parts of its rural and urban economies.

Why should economic growth lead to an increase rather than a reduction in emigration? It is because capitalist economic development changes the structure of production, upsets working relationships between people and transforms communities. Economic development in rural areas of the third world frequently leads to the replacement of traditional, customary communities by modern commercial arrangements. Where formerly peasants had access to enough land to provide for their subsistence, now employers hire a labor force and cut employment if it is not cost-efficient. Where once the land was used to produce subsistence for the local population, now it is dedicated to producing food and agricultural raw materials for export, either to international markets or to the growing cities in the same country. Land once divided into small plots is now consolidated, for efficiency. Where once many people worked in primitive conditions, now machinery, herbicides and fertilizer take their places. Some peasants find that they cannot compete with the more efficient commercial growers. Paradoxically, therefore, as agricultural production is rising, agricultural workers are forced off the land.

People forced off the land are not necessarily forced out of the country, since manufacturing and other urban jobs are expanding. Once they have left their home communities and are searching for new places, however, the nearby city may hold no particular attraction for them. Many third world cities are chaotic, dangerous places where social connections are easily broken. Many rural migrants make the longer journey to the United States.

Moreover, urban job growth is generally insufficient to absorb the outflow of rural people plus the natural population growth. Factories in Mexico and in East Asia tend to hire young women who are unskilled, low paid and have "nimble fingers." Many are hired for a few years, then laid off to make way for still younger workers. This employment pattern has the effect of leaving many of the men unemployed and also many of the older women. Most third world cities are now plagued by growing urban slums, populated by people who have been rejected by both the rural and the urban economies. The slum populations are growing at the same time that production of goods and services is increasing. More people are trapped in the "informal" economy, hawking goods on the street, scavenging, carrying bags at airports, hiring out occasionally for substandard pay and struggling to stay just at the margin of existence. Prostitution has expanded greatly in many areas. These labor patterns are not "traditional"; they are the result of the dislocation of social life caused by economic growth, population growth, capitalist penetration and commercialization.

In a world of rapid population growth, the commercialization of production may be a necessity. It may be that only the application of capitalist organization and technology can provide the food and the other goods and services that are needed. Some hopeful signs exist in countries such as Korea and Taiwan, which have embraced market capitalism and have been rewarded by growing output and an improved standard of living for their people. At the very least, however, one can say that the transition to commercial capitalism is painful, disruptive and dislocating. One need look no further than the agony of the former Soviet Union for confirmation of this. Among many other effects, the triumph of commercial capitalism creates a group of people whose ties to their former communities have been eroded and who are therefore prime candidates for emigration.

Although some authors, like Sassen, insist on the close connection between American foreign investment and social dislocation, the actual connection has often been weak, particularly in recent years. From the end of the Second World War until about 1980, the outflow of capital from the United States to the rest of the world, including the third world, was massive. Since 1980, however, the balance of foreign investment has been strongly in the reverse direction, from other countries into the United States. During the 1980s, the international debt crisis resulted in almost a complete cessation of foreign investment in Mexico, Venezuela, Brazil and other Latin American countries and a sharp slowdown in economic growth. Social upheaval did not stop, however, and emigration increased. The kind of economic change that uproots people and makes emigrants of them should be understood, therefore, as resulting from many causes, not just foreign investment.

Social upheaval has been a large part of the reason for the acceleration in emigration from Mexico. Early in the century came the Mexican Revolution, a massive movement that arose in response to severe inequalities in landholding and power but failed to reverse those inequalities. Later came rapid population growth, accompanied by terribly uneven economic change and commercial penetration.

The growth rate of the Mexican population has been particularly high. In the 1960s, it reached the extraordinary level of 3.5 percent a year, enough to cause the population to double in twenty years, if sustained. Eventually birth rates fell, causing the population growth rate to abate to 3 percent in the 1970s and 2 percent in the 1980s. The population grew from 14 million at the turn of the century to 26 million in 1950, 48 million in 1975 and 85 million in 1992, with figures of 99 million projected for 2000 and 136 million for 2025.[11] The growth was so fast that it contributed to tremendous upheavals: huge numbers migrating from the countryside, the growth of urban slums, the multiplication of the population in Mexico City, growing joblessness and poverty. An elite of landholders, industrialists and privileged workers steadily distanced themselves economically from the majority of the people. Successive presidents failed to take the sorts of actions that might have improved the standards of living of the poorest. The Mexican government allowed the country to run up one of the biggest external debts in the world, and it was then forced almost to the international equivalent of bankruptcy. As the government dealt with its debt crisis in the 1980s by instituting an austerity program, millions of people were pushed out of their comfortable middle-class lives—and malnutrition and poverty rose.

In the 1990s, Mexico plunged into a new series of economic and political crises. In the early years of the decade, the country turned away from a state-managed economy to the free market, away from an inward-looking, self-sufficient strategy to competition in export markets, away from high tariffs to free trade. The shift in economic strategy advantaged some sectors but disadvantaged others, particularly areas of agriculture, which could not compete against more efficient foreign producers. Once again, jobs were lost and communities were battered. When combined with long-standing discrimination against Indians, expulsions from the land and human rights abuses, these economic changes led both to the emigration of Indians[12] and to the rebellion in the southern state of Chiapas that broke out in early 1994. In 1995, the values of the Mexican peso and the Mexican stock market both plummeted, as foreign investors lost confidence in government policies and in the strength of the economy. All this turmoil disrupted the lives of poor and middle-income Mexicans, lowering their incomes, destroying their jobs and disrupting their communities.

Whereas the Harris-Todaro model predicts that economic growth in the third world will reduce the pressure for international migration, the social dislocation perspective sees economic growth as generating emigration. A good example of the two perspectives can be seen in the debate over the consequences of the North American Free Trade Agreement (NAFTA).[13] Beginning in 1994, NAFTA eliminated tariffs between Mexico, Canada and the United States. The hope of the signatories was that NAFTA would raise income levels in all three countries, but most analysts expected Mexico, with a relatively small and poor economy, to gain the most. If this prediction turns out to be correct, and if immigration responds mostly to the gap in living standards, as in the Harris-Todaro formulation, NAFTA will reduce Mexican immigration to the United States. Some proponents of NAFTA argued for it on exactly these grounds: Americans had the option, they said, of accepting Mexican goods in their markets or Mexican people on their soil.

It is possible, however, that NAFTA will have the opposite effect, that it will increase immigration. NAFTA is one component of the intensification of economic integration between the United States and Mexico. With it will come increased trade of goods and services and increased flows of investment capital. Production of more goods will be shared by the two countries, some components produced in Mexico and some in the United States. The commercialization of Mexican agriculture will accelerate, as will the growth of low-wage factory jobs, particularly for young women. Although some sectors of the Mexican economy will expand because of the new opportunities for export, other sectors will contract because of U.S. competition. Mexican producers of corn and beans, for example, may not be able to compete with U.S. producers and may have to lay off much of their labor force. In the long run, these workers (or their children) may find employment in sectors of the economy that are stimulated by NAFTA—but meanwhile, they will be unemployed or underemployed. All these changes will buffet Mexican communities, dislocate their people and produce more emigrants.

The conventional wisdom about NAFTA is that although the adjustments to free trade may increase emigration from Mexico in the short run, the higher rate of economic growth that is likely to ensue will reduce emigration in the long run. This may turn out to be true, but the long run may be very long. A doubling of the standard of living in Mexico will probably not do the trick, at least if the example of Korea is relevant. As Table 4.1 showed, incomes in Korea are twice those in Mexico, yet migration from Korea to the United States has accelerated in recent years.

A different sort of example of dislocation leading to migration is the Vietnam War. Decades of French and then American involvement in what was really a Vietnamese civil conflict led to hundreds of thousands of deaths and injuries, enormous property damage, the destruction of whole villages, the decline of a once rich agricultural sector and, once the Americans and their allies were defeated, political retribution. The war's destruction was not confined to Vietnam but extended to Cambodia and Laos, even to the isolated mountain Hmong people.

The war created in its wake a flow of immigration to the United States. The flow became significant in 1975, just as the southern regime that was supported by the Americans was falling to the forces of the north. Many military officials and others who had worked with the Americans were able to leave at that time and avoid the consequences of the defeat. In the succeeding years, a stream of refugees, mostly from the south, escaped from the regime that they regarded as their captor and oppressor. The desperate stories of the "boat people" became numbingly familiar. Refugees left secretly in small, often unseaworthy boats, hoping to reach port in the Philippines, Malaysia, Singapore, Thailand, Indonesia, Japan or Hong Kong. Some were intercepted by the Vietnamese authorities; others were captured and robbed, raped or murdered by pirates and still others were lost at sea. Some arrived at their destinations only to be confined to refugee camps, and many of those people were returned against their will to Vietnam.[14] Some succeeded in making the entire journey, arriving at last in the United States.

It is true that Vietnamese incomes are less than American, but this was hardly the cause of the emigration. The income gap had existed for decades without causing a migrant flow. The cause of the emigration was the military destruction of the way of life the migrants had known.

The Destination: Pull Forces

What explains the destination of the migrants? Why do some choose the United States and others choose Canada, a European country or another third world country? Income gaps cannot explain the choice, since there are many countries with relatively high average incomes. Proximity doubtless has something to do with the choice; Mexicans choose the United States at least in part because of the long common border. Proximity cannot be the whole explanation, though, since many migrants travel great distances.

Part of the answer has to do with the links that have been established between economically advanced countries and certain third world areas, links that serve to pull the migrants along particular paths. The forces from abroad that destroyed old communities and ways of life have become familiar to the victims. The world has been interconnected for centuries, since the formation of the great European empires. An enormous variety of bonds have been built up in such spheres as trade, foreign investment, technology transfer, language, ideology, education, warfare and the memory of imperialism.

Before 1960, when Vietnamese migrants left their country, they frequently went to France, because most parts of Vietnam had been part of the French empire for a century. Many Vietnamese spoke French, understood something of French culture and had personal connections with people in France. After the massive American involvement in the war, however, Vietnamese refugees came overwhelmingly to the United States, not to France. The American connection was dominant.

The links created by economic penetration are less dramatic than those of warfare, but they are more pervasive and longer lasting. The European empires were built in part to support the export of primary products, both agricultural and mineral, from the third world to Europe and the United States. Public and private institutions were set up to facilitate the trade, and extensive transportation networks carried the goods. The formal empires are behind us, but the trading patterns remain, supplemented now by networks of foreign investment. For potential migrants, these economic links create a familiarity with a particular developed country; the local people use the foreign products, absorb the advertising and perhaps even work in the factories that have been designed abroad. The transportation networks established for trade create a communications link with the foreign country and reduce the travel costs to that country.

Ideological and cultural links are just as important. Many West Africans learned French in schools that were designed on a French model, so they feel more comfortable immigrating to France. The Indian subcontinent was ruled by the British, with the consequence that the English language and English schools predominated; hence Indians and Pakistanis have been drawn to Britain. The Americans did less exporting of educational models, but they have dominated international popular culture with movies, television programs, magazines and mass advertising. As communications and media links have expanded in Mexico and throughout Latin America, migrants from those areas have been drawn increasingly to the United States.

The attraction the United States has for migrants is a consequence not only of economic and cultural linkages to third world areas but also of the structure of American industry and the demand for labor in the United States. Many individuals, groups and broader social forces in the United States actively encourage particular streams of immigration.

In previous eras, American companies sent recruiters to foreign countries to seek out unskilled, low-paid labor. Employers sometimes ordered immigrant workers just as they ordered raw materials and supplies. Historian Ronald Takaki has found bills from Hawaiian employers around the turn of the twentieth century for commodities such as tobacco, Portuguese laborers, lumber, canvas, Japanese laborers, fertilizer and Filipinos, all apparently undifferentiated.[15] When the first railroads were built from the U.S. border to the interior states of western Mexico in the late nineteenth century, representatives of U.S. firms rode them, trying to entice people north to work in the farms and the factories. The patterns that were established at that time persist; western Mexico, which is not the poorest area of the country, is still the source of a disproportionate share of Mexican immigrants to the United States.

Chapter 3 showed that there are two fairly distinct types of immigration into the United States—one predominantly Asian, composed of people who are generally well educated and able to compete for good jobs, the other predominantly Mexican and Caribbean, made up of people whose skills qualify them for only the worst-paying jobs in the country. American firms have been fairly passive in response to the first group, but they have actively sought the low-paid Latino immigrants.

Today, American firms seldom send recruiters abroad, but they encourage immigration in other ways. Companies were the most active group arguing for the amnesty provisions of the 1986 Immigration Reform and Control Act (IRCA), provisions that allowed 3 million undocumented immigrants to legalize their status. Agribusiness interests were particularly successful, achieving lenient terms for agricultural workers. Business lobbyists also pressured for the increase in immigrant numbers that was permitted in the 1990 Immigration Act.

A wide range of economic sectors in the United States depends on low-wage immigrants: immigrants dominate the workforce in such areas as agricultural labor, canning and packing, textiles and hotel service. These are among the sectors that do not require highly trained and skilled workers but are under great competitive pressure to keep their costs low. Firms whose survival and profits depend on cheap labor frequently seek immigrants. Many immigrants are willing to work for wages that are low by American standards, and they are less apt to unionize than are American workers. These businesses frequently place the responsibility for hiring in the hands of an immigrant, who in turn provides jobs for his or her kin and neighbors from back home, thereby encouraging the flow of new entrants.

The type of immigration is influenced by the sectors of the U.S. economy to which the migrants move. Durand and Massey point out that the character of Mexican immigration is different, depending on whether the migrants are bound for rural or urban occupations.[16] Migrants working in agricultural jobs are more likely to have legal documents, and migrants working in urban jobs are more likely to be undocumented. The reason for this is that growers have a long history of working collectively and politically to assure a steady stream of legal migrant labor. Their success in shaping the IRCA legislation was not their first; it was preceded by the Bracero program. Mexican migration to rural areas also includes a higher proportion of women and children than does migration to urban areas.

Still, the majority of today's immigrants come to cities, not rural areas: to New York, Los Angeles and Miami in particular. Sassen calls these "global cities," not just because of their immigrants but because of their strategic role in the emerging transnational economy.[17] They are the hubs of planning, managing, marketing and banking, with connections to every continent and almost every country. The linkages that promote immigration from the third world are more direct to those three and a few other cities than to the United States as a whole. These global cities are not generating new blue-collar manufacturing jobs; those jobs are disappearing, to other parts of the country and abroad. The global cities create a tremendous demand, though, for low-paid workers: for the service workers who support the business functions and the lifestyles of the global managers, and for the sweatshop workers who toil in textile and other industries that compete directly with imports from low-wage countries. As immigrants are pulled into the global cities, they play a role in the new international economic division of labor.

The cities have particular niches for immigrant women. Until recently, not a great deal of research was done on the economic role of women immigrants; it was assumed implicitly that they came simply to be with their husbands and families. For many of them, however, this is not true. Many adult female immigrants are single, and even for the married women, work is a principal motive for immigration. An interesting survey, administered over six years to undocumented women passing through the border city of Tijuana, found that fully 70 percent said that they were going to the United States to seek work. Many were also crossing the border to reunite with a spouse or other family members, but the most important goal was work.[18] In the cities, those with the fewest skills and/or without documents find housekeeping and child-care jobs, sometimes as live-in maids, sometimes on a day-work basis. They clean rooms in hotels, do janitorial work in offices and work in restaurants and in low-skill manufacturing jobs. They do the low-paid "women's work" that technology has not found a way to modernize.

Dual Labor Markets

A well-articulated way of thinking about the "pull" forces affecting immigration to the United States is the hypothesis of the "dual labor market."[19] According to this view, some jobs in the U.S. economy are desirable to residents. These jobs are stable, they pay well, they require skills and they often involve working with expensive capital equipment. Other jobs are undesirable to residents. They are temporary and inse-cure, are low paying and carry low status. They are necessary jobs, but American residents would prefer not to perform them—and to the maximum extent possible, they do not. Since businesses have to get the work done, they hire immigrants to be busboys, crop pickers, dish-washers, day laborers, and so on. Immigrants are willing to perform these jobs because, although the pay is low and the working conditions are bad in comparison to other American jobs, both are better than they can obtain at home in, say, Mexico.

Proponents of the dual labor market theory argue that the real force behind immigration is not the individual decisions of the migrants or the conditions of life in the third world, but rather the requirements of American employers. Fearful of a labor shortage, they seek out immigrants to fill the jobs, often aggressively.

An implication of the dual labor market theory is that immigration into the United States is beneficial not only for the immigrants but also for Americans generally. Immigration gives firms access to the labor that they need and that American residents are unwilling to provide. The fact that immigrants are available relieves Americans from the necessity of performing unpleasant jobs. Instead, they are released to fill more attractive jobs. Thus everyone—immigrants, American firms and American workers—benefits.

The dual labor market theory is controversial. Even if it is an accu-rate description of the American workplace, it is relevant only to the immigration of low-skilled, low-wage people, not to the relatively well-educated, predominantly Asian group. The critique goes beyond this, however.

One line of attack maintains that the jobs typically filled by immigrants are insecure and low paying not because they need to be, not because modern technology demands that they be, but only because immigrants are available to fill them. "The presence of [low-skilled] immigrant labor exerts a narcotic effect on employers in low wage industries," writes economist Vernon Briggs. "They become addicted to their presence and become convinced that citizens and permanent resident aliens will no longer do this type of work. But it is the presence of substantial numbers of unskilled immigrant workers in these low wage labor markets that makes these conclusions of employers little more than self-fulfilling prophesies."[20]

This refutation is persuasive. If immigrants were not available, employers would be forced to raise wages and offer better working conditions in order to attract domestic labor. As they did so, and as the cost of labor rose, employers would have an incentive to substitute capital and technology for labor in these areas. This is the story of road building in the United States. Where once it was done by poorly paid immigrant workers using picks and shovels, now it is done by earthmoving equipment operated by well-paid workers. The same would happen in agriculture in the Southwest and in restaurants were the supply of immigrants to dry up: wages would rise, technology would be developed, productivity would increase and domestic residents would be attracted into those areas. If capital and technology could not be substituted for labor in some sectors, those sectors would disappear in the U.S. economy and reappear in low-wage countries, and they would be replaced in the United States by enterprises in which labor was more productive.

A different sort of attack on the dual labor market theory of immigration comes from people who say that there are enough residents in the United States willing to perform these menial jobs, even without improvements in wages and working conditions. Many women, teenagers, African Americans and other poor people are available to take the jobs. The immigrants displace such people from employment. If immigration were cut back, the jobs would still exist and the employment prospects of the most disadvantaged American residents would improve greatly. Chapter 6 returns to this question.

These two criticisms of dual labor market theory have considerable weight. In this age of high technology, the demand for unskilled labor is not inevitable. Were the supply of low-wage, unskilled labor to dry up, the American economy would be able to survive nicely by substituting capital and technology for labor. Moreover, the country has plenty of unskilled labor at home, without having to look abroad.

So dual labor markets are probably not a necessary feature of American industry, and even if they were, they could survive without immigration. The argument that low-skilled immigrants perform jobs that are critical to the long-term health of the U.S. economy does not hold up. The dual labor market theorists are correct to point out, however, that whether or not the connection is inevitable, a massive demand for unskilled labor in fact exists, immigrants fill a large portion of it and many employers are completely convinced that their prosperity depends on a continued flow of cheap labor from abroad.

Individual Decisions:
The Human Capital Approach

Macroeconomic and macrosociological approaches, such as have been discussed so far, can provide insight into why migration streams begin, where they originate and what their destinations are. Today's immigration results partly from the gap in income and employment opportunities, partly from the ways in which commercial economic development has overturned more traditional ways of life, partly from the international connections established between the United States and those areas of the world and partly from the demand for unskilled, low-wage labor in the United States.

None of these approaches illuminates individual decision making very clearly, however. No matter how strong the forces are that lead to international migration, the actual decision to migrate is made by individuals or at most by families, not by countries, and still less by "averages." Economists and sociologists have devoted a lot of attention to understanding the processes by which individuals decide to migrate.

To take just one example, the Harris-Todaro model focuses on the average wage in the sending and the target countries, but the potential migrant earns a particular income at home, not the average income, and has reason to expect a particular job with a particular wage in the United States. Although the average income figures in Table 4.1 may give a hint of the factors that induce migration, they are too general to give the complete picture.

Economists focusing on individual decisions to migrate often do so in the context of what is called human capital theory, a way of thinking about decision making that was pioneered by Nobel Prize winner Gary Becker.[21] According to this framework, people are held to make decisions that will maximize their likely lifetime earnings or wealth. In order to increase their lifetime earnings, they may have to make an investment in themselves, that is, an investment in human capital (as opposed to the more familiar investment in physical capital). This investment is an expense and will be undertaken only if the benefits are thought to outweigh it.

According to this kind of analysis, migration is an investment made for the purpose of increasing lifetime earnings. A person who is considering whether or not to migrate is characterized as estimating his or her potential lifetime earnings after migration and subtracting from them the likely lifetime earnings that will be received if migration is not undertaken. In both cases, future earnings are discounted by a "time preference" factor that takes account of the fact that income in the future is less certain and less desirable than income today. This difference in earnings is the payoff from migration. It is compared with the costs of migration: the transportation costs as well as the psychological costs of living in an unfamiliar environment, learning a new language, leaving one's friends, and so on. If the payoff exceeds the costs, the investment is justified and the migration will be undertaken.

To forestall the most immediate skepticism about this sort of approach, it should be said that few economists think that people actually make these sorts of calculations explicitly. Rather, an economist sets up an explicit, even mathematical, model in order to understand and predict the decisions that people make intuitively. The human capital approach can provide valid insights if people, for the most part, try to do the best they can for themselves in terms of their lifetime incomes. Even this assumption may be incorrect, of course, and it is possible that the human capital approach is misleading, but one should not dismiss it simply on the grounds that people do not make specific mathematical calculations about their future prospects.

The human capital approach is compatible with the macro approaches already discussed. Like the Harris-Todaro model, it predicts that people will move from low- to high-wage areas, in search of higher incomes. Like the social dislocation approach, it predicts that people whose life patterns have been upset may seek greater certainty by moving abroad. The human capital approach offers additional clues about who in the sending countries will emigrate. Emigration is a selective process; usually only a minority of people in a region engage in it. Why them and not others? Perhaps because they have more to gain than those who choose to stay at home.

George Borjas, a student of migration who uses human capital theory, has focused on the role of education.[22] In every country that has been examined, he shows that an additional year of education is associated with additional earnings. Yet the quantitative relationship differs greatly in different countries. For example, Borjas reports a study showing that an additional year of higher education raises income by 5 percent in Germany, 15 percent in the United States and 29 percent in Mexico. Why should such differences exist? One reason is the differences in the relative supplies of well-educated people. Germany enjoys universal high-quality education, so there is a relative oversupply of people with top skills, and this tends to push their earnings down. Mexico, with a weaker educational system, has a shortage of highly qualified people and consequently pays them well. Another possible explanation is the tax system. European countries tend to tax more heavily than other countries; in particular, they tax upper-income people in order to support their comparatively generous welfare systems. As a result, a significant fraction of the additional income that comes with increased education is taxed away. In terms of returns on education, the United States falls roughly in the middle.

How does this relate to the selectivity of immigration? It leads one to predict that those migrating from Europe to the United States will be well educated and highly skilled, and that those migrating from Mexico will be relatively uneducated. A young, well-educated western European is likely to get less reward for additional schooling at home than he or she will get by coming to the United States. But a poorly educated western European is protected by a more complete safety net at home than is available in the United States. For potential migrants in Mexico, the situation is the opposite. In that country, the returns on higher education are high, so a well-educated Mexican can hope to do very well by staying at home. Poor Mexicans may be in desperate straits at home and can reasonably expect higher earnings in the United States. The low skill levels of Mexican and Central American immigrants is a consequence, therefore, not so much of low average incomes in the area—for it is an area of moderate average incomes—but rather of the severely unequal domestic social structure.

The same sort of reasoning helps explain the relatively high skill levels of many Asian and Cuban immigrants. In both Korea and Taiwan, for example, extensive land reform helped bolster the income of the poorest people and ensure that economic development would proceed along a path of fairly high wages. Income surveys in the two Asian giants, India and China, show a relatively small gap between the rich and the poor. The gap in the Philippines is greater, but not remarkably so.[23] In Cuba, the revolutionary regime has been successful in improving the living standards of the poorest.[24] The evening out of economic prospects in that country has come at the expense of the upper-income people, the professionals, the entrepreneurs and the landowners. The result has been that emigration from those countries to the United States has been a relatively attractive prospect for skilled workers, but less so for the poor.

The human capital method can be used to understand migratory flows between Puerto Rico and the mainland. Puerto Rican migration is a particularly interesting case study because, since the migrants are U.S. citizens, the flows result purely from decisions made by the migrants, uncontaminated by legal and administrative constraint. Fernando A. Ramos has shown that income distribution is more unequal in Puerto Rico than on the mainland and that the returns on education are higher in Puerto Rico.[25] Consistent with this, he finds that the Puerto Ricans who choose to move to the mainland are relatively unskilled. Further, of those migrants, the ones who choose to move back to Puerto Rico at a later date are the most skilled. Finally, among the people of Puerto Rican background born on the mainland, those who choose to migrate to Puerto Rico are on average the most skilled. Migration between Puerto Rico and the mainland is a sorting mechanism, allowing those with higher education and skill levels to receive higher rewards on the island and allowing those with lower skill levels to take advantage of the somewhat more egalitarian social structure on the mainland.

Family Strategies

The experience of Mexican immigration has led social scientists to develop new theories of immigration that focus on family decision making.[26] More than any other stream of immigrants in American history, Mexicans come to the United States without breaking their personal and family connections at home. Many travel back and forth across the border frequently. They come to the United States intending not to make a permanent home but to increase their incomes to make better lives for themselves and their families in Mexico. Many urban and rural communities in the Southwest are now dominated by people who feel a more permanent commitment to Mexico than to the United States—and, correspondingly, many communities in Mexico are populated by a majority of people who have spent some significant part of their lives in the United States. Still, this sort of migration leads inevitably to at least some permanent immigration. Even if migration to the United States is seen at the time as temporary—simply a strategy to improve one's prospects at home—it often turns into a permanent commitment.

Some students of migration view families in the source country—frequently Mexico—as making a series of decisions whose purpose is to improve their income and security. One possible strategy is to send one or more family members away—possibly a short distance, possibly to the capital city or possibly to the United States—in the hope that they can earn a better income and use it to help support the entire family back home. The person sent abroad may be gone for only a short time, or perhaps for a long time or even permanently, but that person never cuts his or her ties with the family.

The idea that emigration is a strategy for a family, the majority or at least some of whose members do not emigrate, is consistent with the earlier theories. Emigration will be advantageous for a family if the earning prospects of the emigrant are greater in the United States than at home in, say, Mexico. It will be particularly attractive if the traditional economic roles of the family have been upset. This perspective opens up some other possibilities as well.

One, which has been analyzed most fully by economist Oded Stark and his colleagues,[27] sees the decision to emigrate as part of a strategy for risk aversion. A family in Mexico may be in a risky situation, because all the available jobs are in the same sector of the economy or because all incomes in the area tend to rise and fall together, depending on the vagaries of the local business cycle. A farm family is dependent on the weather, for example, and on changes in commodity prices, over which it has no control. The family can reduce its risk by sending one or several of its members away, to work in a sector that is unconnected to the occupations at home. The new job may have its own risks, but those risks are probably uncorrelated with the risks at home. If the third son stays home, for example, his income will likely fall just when the family needs his income most. If he emigrates, his bad times may come when the family at home is doing well, and when the family is in trouble, his income may help carry them through.

Migration for risk aversion is likely to be most prevalent in poor countries, where the insurance market is less developed than in rich countries. In the United States, for example, farmers can guard against crop losses by taking out crop insurance, and most employees are protected against unemployment, at least for a time, by unemployment insurance. This kind of insurance coverage is much less available in Mexico. So Mexicans may turn to their own solutions, such as the emigration of a family member.

If emigration is a strategy for minimizing risk, it may proceed even in the absence of income differences between countries. For emigration to be attractive to a Mexican family, it is not necessary that the American wage be higher than the Mexican, although that would be an added bonus. It is only necessary that the causes of economic downturns in the two areas be uncorrelated.

Networks

The perspectives examined so far can help explain why migration streams start, why people from some relatively poor areas of the world migrate to the United States while people from other equally poor areas do not and why poor people emigrate from some areas while higher-income people emigrate from others. Douglas Massey has shown, however, that it is one thing to understand the reasons why migration from a community begins initially and quite another to understand how it develops over time.[28] Flows of migration frequently build up, developing their own self-reinforcing logic. The longer a migration stream has been in existence, the broader the group of people who are attracted to participate in it and the more similar the flows look. Migration from one area may initially consist predominantly of young single men, from another area, women, from another, people with some land and from another, the poorest in the community. Over time, these distinctions blur as wider cross sections of communities are enticed to become migrants.

It is networks that broaden the migration streams. The first migrants attract others from their home community. The others attract still others, until the route from the home community to the immigrant community in the United States is well known and well traveled. These networks are an old part of American immigration; the evidence for them is everywhere. European immigrants did not scatter randomly over the country; for the most part, the Germans went to Pennsylvania, the Irish to Massachusetts, the Swedes to Minnesota and the Jews to New York City. Often the migratory patterns were much more particular than that. Migrants from one village in the home country would all move to the same community in the United States.

The pattern is repeated in the latest wave of immigration. In the part of the country that I know best, officers of the South Vietnamese Air Force have settled in a neighborhood of San Jose, California. Residents of several small towns in the Mexican state of Michoacan have moved to Watsonville. A friend of mine from a town in Michoacan says that most of his small community has moved to Watsonville. He had left Michoacan some years back but only recently arrived in the United States. Upon visiting Watsonville, he was amazed to find virtually all his boyhood friends. They do not necessarily intend to stay in the United States. They travel back and forth often, and many of them are without legal documents, but nevertheless, over the years, his childhood community has relocated to a specific point on the central California coast.

The networks consist of more than just the immigrants themselves. The immigrants meet a labor market need in the United States, so American employers have an incentive to reinforce the networks. Some employers make it known that they are happy to hire people who come from the communities of the existing employees and who are known to the local people. An employer may use an immigrant foreman, with the understanding that he will hire his neighbors from home. The employer may be passing the responsibility for illegal labor practices off to a foreman or an independent contractor.[29] The consequence is that a potential migrant knows that his or her chances of landing a job are significantly increased by going to the area where people from the same community are already located.

The formation of networks is reinforced by American immigration laws. The legal bias in favor of family reunification has the effect of attracting people from the same sending community to the same destination. The networks would exist without this legal support, however. They existed in earlier centuries in the absence of immigration laws, and in any case, many of today's network participants are undocumented.

Networks cut the costs of migration. They reduce the uncertainty and the likelihood of being unemployed. They provide a home away from home until the newcomer can get on his or her feet. They increase the likelihood that the immigrants will end up in a community where people speak their language, understand them, know their life problems and like them. The networks significantly reduce the trauma of immigration. They also reduce the demands made on immigrants to change culturally: to learn a new language and develop new skills and new ways of thinking. The networks can seldom protect the newcomers totally from these pressures, but they do so partially, easing the transition into the new society.

The networks are not strong enough to provide an easy transition for everyone. They fail, for example, to protect many women, particularly undocumented women, from harassment and assault during their journey to the United States. Once in their American communities, some women report feeling much more isolated than they did in their home communities. In an ethnography of a Mexican community in the San Francisco Bay area, for example, Pierrette Hondagneu-Sotelo shows how single women working in domestic service are cut off from meaningful social contact with friends and family, sometimes even when the employer is Mexican.[30] Furthermore, not all migrants stay within the confines of their network. Some move out, sooner or later, and interact more fully with other parts of American society.

Still, the networks are strong and growing. After a while they sometimes dominate and even obliterate the original causes of immigration. Once the network is established, the attraction of migration is no longer a specific economic problem at home but rather the existence of so many friends and relatives in the American neighborhood. The network so reduces the costs and raises the payoff to immigration, both economically and psychologically, that it makes migration attractive to a broader group of people.

The closer one looks at the circumstances under which people immigrate to the United States, the more varied and complicated the picture becomes. Different kinds of people decide to relocate, they make varying sorts of commitments to their new country and they come for all sorts of reasons. This is not surprising. The decision to immigrate is made by millions of individuals and their families; there is no reason to think that their circumstances are similar, or that they go through the same thought process. Nevertheless, one can make a few generalizations.

In spite of all the differences, most immigrants are attracted to the United States because it is a prosperous country and also because, compared with other prosperous countries, its doors are relatively open to newcomers. If the United States were not prosperous, with comparatively high wage rates and a normally expanding job market, most people would not want to move there. Other countries are well off, however; the World Bank lists four European countries plus Japan that have higher per capita incomes than the United States.[31] Immigrants come to the United States instead of to those countries because the United States welcomes them—not all who wish to come, but many more than other countries do.

One can return to Ravenstein, push-pull and the Harris-Todaro model to understand a centrally important dynamic of migration. Those approaches fail to tell us much about what regions of the world will send migrants to the United States and what particular people will choose to migrate, but they do lead us to conclude that as long as the United States remains one of the world's most prosperous countries, it will continue to attract immigrants. At least some people will want to come to the United States as long as the earnings they can expect to obtain after immigration exceed current earnings in their countries of origin.

Push-pull is a blunt theory, however. An understanding of exactly who decides to move to the United States requires detailed knowledge of the changing social conditions in source communities, the changing interactions between the United States and other countries, the changing opportunities available to people to improve their life situations and to ensure against catastrophes and the ebb and flow of networks that facilitate international migration.

Notes

1. Quoted in Seth Mydans, "At the Border With Mexico, Agents Push against a Tide," *New York Times* (February 19, 1994), A1.
2. Quoted in Kathleen Deveny, "Immigrants: Still Believers after All These Years," *Wall Street Journal* (July 12, 1994), B1.
3. Jorge Durand and Douglas S. Massey, "Mexican Migration to the United States: A Critical Review," *Latin American Research Review* 27 (1992):3–42. See also Douglas S. Massey, Luin Goldring and Jorge Durand, "Continuities in Transnational Migration: An Analysis of Nineteen Mexican Communities," *American Journal of Sociology* 99 (1994): 1492–1533.
4. Douglas S. Massey, Joaquin Arango, Graeme Hugo, Ali Kouaouci, Adela Pellegrino and J. Edward Taylor, "An Evaluation of International Migration Theory: The North American Case," *Population and Development Review* 20 (1994):699–751; Timothy J. Hatton and Jeffrey G. Williamson, "What Drove the Mass Migrations from Europe in the Late Nineteenth Century?" *Population and Development Review* 20 (1994):533–59.
5. E. G. Ravenstein, "The Laws of Migration," *Journal of the Royal Statistical Society* (1889):241–301.

6. John R. Harris and Michael P. Todaro, "Migration, Unemployment and Development: A Two-Sector Analysis," *American Economic Review* 60 (1970):126–42. The theory is explained in simpler terms in Michael P. Todaro, *Economic Development*, 5th ed. (New York: Longman, 1994), ch. 8.

7. Massey et al., "An Evaluation of International Migration Theory"; Hatton and Williamson, "What Drove the Mass Migrations."

8. A good survey of the theories of international migration is contained in Douglas Massey, Joaquin Arango, Graeme Hugo, Ali Kouaouci, Adela Pellegrino and J. Edward Taylor, "Theories of International Migration: A Review and Appraisal," *Population and Development Review* 19 (1993):431–66. Empirical verification of the theories is considered in a second paper by the same authors, "An Evaluation of International Migration Theory." I am indebted to these papers for many of the ideas in this chapter.

9. See, among other writings, Saskia Sassen, *The Mobility of Labor and Capital, a Study in International Investment and Labor Flow* (Cambridge: Cambridge University Press, 1988); Saskia Sassen, "U.S. Immigration Policy toward Mexico in a Global Economy," *Journal of International Affairs* 43 (Winter 1990):369–83; Saskia Sassen, "Why Immigration?" *Report on the Americas* 26 (1992):14–19.

10. World Bank, *World Development Report 1994, Infrastructure for Development* (New York: Oxford University Press, 1994), 165.

11. World Bank, *World Development Report 1994*.

12. Carol Zabin, Michael Kearney, Anna Garcia, David Runsten and Carole Nagengast, *Mixtec Migrants in California Agriculture* (Davis, Calif.: California Institute for Rural Studies, 1993).

13. One analysis of the likely effects of NAFTA upon immigration is contained in Dolores Acevedo and Thomas J. Espenshade, "Implications of a North American Free Trade Agreement for Mexican Migration into the United States," *Population and Development Review* 18 (1992):729–44.

14. "Kon-Tikis Go Home," *The Economist* (September 2, 1989), 32–33.

15. Ronald Takaki, ed., *From Different Shores, Perspectives on Race and Ethnicity in America*, 2d ed. (New York: Oxford University Press, 1994), 4.

16. Durand and Massey, "Mexican Migration to the United States."

17. In addition to Sassen's works cited earlier, see Saskia Sassen, *The Global City, New York, London, Tokyo* (Princeton, N.J.: Princeton University Press, 1991); Saskia Sassen, "Rebuilding the Global City: Economy, Ethnicity, and Space," *Social Justice* 20 (Fall-Winter 1993):32–50; Saskia Sassen and Alejandro Portes, "Miami: A New Global City?" *Contemporary Sociology* 22 (1993):471–80.

18. Ofelia Woo Morales, "Undocumented Migrant Women Migrating to the United States," testimony presented to the California Assembly Select Committee on Statewide Immigration Impact (Sacramento, July 19, 1994).

19. An elegant exposition of this view is Michael J. Piore, *Birds of Passage, Migrant Labor in Industrial Societies* (Cambridge: Cambridge University Press, 1979).

120 / THE IMMIGRATION DEBATE

20. Vernon M. Briggs Jr., "Immigrant Labor and the Issue of 'Dirty Work' in Advanced Industrial Societies," *Population and Environment* 14 (1993):512.

21. Gary S. Becker, *Human Capital, a Theoretical and Empirical Analysis, with Special Reference to Education*, 2d ed. (Chicago: University of Chicago Press, 1975).

22. George J. Borjas, *Friends or Strangers, the Impact of Immigrants on the U.S. Economy* (New York: Basic Books, 1990), especially ch. 1.

23. For the distribution of incomes in China, India, Korea, Mexico and the Philippines, see World Bank, *World Development Report 1994*, table 30.

24. The World Bank estimates that in 1992, life expectancy was seventy-six years in Cuba and seventy in Mexico; in 1990, 6 percent of the Cuban population and 13 percent of the Mexican population were illiterate. *World Development Report 1994*.

25. Fernando A. Ramos, "Out-Migration and Return Migration of Puerto Ricans," in *Immigration and the Work Force, Economic Consequences for the United States and Source Areas*, ed. George J. Borjas and Richard B. Freeman (Chicago: University of Chicago Press, 1992), 49–66.

26. Massey et al., "Theories of International Migration," is a comprehensive survey.

27. See, for example, Oded Stark and David E. Bloom, "The New Economics of Labor Migration," *American Economic Review, Papers and Proceedings* 75 (1985):173–78, and Oded Stark and D. Levihari, "On Migration and Risk in LDCs," *Economic Development and Cultural Change* 31 (1982):191–96.

28. Massey et al., "Theories of International Migration"; Douglas S. Massey, "Economic Development and International Migration in Comparative Perspective," *Population and Development Review* 14 (1988):383–413.

29. Philip Martin and J. Edward Taylor, "Immigration Reform and Farm Labor Contracting in California," in *The Paper Curtain: Employer Sanctions' Implementation, Impact and Reform*, ed. Michael Fix (Washington, D.C.: Urban Institute Press, 1991), 239–61.

30. Pierrette Hondagneu-Sotelo, *Gendered Transitions: Mexican Experiences of Immigration* (Berkeley: University of California Press, 1994).

31. World Bank, *World Development Report 1994*, table 1.

5

Projecting the Future

This chapter looks into the future. The first question to be taken up is whether the pressure for immigration is likely to continue into the twenty-first century. The answer is yes. Americans may try to reduce immigration and they may be successful, but they will not be able to eliminate the aspirations of millions of foreigners to move to the United States. That being the case, the rest of the chapter considers the demographic implications of high levels of immigration continuing into the twenty-first century. What effects will it have over the long run on the size of the U.S. population, its age distribution and its ethnic composition?

Will the United States Continue to Be a Magnet for Immigrants?

The trend toward high immigration to the United States is not new. Although immigration has been subject to cyclical fluctuations, the number of people wanting to come to the United States has been high since the early nineteenth century.

The United States is once again on the eve of large ethnic transformations.

—Barry Edmonston and Jeffrey S. Passel[1]

Because we have allowed our nation to become seriously overpopulated we are in deep trouble. . . . To start on the path toward a smaller, more sustainable population, we must halt illegal immigration and sharply reduce legal immigration.

—Negative Population Growth, Inc.[2]

121

The fact that immigration fell to low levels in the middle of the twentieth century was a consequence mostly of the restrictive legislation that was passed in the 1920s as well as the extraordinary circumstances of the depression and the Second World War. The legislation of the 1920s was passed precisely because the pressure from foreigners to enter was strong and Americans were afraid of the transformation that might ensue if the potential immigrants were allowed in. As the restrictions on immigration were eased in the latter part of the twentieth century, large-scale immigration resumed.

Chapter 4 looked at the causes of immigration into the United States. None of the causes identified there is likely to disappear, although they will change. As that chapter showed, the Harris-Todaro model of immigration, although so simple that it misses many of the relevant nuances, nevertheless focuses on a central dynamic of immigration. It asserts that immigration will continue as long as expected earnings in the country of destination exceed earnings in the source country. This section examines whether the gap in earnings between the source countries and the United States will be sustained well into the twenty-first century. The first question to ask is whether the standard of living in the third world is likely to rise to the U.S. level.

It is not impossible; it has happened in some countries in the past. Throughout American history, until the 1960s, most immigrants came from Europe. After the Second World War, however, western European economic growth carried most of its countries to income levels that were equivalent to those of the United States or even higher. As a consequence, Europeans now come to America to visit more often than they used to, but not to stay.

Could the same thing happen in the third world? It may happen in parts of it. Economic growth rates in the third world have been marked by enormous variation in recent decades. As historian Paul Kennedy points out, in the 1960s, South Korea and Ghana had similar economies: agrarian-based and poor, with average annual incomes equivalent to just over $200 in American terms.[3] In the intervening three decades, the Ghanaian economy has stagnated, along with most of the rest of Africa, while Korea has grown at such a fast rate that its income is now approaching that of the developed countries. One would not be surprised to see Korea become a magnet for immigrants rather than a source country sometime in the twenty-first century. The same may hold true for some other Asian countries—Taiwan, Singapore, Malaysia and perhaps others.

These will surely be exceptions, however. It is hardly possible that most of the third world could be transformed to such an extent that the gap with the United States and other developed countries will disappear. For one thing, the ecological carrying capacity of the earth may not permit it.[4] Even if that ultimate constraint does not apply, the current trajectories of economic growth in most of the world's relatively poor countries give no hope that they will catch up to the privileged rich. India and China, for example, had remarkable success in the period 1980 to 1992, with the former's per capita income growing at an annual rate of 3.1 percent and the latter's at 7.7 percent. Yet they remained among the world's poorest countries, with average annual incomes still between $300 and $500 in American terms.[5] If the past history of other countries is any guide, their high growth rates will not be sustainable decade after decade. Even if they were, the gap with the rich countries would not be closed in the foreseeable future unless the economies of the latter collapsed.

Turning to other areas of the third world, Latin America, the Middle East and Africa have not, for the most part, enjoyed the economic growth that some parts of Asia have. In the recent past, Latin America has been trapped in an international debt crisis, and the Middle East has been unable to separate its fortunes from the amazing swings, both up and down, in the price of oil. Many African economies have, if anything, declined since the period of independence in the 1960s. No country in these regions is poised to approach the American standard of living in the twenty-first century.[6]

At the time of writing, eastern Europe and the former Soviet Union are in a state of enormous flux, as they attempt to make the transition from communism to an unknown future. In some parts of the area, including, ominously, Russia, recent economic growth has been negative, and suffering has been widespread. Some areas of eastern Europe will likely achieve a reasonable integration into western Europe and will enjoy an improving standard of living, but many will not.

Will the United States remain an attractive target country for international migrants? In all likelihood it will, unless an economic catastrophe occurs. The Harris-Todaro model reminds us to consider at least two features of the American economy: wage rates and the probability that newcomers to the labor market can get jobs at those wage rates.

The principal determinant of wage rates is productivity, or output per worker. Wages are relatively high in the United States because American workers are productive. They are productive because of their skills, training and education, because of the large amount of capital equipment that they work with and because of the advanced technology that is typically used in the American workplace. Will American workers continue to have these advantages?

For quite a long time, the lesson of economic theory was that large international differences in worker productivity could not be maintained, because economic growth would inevitably be transferred from richer to poorer countries. Take, for example, the role of capital. Economic theory concluded that in the rich countries, with a lot of capital per worker, it must become increasingly difficult to find profitable, productive outlets for more capital investment, whereas in the poor countries, with a low capital-labor ratio, the productive opportunities for additional capital investment must be more plentiful. Even if there were no transfer of capital from one country to another, the higher productivity of capital investment in the poor countries would eventually lead the economies of the rich and poor to converge. In addition, the presumption that investment is more profitable in the poor countries than in the rich countries would lead investors to transfer capital funds from the rich to the poor, and this would accelerate the convergence. Similar arguments can be made about the productivity of additional technology and additional education. Logic seemed to indicate that productivity, wages and standards of living in the world would converge, with the poor catching up to the rich.

History tells another story, however. If anything, the world has experienced divergence, not convergence, in the economic fortunes of its various countries. The rich have been able to increase their productivity and grow at a steady rate, but many of the poor have not. During the colonial era, the standards of living of the rich and poor parts of the globe grew further apart. Statistical evidence for the latest quarter century shows that although the world's economies may no longer be diverging, neither are they converging.[7]

If economic theory predicts that poor and rich economies must converge, but history shows no convergence, something must be wrong with the theory. A new generation of economic growth theorists now assert that a critical piece was missing from the old theories. The new theorists, among them Paul Romer, think that advanced, productive economies generate their own new technology at such a rate as to keep them growing and to keep the poorer countries from catching up with them.[8]

Productivity grew quickly in the United States in the immediate postwar period, then slowed to a crawl in the 1980s. Also in the 1980s, the ratio of wages to total income fell. The result of these two trends was that real wages in the United States, adjusted for inflation, stayed more or less constant. Although this slowdown represented a serious setback for American workers, most economists believed that it was temporary and that both productivity and wages would resume a growth path in the future. The early evidence from the 1990s is that this is so, that economic growth is occurring and that real wages are once again increasing.[9]

One can expect, therefore, that the American economy will continue to grow into the indefinite future and that both labor productivity and wages will rise. No theoretical or empirical reason exists to think that growth in the American economy will be any less than growth in the world's poorer regions. Therefore the gap in earnings that drives much of the migration from poor countries to the United States will probably remain well into the twenty-first century, if not beyond.

The Harris-Todaro model identifies an additional factor that might influence immigration into the United States: unemployment. Is it possible that, over the long run, the American unemployment rate might be high enough to discourage immigration?

It is possible, but unlikely. The United States has known at least one period, the Great Depression of the 1930s, when unemployment rates were devastatingly high, perhaps around 25 percent of the labor force in some months. Economists and policymakers have learned a great deal about economic management since that time, however, largely in response to that disaster. Governments now have many more tools, of fiscal and monetary policy, to influence unemployment rates if not control them completely. Furthermore, the electorate holds the federal government responsible for guiding the economy. Nothing is more damaging to a president's prospects for reelection than a stagnating economy and a rising unemployment rate, as George Bush found in 1992. It is unlikely, therefore, that an American government would allow the economy to get so out of hand that unemployment rose to such high rates, over an extended period of years, that immigration into the country would be seriously discouraged.

The American unemployment rate will probably continue to fluctuate around the relatively low levels that have been experienced since the Great Depression. The probability of an immigrant's finding a job will fluctuate with it. These sorts of modest changes in unemployment appear to have virtually no effect on immigration, however. Fix and Passel point out, for example, that although the unemployment rate for immigrants in the United States rose between 1980 and 1990 (from 5.8 percent to 6.4 percent for men, and from 5.7 percent to 8.4 percent for women), the number of immigrants actually increased.[10]

Still, within the context of the Harris-Todaro model, one more possibility remains for reducing immigration to the United States. If immigration itself were so extensive that the competition for jobs drove wage rates in the United States down to third world levels and raised the pool of the unemployed, immigration might cease to be attractive.

Could such a result occur over the long run in the United States? Perhaps. It might seem to be in the interest of some groups in the country. Some industries and owners might welcome a regime of low wages, in the expectation that it would generate high profits. It is not likely, though. Such a social arrangement is probably not even in the long-run interest of the owners of capital in the country. One of the lessons of the depression was that if workers are impoverished, they cannot afford to buy the goods that are being produced, so profits fall, not rise. One could argue that the world of tomorrow will be different, with more international markets, so that American businesses will not have to depend so much on the home market, but in a country in which exports are still only about 10 percent of total output, this is a leap of imagination. Even if a weak domestic market is not a serious problem for American industry in the future, unproductive labor surely would be. A low-paid, high-unemployment labor force would be unproductive. Finally, the United States is likely to remain a democracy, so even if business interests would like a large, low-paid and unskilled labor force, this will not be in the interest of American workers, who make up the majority of the electorate. In all likelihood, therefore, Americans, acting through their government, will take steps to curtail immigration long before it destroys their standard of living.

The necessary condition for immigration, the fact that expected earnings are higher in the United States than in the source countries, is therefore unlikely to disappear in the twenty-first century.

None of the other causal factors is likely to be reversed either, although they will certainly shift among geographical regions. The internationalization of economic relations—trade, foreign investment, technology transfer and the rest—will surely intensify, not diminish. Economic growth will continue to be uneven and erratic. As a consequence, people will continue to be uprooted from their familiar social and work relationships and will have to find new ways to survive. Some of the regions that have been most affected by these sorts of changes in the past may find a new stable social equilibrium, but if so, they will be replaced by other regions. To venture a guess, South Korean economic growth may proceed to such an extent that whatever social dislocation ensues can be handled better at home than through immigration to the United States. Even this is not certain, of course, particularly if the two halves of the Korean peninsula reunify and face the problems of integrating two completely different societies. In any case, one can expect further social conflict and social change in Africa, Latin America and the Arab world, leading to increased emigration from those areas.

Neither is the demand for low-wage labor in the United States likely to decline. If American productivity and wages continue to rise, American firms will face ever-stiffening international competition from low-wage countries and will search continuously for ways of reducing their costs.

It is less certain, but still probable, that the bifurcation of migrant flows will continue: immigrants with low skills coming from countries with large gaps between the rich and the poor, and immigrants with higher skills coming from countries with more equitable income distributions. The numbers seeking to enter the United States from different countries will rise and fall over time, but the list of major source countries will probably continue to include some with high and some with low disparities in income distribution.

The largest group of low-skilled immigrants has come from Mexico. One would be surprised to see a major change in the character of Mexican immigration, although it is possible. Mexico is unlikely to become a more egalitarian society any time soon. It has chosen a path of capitalist, free-market, export-oriented development that will reward the most favored disproportionately. One might object that Korea and Taiwan also chose export-oriented capitalist development and were able to combine this approach with a relatively egalitarian social structure. In both of those Asian countries, however, land reform and other rural programs raised the incomes of the former peasantry and effectively created a floor beneath which few were allowed to fall. In spite of its rhetoric, the Mexican government has not given comparable treatment to its rural poor and is unlikely to do so in the future. Meanwhile, with intensified economic relationships between the United States and Mexico, the pressure for Mexican immigration will grow.

Finally, no sign exists that political and cultural repression is diminishing in the world. For each civil conflict that comes to an end, two seem to replace it. The number of refugees is likely to grow.

Taking all these factors into consideration, one must predict that the United States' attractiveness to migrants from outside its borders will not subside in even the fairly distant future. The particular sources of immigrants may change, as they have quite regularly in the past. It is therefore realistic, even urgent, to consider what the long-run impact on the U.S. population, economy and society will be, should immigration proceed, decade after decade, at the current rate. The rest of the chapter deals with the future demographic effects of such immigration.

Population Projections

Immigration will have a marked effect upon the size, age distribution and ethnic composition of the American population if the immigration rate of the late 1980s and early 1990s continues into the twenty-first century. This can be seen through a series of population projections.

Population projections are not quite the same as predictions. They draw logical conclusions about future population, given certain assumptions about fertility, mortality, immigration and emigration. Even if the projections are prepared accurately, one cannot be certain that the assumptions will turn out to be correct.

The U.S. Bureau of the Census periodically prepares population projections. In 1992, it projected the U.S. population to the year 2050.[11] Although the Census Bureau's are not the only available projections,[12] they are both comprehensive and carefully thought out; they serve well to show the possible future structure of the U.S. population.

The Census Bureau presents several population projections, using combinations of different assumptions about future fertility, mortality and net immigration. For each variable, it has a low, a middle and a high assumption. In the projection that uses the middle assumptions, the U.S. population grows from 249 million people in 1990 to 382 million in 2050, an increase of 133 million, or 53 percent. The projected average rate of increase over this sixty-year period is 0.7 percent.

In this middle projection, the Census Bureau assumes that the fertility of American women will rise slightly, from 2.05 children per woman in 1990 to 2.12 in 2050. This increase is expected to occur because the proportion of Latina and non-white women in the population will increase; they typically have more children than Anglos do. Mortality is expected to improve, with average life expectancy at birth rising from 75.8 years in 1990 to 82.1 years in 2050. Net immigration is projected to stay constant throughout the sixty-year period, at 880,000 a year. The figure of 880,000 is arrived at by subtracting 160,000 emigrants from 1,040,000 immigrants. It is intended to represent roughly the underlying level of net immigration, both legal and unauthorized, into the United States in the late 1980s and early 1990s.

Table 5.1 Four Levels of Annual Net Immigration

Projection	Net Immigration (in Thousands)
Zero immigration	0
Low immigration	350
Middle immigration	880
High immigration	1,370

Fertility, mortality and immigration have fluctuated in the twentieth century, and they may change in the twenty-first. This chapter leaves unexamined the consequences of changing fertility and mortality, above or below their middle levels. It shows, however, how changing the levels of net immigration (Table 5.1) would change the future population.

The projection with zero immigration is certainly unattainable, even if American policymakers should wish it, because of the continuation of illegal immigration. This projection is interesting to consider, however, to see the full effect of immigration on the size and structure of the population in the future. The low immigration projection assumes that legal immigration will fall to about the levels of the late 1970s and early 1980s (around 500,000 a year), that net illegal immigration will fall to 100,000 a year because of more effective enforcement and that net emigration will rise to 260,000. It can be thought of as setting the lowest reasonable limit to net immigration. The high projection assumes that legal immigration will increase substantially because of a rise in family sponsorships, that the emigration of legal immigrants will fall and that the flow of refugees and illegal immigrants will increase. Table 5.2 shows the growth of the American population, from 249 million in 1990, using these four assumptions about net immigration.

The table shows that, in the absence of immigration and with intermediate levels of fertility and mortality, the population would increase by 52 million people, to 301 million, by 2050. Over the sixty-year period, this represents an average annual growth rate of 0.3 percent, but by the end of the period, population growth would slow to almost zero. Without immigration, the United States would reach almost zero population growth in the middle of the twenty-first century, at a population size about 20 percent greater than it is in the early 1990s.[13] The only reason the population is projected to grow in the short run is that there is a disproportionate bulge in the middle, child-bearing,

Table 5.2 Growth of the U.S. Population (in Millions) to 2050

Immigration	Population in 2020	Population in 2050	Increase 1990–2050	Annual Growth Rate 1990–2050	Annual Growth Rate in 2050
Zero	289	301	52	0.3%	0.04%
Low	304	339	89	0.5	0.3
Middle	323	383	133	0.7	0.5
High	340	424	175	0.9	0.6

Some figures may not total correctly, because of rounding.

low-mortality years, a bulge caused by the baby boom a generation ago. Once this bulge and its echoes in subsequent generations disappear, the underlying fertility and mortality schedules will cause births to equal deaths and the population to be unchanging.

The third row of Table 5.2, labeled "middle," shows the projected population if immigration stays constant at roughly the current level. The population will grow by 133 million over the sixty-year period; 81 million of these people will be immigrants or the offspring of immigrants. Put differently, 61 percent of the growth in the U.S. population will be due to immigration, according to this projection. The population will grow at an average annual rate of 0.7 percent over the period, and even at the end of the period it will still be growing at 0.5 percent.

The second and fourth rows show the consequences of low and high immigration, respectively. With low immigration, the population will rise by 89 million people, 37 million (or 42 percent) of whom will be accounted for by immigration. With high immigration, the population will rise by 175 million, with 123 million, or 70 percent, caused by immigration.

Earlier, Chapter 2 showed that over the course of American history, although immigration has been massive at times, it has not accounted for most of the country's population growth. The projections reported in this chapter show how the effect of immigration on population growth is likely to become more important in the future. Using the middle assumptions in Table 5.2, 61 percent of the population increase between 1990 and 2050 will be accounted for by immigration, and only 39 percent by the population resident in the country in 1990. After the middle of the twenty-first century, almost all the growth will be caused by immigration. The change in the demographic impact of immigration is a consequence of the dramatic reduction in the rate of natural increase of the resident population.

A comparison between the first and third rows of Table 5.2 shows the overall demographic impact of immigration if it continues at its current levels. From the point of view of the effects of public policy, however, a more revealing comparison may be between the second and the third rows, since zero immigration is completely impossible. If the nation were to make a major commitment to reducing immigration, something like the second row might occur. This would result in a population in 2050 that was 44 million, or 11 percent, less than in the middle projection. In 2050, the population would still be growing, but at a rate considerably slower than if current levels of immigration prevail.

Age Distribution

Immigration will have a perceptible although modest effect on the age distribution of the American population over the next sixty years. Compared with the resident population, immigrants are concentrated in the age groups from fifteen to thirty-nine, with relatively fewer children and older people. The deficit at the older ages is greater, however, so the median age is significantly lower for newly admitted immigrants than for residents: in 1993, 27.8 years for immigrant men, compared with 32.5 for all men in the United States; and 28.7 for immigrant women, compared with 34.9 for all women.[14] The consequence of this is that immigration will help slow the aging of the American population.[15] The figures are shown in Table 5.3.

In 1990, 25.7 percent of the U.S. population was under the age of eighteen, and 12.5 percent was aged sixty-five or over. The ratio of these two groups to the population of prime working ages, (eighteen to sixty-four), or the dependency ratio, was 62.0 percent. The median age of the population was 32.8 years.

Comparison of the first and second rows of Table 5.3 shows the remarkable changes that would occur in the American age distribution in the absence of immigration. The median age would zoom to 41.1, the proportion of young people would decline somewhat, the proportion of the elderly would almost double and the dependency ratio would increase sharply. This aging of the population would be caused partly by improvements in mortality at old ages but more fundamentally by the decline in fertility from the baby-boom high. A lower

Table 5.3 Age Distribution of the U.S. Population

Projection	Percentage 0–17 Years	Percentage 65+ Years	Dependency Ratio (%)	Median Age (in Years)
1990	25.7	12.5	62.0	32.8
2050				
Zero immigration	22.2	22.8	81.7	41.1
Low immigration	22.9	21.4	79.5	39.9
Middle immigration	23.2	20.6	77.8	39.3
High immigration	23.4	20.0	76.6	38.8

birth rate necessarily leads to the aging of the population, whatever the death rate.[16]

The last three rows, with varying levels of immigration, show that these tendencies will occur in any case but that they will be attenuated, if only a little, by immigration. The fact that immigrants are typically younger than residents will slow the aging of the population somewhat.[17]

Ethnic Composition

The most startling changes are projected to occur in the ethnic composition of the population. Table 5.4 contains a summary of the Census Bureau's projection by ethnic or racial group.

In the table, "Anglo" means non-Hispanic white. Hispanic is a national origin, not a race; Hispanics can be of any race. It should be understood, therefore, that the figures for blacks, Asians and Indians in Table 5.4 are all underestimates, because they omit the Hispanics in those categories.

The Census Bureau cannot—or at least chooses not to—deal with the issue of mixed ethnicity in its projections, in spite of the fact that this is a major feature of American race relations. To take one example, the great majority of Mexicans and Mexican immigrants regard themselves as mestizo, of mixed white and Indian ancestry. Yet the Census Bureau, which is committed to assigning Hispanics into one of four racial groups, classified 91 percent of Hispanics in the United States as white in 1990, just 1 percent as Indian and none as mestizo.

Since children are in fact born to parents of different races—at a significant and increasing rate—the Census Bureau needs a methodology

Table 5.4 Ethnic Composition (%) of the Population

Year	Anglo	Black	Hispanic	Asian/Pacific Islander	American Indian
1950	86.6	10.1	2.6	0.5	0.2
1990	75.7	11.8	9.0	2.8	0.7
2050					
Zero immigration	62.1	17.1	15.8	3.7	1.4
Low immigration	56.1	16.0	18.5	8.2	1.2
Middle immigration	52.7	15.0	21.1	10.1	1.1
High immigration	50.1	14.2	23.1	11.7	1.0

for assigning them to a racial category when making projections. Beginning in 1990, it assigned a newborn to the race of his or her mother. This is the method underlying the projections in Table 5.4. The larger issue of mixed-race ancestry is left unexamined by these projections, however.[18] As the mixtures continue and become more complex over generations, an increasing proportion of people will have difficulty identifying themselves unambiguously as belonging to one or another group, and the Census Bureau's convention of assigning the race of the mother will not help. Ethnic mixing may blur what seem to be rigid racial categories. The Census Bureau is considering introducing some mixed-race categories, but at the date of writing it has not yet come to a decision.

A comparison of the first two rows of Table 5.4 shows that the ethnic composition of the population has changed considerably in the latter part of the twentieth century; this was discussed in Chapter 3. Between 1950 and 1990, Anglos fell from 87 to 76 percent of the population, while the proportion of all the other ethnic groups increased. In part, this was because of higher fertility among the non-Anglos; this is the principal explanation for the increasing proportions of African and Native Americans. The increase in the proportion of the two groups heavily represented in the new immigration—Hispanics and Asians—was more dramatic.

A comparison of the second and third rows of Table 5.4 shows that even in the absence of further immigration, these trends will continue, driven by the fertility differential. Anglos will fall from 76 to just 62 percent of the population by 2050, and the other categories will increase.

In 1990, non-Hispanic white fertility was actually below the replacement level. In all the projections, therefore, this segment of the population declines in the twenty-first century, in absolute numbers as well as proportionately, assuming that their fertility stays constant. The other ethnic groups become larger, both numerically and proportionately, even though the Census Bureau projects that both Hispanic and Asian fertility will decline by 10 percent after 2000.

These trends in ethnic composition will be accentuated by immigration. To the ethnic differential in fertility will be added a much sharper ethnic differential in immigration. The Census Bureau assumes, reasonably, that the ethnic composition of immigrants in the early 1990s will persist into the next century.

The fifth row of Table 5.4 shows the expected ethnic consequences of immigration continued at its current level. The Anglo population will fall from more than three-quarters of the total population to just over one-half by 2050. If the trends are continued beyond 2050, this group will become a minority at some point in the second half of the century. The biggest proportional increase will come among the Hispanic population, which will rise to more than one-fifth of the total. By 2050, Hispanics will considerably outnumber African Americans. The latter group will have grown, proportionately, since 1990, but not nearly as quickly. Immigration will also lead to a large increase in the proportion of Asians.

All these trends will be accentuated by unusually high immigration and reduced by low immigration. The table shows, however, that even with low immigration, Hispanics are likely to outnumber blacks in 2050.

In all likelihood, the different ethnic groups will be located unevenly around the country in future years, as they are now. Some regions may retain a clear Anglo majority, but if so, those regions will be balanced by others in which that formerly dominant group is a relatively small minority. According to Leon Bouvier's projection, using medium assumptions for fertility, mortality and immigration, California's population in 2020 will be just 36 percent Anglo and 40 percent Hispanic. Asians will account for 17 percent, and blacks just 7 percent.[19]

In terms of the country's ethnic composition, then, the two most striking consequences of immigration's continuing at its current level are these: First, the United States will approach a situation in which it is a country of minorities, with Anglos falling toward less than half. Second, blacks will be displaced by Hispanics from the position of principal non-Anglo ethnic group.

Not everyone agrees that whites are headed for minority status in the country. Peter Salins, a scholar at the Manhattan Institute for Policy Research, writes, "The Latino cohort is very racially mixed. . . . The vast majority, however, including most Mexicans, have mixed racial background, and—not that it matters—don't look very different from Americans of Southern European descent, and classify themselves as white in surveys. The same is increasingly the case for Asians."[20] Historian Stephan Thernstrom argues that the fertility levels of the different ethnic groups will converge and that immigration will be reduced and/or shifted toward whites long before whites become a minority. In any case, he writes, the issue will be unimportant, since the new immigrants will assimilate into American society, as previous immigrants did.[21]

Perhaps. The United States has not done an impressive job of assimilating non-whites into its majority consensus, however, and it may not do so in the future.

The first two debates of Chapter 1 centered on the demography of immigration: (1) Is the current wave unusually large? (2) Will it transform the ethnic composition of the American population? This chapter helps resolve those debates.

Chapter 2 showed that partisans looking at today's immigration could choose numbers to buttress either side of the first argument. They could say, for example, that current immigration is close to the highest in the country's history in terms of absolute numbers or, alternatively, that it is relatively modest in proportion to the population.

When considering the question from the perspective of the future, however, there is little doubt that the current wave of immigration is major. It will probably continue without letup, unless the U.S. government takes strong actions to reduce it. If the present level of immigration continues, it will become the principal source of population growth in the country—eventually, the only source. There is therefore no question that today's immigration is significant in terms of the overall size of the U.S. population.

It is even more significant to the changing ethnic balance of the population. Chapters 2 and 3 showed how recent immigration has shifted sharply to non-Anglo source countries. The proportion of Anglos in the country has already begun to fall and the proportion of Latinos and Asians to rise. In the absence of future immigration, the Anglo proportion is projected to continue falling and the non-Anglo proportion to continue increasing, because of differential fertility. These changes will be relatively modest, however. They will be accelerated by future immigration, to such an extent that Anglos will cease to constitute a majority of the population by the second half of the twenty-first century.

Over the next hundred years, the very meaning of ethnicity and the nature of race relations in the United States may change a great deal, as they have over the last century. Perhaps the distinctions that are so important today will seem unimportant or even silly in the future. Demographic analysis has nothing to contribute to those sorts of questions. It simply shows that, given the distinctions that are primary in American society today, immigration is projected to transform the ethnic structure of the country.

Although projections are not exactly predictions, the numbers presented in this chapter are more than just random guesses. Immigration is remaking America.

Notes

1. Barry Edmonston and Jeffrey S. Passel, "The Future Immigrant Population of the United States," in *Immigration and Ethnicity, the Integration of America's Newest Arrivals*, ed. Barry Edmonston and Jeffrey S. Passel (Washington, D.C.: Urban Institute Press, 1994), 317.
2. Negative Population Growth, Inc., advertisement in *New Republic* (February 13, 1995), 25.
3. Paul Kennedy, *Preparing for the Twenty-First Century* (New York: Random House, 1993), 193.
4. See John Isbister, *Promises Not Kept, the Betrayal of Social Change in the Third World* 3d ed. (West Hartford, Conn.: Kumarian Press, 1995), ch. 8.
5. World Bank, *World Development Report 1994, Infrastructure for Development* (New York: Oxford University Press, 1994), tables 1, 2, 25.
6. For overall assessments of prospects in the third world, see Isbister, *Promises Not Kept*, and Kennedy, *Preparing for the Twenty-First Century*, chs. 9, 10.
7. A large new literature, both theoretical and empirical, deals with comparative economic growth and the sources of growth. See Paul M. Romer, "The Origins of Endogenous Growth," *Journal of Economic Perspectives* 8 (Winter 1994):3–22.
8. For discussions of the new growth theory, see the following papers, all from *Journal of Economic Perspectives* 8 (Winter 1994): Romer, "The Origins of Endogenous Growth"; Gene M. Grossman and Elhanan Helpman, "Endogenous Innovation in the Theory of Growth," 23–44; Robert M. Solow, "Perspectives on Growth Theory," 45–54; Howard Pack, "Endogenous Growth Theory: Intellectual Appeal and Empirical Shortcomings," 55–72.
9. *The Economic Report of the President* (Washington, D.C.: U.S. Government Printing Office, 1995), table B-47.
10. Michael Fix and Jeffrey S. Passel, *Immigration and Immigrants, Setting the Record Straight* (Washington, D.C.: Urban Institute Press, 1994), 35.
11. U.S. Bureau of the Census, *Population Projections of the United States, by Age, Sex, Race, and Hispanic Origin: 1992 to 2050* (Washington, D.C.: U.S.

Government Printing Office, 1992). Unless otherwise noted, all the data and projections in this chapter come from this source.

12. Two other projections that focus on the effects of immigration are Edmonston and Passel, "The Future Immigrant Population of the United States," and Ansley J. Coale, "Demographic Effects of Below-Replacement Fertility and Their Social Implications," in *Below-Replacement Fertility in Industrial Societies, Causes, Consequences, Policies,* ed. Kingsley Davis, Mikhail S. Bernstam and Rita Ricardo-Campbell, a supplement to *Population and Development Review* 12 (1986):203–16.

13. Other Census Bureau projections, not shown here, demonstrate that if fertility were to fall along with immigration, the United States could enter a period of declining population growth in the twenty-first century.

14. U.S. Immigration and Naturalization Service, *1993 Statistical Yearbook* (Washington, D.C.: U.S. Government Printing Office, 1994), 22.

15. On the effects of immigration on age structure, see Coale, "Demographic Effects of Below-Replacement Fertility," and Thomas J. Espenshade, Leon F. Bouvier and W. Brian Arthur, "Immigration and the Stable Population Model," *Demography* 19 (1982):125–33.

16. Ansley J. Coale, "How a Population Ages or Grows Younger," in *Population, the Vital Revolution,* ed. Ronald Freedman (Garden City, N.Y.: Doubleday, 1964), 47–57.

17. Thomas J. Espenshade makes the point that the effect of even high immigration on the age distribution will be so small that Americans should not think that they can rely on immigration to solve the social problem of an aging population. "Can Immigration Slow U.S. Population Aging?" *Journal of Policy Analysis and Management* 13 (Fall 1994):759–68.

18. An as yet uncompleted project at the Urban Institute is examining the demographic consequences of ethnically mixed marriages. See Edmonston and Passel, "The Future Immigrant Population of the United States."

19. Leon F. Bouvier, *Fifty Million Californians?* (Washington, D.C.: Center for Immigration Studies, 1991), 24.

20. Peter D. Salins, "Take a Ticket," *New Republic* (December 27, 1993), 13–15.

21. Stephan Thernstrom, "The Minority Majority Will Never Come," *Wall Street Journal* (July 26, 1990), A16.

6

Wages, Employment and the Public Finances

The economic impact of immigration on Americans can be divided somewhat arbitrarily into short- and long-run effects. This chapter looks at the short run: what effects do recent immigrants have on the wages and employment of American residents and on the taxes and expenditures of American governments? Chapter 7 takes a longer-run perspective, considering the potential effects of immigration on the industrial structure and international competitiveness of the American economy and on the natural environment.

Many restrictionists argue that by increasing the U.S. labor supply, particularly the supply of low-skilled and poorly educated workers, immigrants lower domestic wages and take jobs away from residents. They harm the least-advantaged Americans by widening the gap between capital and labor incomes and between the rich and the poor. They further argue that immigrants impose unacceptable burdens on taxpayers. Most expansionists deny all these propositions. At the very least, they claim, immigrants do no harm to Americans' incomes and may actually improve them. Moreover, they pay more in taxes than they cost in public expenditures.

Ignorant, unskilled, inert, accustomed to the beastliest conditions. . . . The arrival on our shores of such masses of degraded peasantry brings the greatest danger that American labor has ever known.
—1892 newspaper article[1]

I also contribute to this society—I pay taxes.
—sign carried by an undocumented activist, San Jose, Calif., 1994[2]

The simplest index of a country's economic welfare is total production, or output, per person. According to the conventions of national income accounting, the money value of a country's output is equal to the value of the income generated in the country. Therefore, output per person is equal to average income, and average income is the best single indicator, although not a perfect one, of a country's material standard of living.

Immigration increases the number of people in the country; by itself, this reduces output per person. Because many of the immigrants work and thereby increase the country's output, however, this counteracts the tendency of immigration to reduce the index. If the increase in output is less than proportional to the increase in population, immigration still reduces the index and probably harms resident Americans. Much of the economic research is directed toward understanding whether this is actually the case, whether immigration lowers the incomes of American residents by, for example, reducing their wage rates or increasing their unemployment rates.

Economic research on these questions takes two directions. In the first direction, that of abstract reasoning, economists construct mental or mathematical models that are intended to be simplified versions of the real world and then manipulate them to see what happens when immigration changes. In the second direction, empirical research, economists employ statistical tests to measure the effects of immigration.

The Simplest Models

A model, in economics as elsewhere, is a simplification, constructed to help an analyst focus on the main issues without being distracted by irrelevancies. A model can be helpful, even essential, to clear thought, but it can also be misleading if some of the features disregarded by the model turn out to be critical in the real world.

We begin with a simple supply-and-demand model.[3] It predicts that immigration will have an effect on the incomes of American residents, helping some and hurting others. To show this, one needs to make some simplifying assumptions. First, assume that the number of workers that employers are prepared to hire depends negatively on the wage rate: the lower the wage, the more people they hire. Second, assume that this relationship between wages and hiring is fixed independently of the level of immigration; immigration will not lead employers to want to hire more workers, unless wages fall. Third, assume that no differences exist among workers; all resident workers and all immigrant workers have exactly the same skills and abilities.

The first assumption is probably correct; employers are likely to increase their workforces when wages fall. The second and third assumptions are incorrect; immigration increases the demand for labor, as is shown later in the chapter, and both immigrant and resident workers are diverse. Nevertheless, it is helpful to begin with the second and third assumptions and later examine how the conclusions of the analysis change as these assumptions are relaxed.

Although it is not necessary to the argument, suppose that, in the absence of immigration, all resident workers are employed. Since they are indistinguishable from one another, they all earn the same wage. These plus a few other technical assumptions that need not be reviewed leave us with what economists call an equilibrium: everyone who wants to work has a job, and employers are hiring as many people as they want to, in view of the wages they are required to pay.

Readers who are unfamiliar with economic modeling may be skeptical of a method that begins by using assumptions that are untrue. The justification for proceeding this way is ease of exposition; the rigid assumptions allow us to sketch a relatively simple model, one that focuses on just a small number of economic effects. Later the assumptions are made more realistic, one at a time, and the model becomes more complex, showing additional economic effects. In the end, the model will illustrate a fairly broad array of ways in which immigration affects the economy. The alternative method would be to consider all the complexities initially; although more realistic, this would require simultaneous consideration of so many different effects that it would risk more confusion than clarity.

The initial model outlined in this section is one that is familiar to every student of introductory microeconomics. As the rigid assumptions of this model are relaxed in subsequent sections, the findings will come closer to those of the current professional research literature.

Using the simple, initial model, what happens when a wave of immigrants arrives? Since employers are already hiring as many workers as they want, at the going wage, none of the immigrants finds jobs; they are all unemployed at first. Perhaps they will succeed in displacing some resident workers from their jobs; whether or not they do, as long as the wage rate stays unchanged, the number of unemployed will be equal to the number of immigrants in the labor force. This is not a stable situation, however, in the context of this model. The unemployed offer to work for a somewhat lower wage. The resident workers, who have no more skills than the newcomers, cannot hold out against the pressure for a wage cut, so the wages of all workers fall. As wages fall, employers find it profitable to hire more workers. Also, as wages fall, some people currently in the labor market become discouraged with their earnings and drop out. The employment level among residents falls. The process of wage cuts and new hiring continues until jobs are provided for all the immigrants and residents who want them.

Immigration, in this initial model, has a number of effects, some of them obvious, others hidden. The incomes of the native workers fall, both because their wages fall and because some of them drop out of the labor force. Employment in the country increases, because the immigrants now have jobs. Perhaps somewhat less obviously, production in the country increases, and with it the national income. This follows from the fact that employers hire more workers, who must be producing something. Another hidden effect is that nonwage income in the country increases. This income can be thought of as profits or as the return to capital; in any case, with lower wages on the one hand and increased production on the other, the share of the country's income that goes to nonworkers must go up.

What can one say about immigration's costs and benefits to Americans in this initial model? Resident workers are hurt, because their wages fall. Capitalists benefit, because their profits rise. The principal economic effect of immigration on American residents, then, is a transfer of income from wages to profits. Since workers normally have less income than profit earners, this is a regressive shift of income, from the poor to the rich. One cannot say in advance whether, among the natives, the gain in profits exceeds the loss in wages—that is, whether Americans as a whole gain or lose income as a consequence of immigration.[4] Whether they gain or lose, however, the change in total income accruing to Americans is quite small, certainly much smaller than the much larger shift in income from workers to the owners of capital.[5] Most people would agree that any event that systematically moves resources from the poor to the rich harms the country.[6]

The counterargument can be made that workers own a great deal of the country's capital stock, through their personal savings and through the investment of their retirement funds, and that they therefore share in the increase in capital income caused by immigration, even if their wages suffer. There is some truth to this, but it remains the case that the owners of capital are on average richer than Americans generally and that the shift in income from wages to profits caused by immigration is regressive. In sum, the simplest economic model of immigration shows that although it affects different residents differently, overall it harms them.

What If Immigration Raises the Demand for Labor?

The second assumption we began with—that immigration by itself does not create incentives for employers to hire more workers—is certainly false. Immigration leads to increased employment and production in the country and, therefore, increased incomes. Although the incomes of the previously resident workers fall, the incomes of both the capitalists and the immigrants rise. The people who earn these increased incomes spend a large fraction of them, thereby creating new demand for goods and services. Firms expand their output, and new firms come into existence, in order to meet that demand. Firms try to hire more workers, even in the absence of a fall in wages.

How does this increase in the demand for labor affect the conclusions of the previous section? It attenuates them. By itself, an increase in the demand for labor would raise wages; in this case, the tendency of wages to fall as a consequence of immigration is lessened. The negative impact of immigration on American workers is reduced.

Is it possible that the two opposite effects completely offset each other, that the tendency of immigration to reduce wages is negated by the increase in demand for labor? Not if the immigrant flow does not affect the amount of capital and other productive resources in the country. Production and the demand for labor would grow at the same rate as the growth of the labor force only if the other nonlabor productive resources grew at that same rate. If they do not, then immigration raises the ratio of labor to capital; to put it differently, immigration reduces the amount of cooperating resources that the average worker has at his or her disposal. Consequently, output per worker falls, and with it income per worker.

This first adjustment to the simple model in the direction of being more realistic does not, therefore, change the overall conclusion. It is still the case that immigration tends to lower wage rates, raise profits and shift the distribution of the country's income from the poor to the rich.

What If Capital Accompanies Immigrants into the Country?

There are some conditions under which the growth of demand for labor will match the inflow of immigrants. This could happen if the immigrants were to bring additional capital with them.

Capital is defined by economists as all previously produced means of production, including plant, equipment, tools, public works and inventories. In a somewhat different sense, capital can also be thought of as the funds that allow for the production of those goods. Workers cannot produce without capital. The more capital that workers have to work with, together with the technology that is embedded in the capital, the more productive the workers are.

In this chapter's model, there are only two factors of production: labor and capital (the influence of land and natural resources is considered in Chapter 7). Suppose that immigration somehow generated additional capital flows into the country, such that the ratio of capital to labor did not decline. There would be no reason for the average output per worker to decline. Each new immigrant would generate as much output and income as the typical resident worker. Since this income would be spent, demand for goods and services would rise at the same rate as immigration. Firms would want to increase their employment at the same rate that immigrants are flowing into the country and demand is increasing, even without the incentive of falling wage rates. The immigrants would all be employed, without there being any downward pressure on wages; therefore, the resident workers would not bear any burden from the immigration. The economic situation of the residents would be unaffected by immigration.

Is this a plausible picture? Can one reasonably think that immigrants cause so much new capital to come into the country that the capital-labor ratio stays constant? Probably not, if one thinks of the immigrants personally bringing capital with them when they arrive. Some immigrants may bring a bit of capital with them in the way of personal savings, but that is only a small fraction of the average capital-labor ratio in the United States.[7]

That is not the only way that immigrants can generate capital flows into the country, however. International investors transfer massive amounts of funds between countries, in response to changes in opportunities to make a profit with those funds. A question arises, therefore. Does immigration make capital investment more profitable in the

United States, such that foreign funds are attracted into the country? The answer may well be yes. Recall how, in the simplest model, immigration tended to reduce wage rates in the United States and increase the earnings of capital. These are precisely the signals that foreign investors might respond to. If immigration makes capital investment more profitable, it may encourage capital to flow into the country and at least attenuate, if not completely eliminate, the negative effects that it would otherwise have on domestic labor.

Although the response of capital flows to immigration is a fascinating and important question, it has not been intensively studied in the United States. As discussed in Chapter 4, Saskia Sassen and others have considered the response of emigration from third world countries to capital inflows into those same countries, but that is a different question. Little work has been done on the relationship of immigration and capital inflows in countries receiving immigrants.

Some preliminary evidence I have compiled indicates that in Canada, capital inflows matched immigrant inflows very closely in the late nineteenth century and somewhat more loosely in the twentieth century, so that the potentially regressive impact of immigration on the income distribution of Canadian residents was at least eased. In the United States, it appears that swings in capital flows and immigrant flows were correlated in the nineteenth century, although not as closely as in Canada. During most of the twentieth century, however, there has not been much connection between immigration and capital flow into the United States.[8]

Throughout most of the nineteenth century, the United States attracted both immigrants and capital from abroad. Whether the immigration caused the capital inflows, whether the two were responding to a common cause or whether they were unrelated are difficult questions to answer, but at least one can say that the inflow of foreign capital into the United States in the nineteenth century eased the impact of immigration on the incomes of resident workers. Around the beginning of the twentieth century, however, the United States shifted from being a capital importer to a capital exporter. From about 1900 until about 1980, investors shipped a great deal more capital overseas than they brought in. Immigration of people continued to exceed emigration, however. The combination of labor moving in and capital moving out had obvious negative impacts on income distribution in the United States. It accentuated rather than mitigated the effects in our simple model, tending to reduce the capital-labor ratio, to the detriment of labor. It is likely, therefore, that the consequences of twentieth-century immigration have been worse for American workers than were those of nineteenth-century immigration.

Interestingly, though, in the 1980s, the United States reverted to its nineteenth-century position of being a capital importer. This shift in the flow of capital was probably not caused to any appreciable extent by immigration. The economic literature points to a complicated series of causes, originating perhaps in the massive federal government deficits, which led to higher than normal interest rates, which attracted the foreign capital.

In the absence of more complete econometric analysis, therefore, we are left with the following picture. In the period since 1980, capital has flowed into the country along with immigrants. The magnitude has been relatively greater for capital than for immigration. From 1983 through 1993, for example, the annual capital inflow was typically between one-half and 1 percent of the domestic capital stock, and annual immigration was usually closer to one-quarter of 1 percent of the U.S. population.[9] The combination of capital and labor flows therefore increased the capital-labor ratio rather than diluted it and, if anything, caused wages to increase and the distribution of income to shift from capital toward labor—the opposite of our simple model's prediction.

This does not necessarily mean, however, that immigration had no negative effects on domestic labor. Recall that although immigration may have attracted some foreign capital, the major causes of the capital inflows since the early 1980s probably lie elsewhere. The foreign capital would have come anyway, in the absence of immigration. If this is correct, one can still reason that resident workers were made worse off by the immigration than they would have been in its absence.

The relationship between immigration and capital flows is in need of further research. In the absence of definitive evidence that the former caused the latter, however, one must conclude that the weight of the abstract reasoning is that immigration raises the ratio of labor to capital in the United States, and therefore lowers the earnings of American workers.

We have now completely abandoned the second assumption in the initial model, that the demand for labor is unaffected by immigration. The demand for labor rises with immigration, because the labor force and the capital stock in the country increase. These increases cause production and income to grow, and the growing incomes cause the demand for goods and services to grow. This, in turn, causes employers to seek more workers. Nevertheless, the basic conclusion of the initial model is still intact: immigration causes the wages of Americans to fall and profits to rise.

The Skills of the Immigrants

The third assumption in the initial model was that all labor is identical; domestic workers and immigrant workers have the same skills and all are equally productive. Obviously this is false. Resident workers are diverse, immigrants are diverse and, even when looking at averages, immigrants differ from residents. The next task is to consider whether abandonment of the third assumption leads to a change in the conclusions.

Chapter 3 reviewed the evidence on skills. The principal conclusion was that immigration is bifurcated into two streams—one with relatively low skills, and one on a par with American residents. Taking recent immigrants as a group, however, on average they are less skilled than residents. They are less prepared, in terms of both education and English-language ability. Their success in the labor market is below that of natives; they earn lower wages, work fewer hours and are subject to more unemployment.

A great deal of the research on the economic impact of immigration has focused on the skills of the newcomers. One of the problems with this research is that it is not clear what sorts of analytical models should be used to capture the effects of less-skilled immigrants on residents. The uncertainty is related to some of the disputes that were outlined in Chapter 1. Some models in the research literature predict that unskilled immigrants will reduce the wages and harm the employment possibilities of unskilled American residents. Others predict the opposite, that unskilled residents will be able to rise on the backs, as it were, of unskilled immigrants.

Critics of immigration tend to be in the former analytical camp. They point to several major changes in the U.S. labor market in recent years: the increase in immigration, the declining skill level of immigrants and the widening wage gap between skilled and unskilled American workers. They fear that these changes are not unrelated coincidences, that an influx of unskilled workers systematically reduces the employment and wages of the least skilled American workers who are in competition with them, particularly racial minorities. This has been called "the replacement hypothesis" by economists Michael Greenwood and John McDowell.[10]

Labor economist Vernon Briggs argues that America may well have been built by unskilled labor in the past, but employment needs are changing and the demand for unskilled labor is falling, just when the country is facing the enormous challenge of providing opportunities for unskilled black and Latino Americans. The arrival of large numbers of unskilled immigrants only makes that task harder and, in fact, destroys the promise of progress for those groups.[11] Economist Philip Martin adds that immigrant networks, described in Chapter 4, effectively squeeze low-skilled American workers out of jobs, because they lead to employer discrimination in favor of network members.[12]

Some proponents of immigration argue that the arrival of unskilled immigrants relieves the natives of the necessity of performing the most unpleasant tasks in the marketplace and allows them to rise to higher positions. This is the view of the "dual labor market theory," outlined in Chapter 4. More generally, it has been called the "segmentation hypothesis" by Greenwood and McDowell.

It is not necessary to adopt either view to the exclusion of the other. Immigration of relatively unskilled workers could lead to all of the following:

1. Wages of unskilled native workers could fall.

2. Some unskilled natives could be displaced from their jobs by immigrants.

3. Immigration could lead to an increase in production, incomes and spending, with the result that the overall demand for labor would increase, and some native workers would be able to upgrade their employment.

One of the most interesting recent analyses is by economists George Borjas, Richard Freeman and Lawrence Katz.[13] It is a particularly careful study that builds on much of the previous work on the subject. The authors observed that during the 1980s, the gap between the earnings of high school dropouts and those of high school graduates in the United States increased by about 10 percent, a major and troubling change. There may have been many different causes of this deterioration. The authors attempted to estimate the proportion of the deterioration that was accounted for by immigration and trade during the decade. Immigration could have depressed the wages of high school dropouts in the way predicted by the replacement hypothesis. The arrival of low-skilled immigrants would have increased the proportion of dropouts in the overall labor force, and this, in turn, would have allowed employers to lower their relative wages. Trade could have had the same sort of effect; to the extent that imports were produced by relatively low-skilled labor, the imports might have substituted for goods made by American high school dropouts and thus lowered the demand for the labor of American dropouts.

The authors measured the increase in unskilled labor caused by immigration and its equivalent related to trade. They were still left with the problem of distinguishing between the replacement and segmentation hypotheses in order to determine the effects of these changes in the labor force. They attempted to solve this problem not by looking at immigration directly but by statistically estimating the overall quantitative relationship between the relative proportion of high school dropouts in the labor force and their earnings. What they came up with is roughly in the middle between the two hypotheses: an increase in the relative proportion of high school dropouts in the labor force decreases their relative earnings, but less than proportionately.

Putting all the pieces of the study together, the authors estimated that about 42 percent of the overall deterioration in the relative earnings of high school dropouts in the 1980s could be attributed to immigration and trade. Of the two, immigration was the most important. In other words, this study indicates that immigration has had a serious negative effect on one of the most critical problems facing the United States at the end of the twentieth century—the decline in relative economic prospects for the least-skilled workers.

In deciding how much weight to put on this one study, however, one should understand that the study did not directly measure the effect of immigration on the incomes of high school dropouts in the country. Rather, it made deductions from a model. The only variable it measured directly was the increase in unskilled labor caused by immigration. Beyond this it deduced, on the basis of an understanding of economic theory and general quantitative relationships in the economy, the effect that this increase in unskilled labor *must have had* on wage rates. The study had no way of looking directly at the relationship between immigration and wage rates, however. Consequently, although it is filled with tables and numbers, it should be thought of as belonging to the first type of research, abstract model building, rather than the second type, empirical estimation.

In sum, when the initial model is made more realistic by abandoning the third assumption and incorporating into the reasoning the fact that the skills of workers are diverse, the conclusions of the model are not reversed. This is true even if capital inflows are such that the average incomes of all workers taken together are not affected by immigration. Even in these unlikely circumstances, the models show that relatively unskilled immigrants will increase the earnings gap between American workers.

Many more examples exist of the model-building, abstract-reasoning approach to understanding the economic effects of immigration, but the approaches outlined so far convey both a flavor of the method and some appreciation of the sorts of conclusions the analyses come to. Although the conclusions are varied, on the whole, the models indicate some cause to worry about immigration, some possibility that immigration may harm resident Americans, particularly those at the bottom of the economic scale.

The Difficulty of Empirical Research

One might well ask why one should bother with the abstract models at all, when data are available. Why not proceed directly to the measurement of the effect of immigration on the wages and employment of resident Americans?

It turns out not to be that simple. Empirical research in all aspects of economic demography is difficult, and immigration studies are no exception. The basic problem is that demographic variables such as immigration—or fertility or mortality—change so slowly, over such a long period of time, that statisticians cannot observe enough change to estimate the impact of the change.

One can see the problem by contrasting research in immigration with another topic, the impact of changes in interest rates on housing construction. Interest rates bounce around a great deal from year to year, even from month to month. Housing starts also tend to fluctuate frequently. An analyst who has access to, say, monthly observations of interest rates and housing starts over a thirty-year period can find many examples of both variables moving up and moving down. It is difficult, but not impossible, to construct statistical tests to see whether there is a correlation between the two data series and what the quantitative impact of interest rates on housing starts might be.

Movements of human populations, however, are much slower. Immigration may change a bit from month to month, but no one thinks that monthly changes will have much effect on wages. Going back over a thirty-year period in the United States, instead of many ups and downs, we can really observe only a fraction of one wave. Immigration was relatively low in the early 1960s and rose steadily through the early 1990s. One-half of one wave is completely inadequate for valid statistical tests; we would need to observe many waves of both immigration and wage rates in order to come to a conclusion that had any validity at all. Time series observations are, therefore, of virtually no use in estimating the effects of immigration on wages and employment.[14]

This is a serious problem, but it has not caused economists to shy away from direct estimation of the economic effects of immigration. Since time series are not usable in the empirical study of immigration, analysts turn instead to cross sections of data. They look, for example, at a wide variety of cities in the United States, all during the same time period. Some cities (especially Miami, Los Angeles and New York) have been impacted heavily by immigration, and some (such as Louisville and Pittsburgh) lightly. The analysts investigate whether the labor markets differ systematically in the different cities, depending on how many immigrants are resident in the cities. Is it the case, for example, that the gap between wages of graduates and wages of dropouts is greater in cities with a large number of recent immigrants? If so, this would constitute some evidence that immigration depresses the wages of unskilled workers.

Unfortunately, however, the evidence from cross-sectional studies cannot be conclusive. Cross-sectional statistical tests only indirectly address the most controversial issues surrounding immigration. We would like to know, for example, whether continued high rates of immigration in the future will depress the earnings of the least privileged American residents. The best evidence with a bearing on this question would come from the past: has high immigration in the past depressed U.S. wages? For the reasons just stated, however, we cannot interpret the time series evidence adequately. So, as a substitute, we ask: have different areas of the country responded differently to different inflows of immigrants? If the answer to this question is yes, we can be reasonably confident that in the future, various areas of the country will respond differently to different levels of immigration. We are on much shakier ground extrapolating from these results that wages in the country as a whole will be affected if immigration into the United States changes.

The economists are behaving a bit like a drunk who has lost his coin in an area of dark shadows but is searching for it under the lamppost because the light is better there. Cross-sectional studies will never tell us exactly what we want to know about the effects of immigration, but cross-sectional studies are what we have available to us.

What the Empirical Studies Show

What do the cross-sectional studies tell us? Briefly, they show that immigration has little if any economic impact on the wages and employment opportunities of residents, even residents who are unskilled, low paid or racial minorities.[15]

As an example, Robert LaLonde and Robert Topel used the 1970 and 1980 censuses to study the effects of immigration in 119 standard metropolitan statistical areas. They found that immigration had only a slight effect on earnings. According to their calculations, a 100 percent increase in immigration to a city would cause only a 3 percent decline in the earnings of the immigrants themselves and a 1 percent decline in the earnings of African American and Latino residents.[16] Joseph Altonji and David Card came up with more ambiguous results. Some of their statistical tests showed virtually no impact of immigration on employment and earnings of low-skilled residents, but other tests showed a significant impact. What the study seems to indicate is that if the effect of immigration on the economic prospects of low-income people is dependent on the type of statistical test chosen, at the least one can say that it is not well established.[17]

At least one study showed a more substantial effect of immigration. Donald Huddle and his colleagues estimated that in the Houston-Galveston area in 1982–83, every hundred undocumented aliens displaced sixty-five American workers from their jobs.[18] This study has been heavily criticized, however; it stands alone, and by itself, it is not persuasive.

Most of the studies use data from no later than 1980, but Kristin Butcher and David Card extended their study through 1989. The additional data yielded no new results; the authors found no significant effect of immigration on wages, even on the wages of the most low-paid workers in the economy.[19]

Although most of the empirical work is based on cross sections of many cities, at least one fascinating piece of research is a case study by David Card of just one city, Miami at the time of Mariel boatlift from Cuba. As Chapter 3 noted, after years of trying to prevent emigration from Cuba, President Castro unexpectedly lifted the restrictions in 1980. From May to September of that year, about 125,000 people left the Cuban port of Mariel for Miami. About half stayed in Miami, causing an almost overnight 7 percent increase in the city's labor force and a 20 percent increase in its Cuban labor force. The Mariel boatlift seemed designed to cause disruption in Miami's labor market. After careful statistical analysis, however, Card found no effect whatsoever. The boatlift appears to have had no effect on the unemployment rates and wages of low-skilled African Americans or other non-Cubans. It seems to have had no effect on the Cubans who were already resident in Miami. The only effect Card could find was on the unemployment rate of the immigrants themselves. Some of the Mariel immigrants had trouble finding jobs when they first arrived in Miami, but their troubles had no effect on other low-skilled, low-paid or racial minority groups.[20]

The rest of the cross-sectional empirical work leads to similar conclusions. The great majority of the studies find that immigration has little or no effect on the wages and employment of natives, even on the wages and employment of disadvantaged subgroups.

Can the Empirical Studies Be Reconciled with the Models?

We are left with a puzzle. Why is it that the theoretical models predict that immigration will harm the employment and wages of resident Americans, particularly disadvantaged Americans, yet most of the empirical research cannot identify such an effect? Normally in such a case, one would treat the models as hypotheses to be tested and conclude that the empirical tests have disproved the hypotheses. In this case, however, the models were not really tested directly, because time series studies were not possible.

It is easy to think of reasons why the cross-sectional empirical studies might be misleading.[21] Perhaps immigration into a city tends to reduce the wages of low-skilled workers, as the models predict, but within a short time the flow of both labor and capital within the United States responds so as to negate the initial effect of immigration in those cities. Americans might move out of cities with high immigration, because their prospects are diminished; capital might flow into those cities from the rest of the country, because of a growing number of low-wage laborers there. If so, immigration would lead to no relative differences in the ratio of capital to labor among the different cities—and no discernible effect of immigration on wages in the cross-sectional studies. Nevertheless, immigration would lead to a deterioration in the capital-labor ratio, and therefore it would lower wages in the country as a whole. The abstract models would be correct for the country, but the statistical tests would reveal no evidence of it.

So far, empirical investigations of such compensating labor and capital movements within the United States have been inconclusive. In the case of labor, the studies are contradictory,[22] and intercity capital flows have not been investigated.

After dozens of sophisticated studies, therefore, we are still uncertain about the short-run economic impact of immigration. Immigration may have negative economic effects that our statistical methods are incapable of detecting. The case is not proved, however. One can certainly come up with an argument to support the validity of the empirical studies. For example, if immigration attracts new capital into the country, it may have no overall effect on wages.

It is frustrating to learn that economists, with all their high-powered methodological tools, cannot give a clear answer to a simple, important question: how does immigration affect the earnings of American residents, in particular the most disadvantaged Americans? Nevertheless, that is the state of the professional literature.

Are Immigrants a Fiscal Burden?

Much of the debate has focused on the public finances. Some restrictionists assert that immigrants impose costs on resident Americans because of their use of government services. The immigrants are seen as exploiting the residents. For some reason, much of the anger has been expressed toward unauthorized immigrants rather than immigrants in general, although, as we shall see, they are probably less of a burden on the residents than their fully documented brethren are.

Immigrants do not, however, necessarily impose a fiscal burden on their resident neighbors. They occasion government expenditures—in such areas as health, education and welfare—but they also generate taxes. They would represent a fiscal burden to other Americans only if the expenditures exceeded the taxes. Some of the loudest voices in the debate look only at the expenditure side and therefore conclude that immigrants are a burden. Immigrants may, however, absorb less government spending than demographically comparable natives. They are less embedded in community social structures than natives tend to be and therefore are less likely to use social services such as welfare and health care. They are legally excluded from many services for five years after arrival. They find it just as difficult as natives, however, to avoid paying taxes. Most work for employers who are required by law to deduct anticipated income taxes from wage payments, and they have no way of avoiding the sales, property and excise taxes that Americans pay. On the face of it, then, one might expect immigrants to represent less of a fiscal burden than natives do. Careful research has been conducted on the question,[23] and the conclusions of the studies are diverse. The subject is a complicated one, not well suited for political stump speeches.

None of the research to date has been adequately designed to provide a fully persuasive answer to the question of whether immigration creates a fiscal burden on residents.[24] The studies are in an accounting rather than an economic mode. They attempt to count the expenditures that are made on immigrants and the taxes paid by immigrants. Even this is exceptionally difficult to do, and every one of the studies can be criticized for being incomplete in one way or another. Few of them even attempt to measure the indirect market effects of immigration on the public finances. For example, if immigration leads to an increase in aggregate demand and the consequent creation of new jobs, some of which are held by previously unemployed natives, the taxes paid by these new employees and the reduction in unemployment insurance payments should be counted as a fiscal benefit of immigration. A study by Donald Huddle takes the opposite tack, assuming that immigration displaces natives from jobs and thus creates new government expenditures for welfare and unemployment insurance, expenditures that should be charged as a cost of immigration even though they are paid to natives.[25] Although Huddle's methods are an advance over those of most other researchers in the field, his particular conclusions are too narrow to be persuasive.[26] Indeed, in view of our lack of understanding of the impact of immigration on the wages and employment of residents (shown in the previous sections), it would be impossible to conduct a fully adequate economic study of fiscal impacts at the present time.

Although incomplete, the research findings on fiscal impact are worth contemplating. The studies look at different levels of government. Some of the studies have tried to assess the fiscal impact of immigrants on all governments in the country. This is difficult—perhaps impossible—to do accurately, because so many governments exist with so many different revenue sources and expenditures. It is hard to identify all the ways in which immigrants affect the revenues and expenditures of the different governments, let alone measure the effects. Taken together, however, most of the studies seem to indicate that immigrants have not been a net burden to U.S. governments—that government expenditures on the immigrants have not exceeded tax revenues paid by the immigrants. Immigrants may even have been a net asset.

For example, from interviews conducted in 1975 with 850 illegal immigrants, David North and Marion Houstoun concluded that at least three-quarters of them had paid taxes, but only about one-quarter had used government services such as hospitals or schools for their children.[27] Using a 1976 Census Bureau survey, Julian Simon found that although immigrant and resident families paid roughly the same amount of taxes, the residents used government services more heavily.[28]

Several studies at the national level compared government expenditures made to immigrants and to natives, without also looking at the revenue side of the equation. They showed that immigrants tend to receive more social insurance payments (for example, workers' compensation, unemployment insurance) than do natives, but that immigrants receive less welfare support than do demographically comparable natives.[29]

The one major study at the national level that shows immigrants to be a fiscal burden is Huddle's, noted earlier. He found that in 1992, immigrants generated fiscal costs of $62.7 billion and revenues of only $20.2, for a net burden of $42.5 billion, certainly a significant amount. Huddle's conclusions are controversial, however. A revision of his study by Fix and Passel shows a net benefit of $28.7 billion rather than a burden.[30]

In sum, the evidence is uncertain, but it seems to indicate that immigrants pay their way nationally.

At the level of state governments, the situation may vary according to the state. Nancy Collins's study of New Jersey showed that immigrants and natives have almost exactly the same impact on the state's treasury, with both groups contributing just a little more than they take.[31] Muller and Espenshade showed that in Los Angeles in 1980, immigrant households headed by Mexicans imposed a burden on the state government that considerably exceeded the impact of other households.[32] Huddle estimated that immigrants in California were a net burden, but again his findings were challenged by Fix and Passel.

Most, but not all, of the studies that have looked at local governments have concluded that immigrants require more in expenditures than they provide in revenues and that they therefore constitute a fiscal burden at that level. In New Jersey, when looking at local finance, Nancy Collins again found no difference between immigrants and natives, but this time she concluded that both groups created a burden because they took more in spending than they paid in taxes. In Los Angeles, Muller and Espenshade found that Mexican immigrants imposed a burden on local government (in large part because they had more children in school) compared with all residents, who were revenue neutral. A study commissioned by Los Angeles County found that immigrants in that jurisdiction had a heavily negative fiscal impact on the county,[33] and a study of undocumented immigrants in San Diego came to a similar conclusion.[34] Other studies are consistent with this general finding.

It appears, therefore, that in the country as a whole, immigrants probably impose no burden on resident taxpayers and may even contribute more than they use. At the state level, however, and even more so at the local level in communities where immigration has been heavy, there are a number of cases of immigrants imposing a fiscal burden. However, because every study to date has been seriously incomplete, we have only hints about the true fiscal impact of immigration, not proof.

Different Groups Have Different Fiscal Impacts

In attempting to understand the effects that immigrants have on government finances in the United States, it is helpful to divide the immigrants in different ways—by permanence of stay, by legal status and by national origin.

Other things being equal, immigrants who are in the country permanently tend to impose greater net costs than those who are temporary, immigrants who are documented impose greater costs than those who are not and immigrants from Mexico and the rest of Latin America impose more costs than Asians. These findings are confusing because, as we have seen, temporary and illegal immigrants tend to be concentrated among Latin Americans. More precisely, then, within each national-origin group, fiscal costs are positively associated with permanence and legal status—but between national groups, Asians still impose fewer costs than Latinos.

Take permanence of stay first. Both temporary and permanent immigrants pay about the same amount in taxes, but the permanent immigrants impose significantly higher costs on governments. A study of Mexican immigrants in California showed that the difference in expenditures is particularly great—more than three times higher for permanent immigrants—in the area of education.[35] Permanent immigrants tend to come in families, and the families expand while they are in the United States, so the permanent immigrants send more children to school. The families of the permanent immigrants also impose more costs for health care, and they are more likely to be involved in the welfare system. Temporary migrants are more likely to leave their families at home. They come to the United States only to work, not to raise a family or to establish roots. As a consequence, they intersect less frequently with government services and impose fewer costs.

Undocumented immigrants also appear to impose less of a fiscal burden than legal immigrants of the same nationality. They avoid entanglements with American bureaucracies in order to protect against the possibility of arrest and deportation. Certainly many of them send their children to school, although they may tend to keep their children out of school to a greater extent than legal immigrants do. They find it difficult to qualify for welfare without revealing their undocumented status to the authorities.

This picture of the behavior of undocumented immigrants receives some confirmation from the research literature, although uncertainty remains. It is difficult to study the undocumented. A study by the Urban Institute on the fiscal impact of undocumented immigrants in seven states showed generally lower expenditures and higher tax revenues than the respective state governments themselves had estimated.[36] A 1984 study showed that undocumented immigrants were a net fiscal asset to the state of Texas.[37] Several studies in California showed the undocumented to be a fiscal burden but did not compare them with legal immigrants.[38] The studies that have been conducted so far certainly do not support the extreme statements made by the governors of California and Florida about the high costs to taxpayers of illegal immigration in those states.

It is also likely that the fiscal burden of immigrants varies by national origin. The question has been studied carefully only in terms of welfare utilization, and here the differences are striking. Among American residents, different ethnic groups have different rates of participation in the welfare system. In every case, welfare utilization is lower among immigrants than among U.S. natives of the same ethnicity, but utilization varies among the immigrants by ethnicity, just as it does among the natives. Borjas and Trejo showed that, according to data in the 1980 census, well under 10 percent of European, Asian and African immigrants received welfare payments, with the exception of Filipinos (11 percent) and Vietnamese (29 percent). Latin American and Caribbean immigrants generally participated in the welfare system more heavily:

the figure for Mexico was 12 percent and for the Dominican Republic 26 percent.[39] The shift in immigration sources toward Latin America is responsible for an increase in the overall participation of immigrants in welfare.

Whether this translates into a heavier overall burden on the fiscal system imposed by immigrants from Latin America and the Caribbean is an open question. Perhaps some compensating factors exist—public programs in which Latino immigrants participate to a lesser extent than other immigrants, or greater tax payments. By itself, however, the evidence on welfare utilization indicates that immigrants from south of the U.S. border may impose a heavier overall burden.

This chapter has restricted itself to the short run, looking at what is known about the impacts of immigrants on the incomes of American residents and the fiscal balance of American governments.

The empirical studies show remarkably little impact of immigration on the incomes of Americans, even the least-advantaged Americans. This finding is not conclusive, however, because of the methodological problems inherent in conducting the research. The theoretical literature is clearer. It predicts that, if immigration is not accompanied by proportional capital inflows, it will transfer income from labor to capital and from low- to high-income people. Further, if immigrant labor is unskilled in comparison to resident labor (as, on average, it is), immigration will lower the wages of low-skilled Americans; this prediction holds true even if capital inflows match immigration. In terms of the fiscal impacts, the studies again are inconclusive; the best guess is that immigrants do not burden the country as a whole but cause problems for some jurisdictions.

It will come as no surprise to learn that people read the research literature in different ways. My own reading is this: The theoretical models, although unconfirmed empirically, point to a negative impact of immigration on the wages of the least-advantaged Americans. The empirical studies cannot reject this conclusion because of problems inherent in their design. I think it is possible, therefore, that the negative impact in fact exists. It seems to me prudent, in a book whose overall argument is in favor of continued high immigration, not to base that argument on economics. It is possible, although unproven, that Americans, especially low-income Americans, pay a price for immigration.

The history of American race relations offers at least some confirmation of these conclusions. From the end of the Civil War until the

1920s, the United States allowed virtually open immigration. During this period, the social predicament of African Americans was abysmal. They were freed from slavery but confined to the South in the Jim Crow system that was almost the functional equivalent of slavery. Between the 1920s and the 1960s, immigration was cut back and the flow of unskilled foreign labor into the country was severely reduced. The industrial demand for unskilled labor remained high, however, so African Americans were induced to migrate from the South to the North to meet that demand. The conditions under which most were forced to live remained disgraceful, but there was some opportunity for improvement. The period culminated in the civil rights movement, which claimed markedly greater rights for African Americans. After 1965, large-scale immigration resumed, but the demand for unskilled labor was falling as the U.S. economy moved away from manufacturing and construction and into the information era. Although a minority of African Americans moved up the educational and social ladder during this period, the majority became worse off, at least after the mid-1970s. The urban underclass grew, and with it the problems of drug abuse, splintering families and homelessness. After falling steadily, the poverty rate began to rise again after the mid-1970s. The gap between the rich and the poor grew in the 1980s.

A causal negative relationship between the two types of changes—large-scale immigration and the social progress of African Americans—cannot be demonstrated with any degree of precision, certainly not statistically. It seems plausible, however.[40] Coupled with the ambiguous results of the analytical economic literature, it leaves one with a suspicion, although not a certainty, that major immigration flows have hurt low-income Americans in the past and may do so in the future.

Notes

1. Quoted in "Return of the Huddled Masses," *The Economist* (May 7, 1994), 25–26.
2. Steve Johnson, "Hispanics Aim Campaign at Anti-Immigration Advocates," *San Jose Mercury News* (May 29, 1994), B1.
3. This sort of model, with variations, was introduced into the literature on immigration in R. A. Berry and R. Soligo, "Some Welfare Aspects of International Migration," *Journal of Political Economy* 77 (1969):778–94. For a recent formulation, see George J. Borjas, "The Economic Benefits from Immigration," *Journal of Economic Perspectives* 9 (Spring 1995):3–22.

4. This indeterminacy disappears if the number of American workers is unaffected by immigration, in which case the income accruing to Americans unambiguously increases.

5. This is demonstrated rigorously in Borjas, "The Economic Benefits from Immigration."

6. Borjas, in the work cited above, takes a different point of view. He argues that if immigration increases the income accruing to all Americans, this represents an improvement in efficiency and a benefit for the country, a benefit that needs to be weighed against the distributional consequences of immigration. This reasoning neglects, however, the differences in the marginal utility of income between the rich and the poor. That is, at the margin, a dollar does a poor person more good than it does a rich person, and so the transfer of money from the poor to the rich lowers the overall well-being of the country's residents, even if there is at the same time a small increase in the aggregate sum they earn.

7. Julian Simon, however, makes the opposite argument in *The Economic Consequences of Immigration* (Oxford: Basil Blackwell, 1989), ch. 7.

8. John Isbister, "Immigration and Income Distribution in Canada," in *Essays in Labor Market Analysis, in Memory of Yochanan Peter Comay*, ed. Orley C. Ashenfelter and Wallace E. Oates (New York: John Wiley and Sons, 1977), 147–77.

9. Calculated from data in the U.S. Immigration and Naturalization Service, *1993 Statistical Yearbook* (Washington, D.C.: U.S. Government Printing Office, 1994), and *The Economic Report of the President* (Washington, D.C.: U.S. Government Printing Office, 1995). As a rough guess, the country's capital stock was taken to be 2.75 times its gross domestic product.

10. Michael J. Greenwood and John M. McDowell, "The Factor Market Consequences of U.S. Immigration," *Journal of Economic Literature* 24 (1986):1738–72.

11. Vernon M. Briggs Jr., "Immigration Policy and Work Force Preparedness," *ILR Report* 28 (Fall 1990); Vernon M. Briggs Jr., *Mass Immigration and the National Interest* (Armonk, N.Y.: M. E. Sharpe, 1992); Vernon M. Briggs Jr. and Stephen Moore, *Still an Open Door? U.S. Immigration Policy and the American Economy* (Washington, D.C.: American University Press, 1994).

12. Philip Martin, *Illegal Immigration and the Colonization of the American Labor Market* (Washington, D.C.: Center for Immigration Studies, 1986), and Philip Martin, "The Missing Bridge: How Immigrant Networks Keep Americans Out of Dirty Jobs," *Population and Environment* 14 (1993):539–65.

13. George J. Borjas, Richard B. Freeman and Lawrence F. Katz, "On the Labor Market Effects of Immigration and Trade," in *Immigration and the Work Force, Economic Consequences for the United States and Source Areas*, ed. George J. Borjas and Richard B. Freeman (Chicago: University of Chicago Press, 1992), 213–44.

14. See, however, one attempt to use time series: Richard Vedder, Lowell Galloway and Stephen Moore, "Do Immigrants Increase Unemployment or Reduce Economic Growth?" *Congressional Record* (September 26, 1990).

15. Several of the studies are noted in the next two paragraphs. Among the others, see Frank D. Bean, Mark A. Fossett and Kyung Tae Park, "Labor Market Dynamics and the Effects of Immigration on African Americans," in *Blacks, Immigration and Race Relations*, ed. Gerald Jaynes (New Haven, Conn.: Yale University Press, 1993); George J. Borjas, "Immigrants, Minorities, and Labor Market Competition," *Industrial and Labor Relations Review* 40 (1987):382–92; Gregory DeFreitas, "Hispanic Immigration and Labor Market Segmentation," *Industrial Relations* 27 (1988):195–214; Jean Baldwin Grossman, "The Substitutability of Natives and Immigrants in Production," *Review of Economics and Statistics* 64 (1982):596–603; Robert J. LaLonde and Robert H. Topel, "Immigrants in the American Labor Market: Quality, Assimilation, and Distributional Effects," *American Economic Review* 81 (1991):297–302; Thomas Muller and Thomas J. Espenshade, *The Fourth Wave, California's Newest Immigrants* (Washington, D.C.: Urban Institute Press, 1985); Francisco L. Rivera-Batiz and Selig L. Sechzer, "Substitution and Complementarity between Immigrant and Native Labor in the United States," in *U.S. Immigration Policy Reform in the 1980s: A Preliminary Assessment*, ed. Francisco L. Rivera-Batiz, Selig L. Sechzer and Ira N. Gang (New York: Praeger, 1991), 89–116; C. R. Winegarden and Lay Boon Khor, "Undocumented Immigration and Unemployment of U.S. Youth and Minority Workers: Econometric Evidence," *Review of Economics and Statistics* 73 (1991):105–12. An annotated bibliography on the labor market impact of immigration is contained in Michael Fix and Jeffrey S. Passel, *Immigration and Immigrants, Setting the Record Straight* (Washington, D.C.: Urban Institute Press, 1994), 77–83. The literature is reviewed in George J. Borjas, "The Economics of Immigration," *Journal of Economic Literature* 32 (1994):1667–1717, and in Rachel M. Friedberg and Jennifer Hunt, "The Impact of Immigrants on Host Country Wages, Employment and Growth," *Journal of Economic Perspectives* 9 (Spring 1995):23–44.
16. Robert J. LaLonde and Robert H. Topel, "Labor Market Adjustments to Increased Immigration," in *Immigration, Trade, and the Labor Market*, ed. John M. Abowd and Richard B. Freeman (Chicago: University of Chicago Press, 1991), 167–99.
17. Joseph G. Altonji and David Card, "The Effects of Immigration on the Labor Market Outcomes of Less-skilled Natives," in *Immigration, Trade, and the Labor Market*, ed. John M. Abowd and Richard B. Freeman (Chicago: University of Chicago Press, 1991), 201–34.
18. Donald Huddle, Arthur Corwin and Gordon MacDonald, *Illegal Immigration: Job Displacement and Social Costs* (Alexandria, Va.: American Immigration Control Foundation, 1985).
19. Kristin Butcher and David Card, "Immigration and Wages: Evidence from the 1980's," *American Economic Review* 81 (1991):292–96.
20. David Card, "The Impact of the Mariel Boatlift on the Miami Labor Market," *Industrial and Labor Relations Review* 43 (1990):245–57.
21. See Borjas et al., "On the Labor Market Effects of Immigration and Trade," and Borjas, "The Economics of Immigration."

22. Butcher and Card, "Immigration and Wages"; Randall K. Filer, "The Effect of Immigrant Arrivals on Migratory Patterns of Native Workers," in Borjas and Freeman, *Immigration and the Work Force*, 245–69; Michael J. White and Yoshie Imai, "The Impact of U.S. Immigration upon Internal Migration," *Population and Environment* 15 (1994):189–209. A study by William Frey is reported in Ann Scott Tyson, "Ethnic, Economic Divisions of U.S. Growing," *Christian Science Monitor* (July 7, 1994), 3.

23. Studies on the topic are well surveyed in Eric S. Rothman and Thomas J. Espenshade, "Fiscal Impacts of Immigration to the United States," *Population Index* 58 (Fall 1992):381–415.

24. For a general critique of the studies, see Borjas, "The Economics of Immigration."

25. Donald Huddle, "The Costs of Immigration" (unpublished typescript, Rice University, Houston, 1993).

26. For a critique, see Michael Fix and Jeffrey S. Passel, "Immigrants and Welfare: New Myths, New Realities," testimony before the U.S. House of Representatives, Committee on Ways and Means, Subcommittee on Human Resources (November 15, 1993).

27. David North and Marion Houstoun, *The Characteristics and Role of Illegal Aliens in the U.S. Labor Market, an Exploratory Study* (Washington, D.C.: Linton and Company, 1976).

28. Julian Simon, "What Immigrants Take from and Give to the Public Coffers," in *U.S. Immigration Policy and the National Interest, Appendix D to Staff Report of the Select Commission on Immigration and Refugee Policy* (Washington, D.C.: U.S. Government Printing Office, 1981).

29. See Francine Blau, "The Use of Transfer Payments by Immigrants," *Industrial and Labor Relations Review* 37 (1984):222–39; George J. Borjas and Stephen J. Trejo, "Immigrant Participation in the Welfare System," *Industrial and Labor Relations Review* 44 (1991):195–211; Marta Tienda and Leif Jensen, "Immigration and Public Assistance Participation: Dispelling the Myth of Dependency," *Social Science Research* 15 (1986):372–400.

30. Fix and Passel, "Immigrants and Welfare."

31. Nancy Collins, "Do Immigrants Place a Tax Burden on New Jersey Residents?" senior thesis, (Princeton University, Department of Economics, 1991); cited in Rothman and Espenshade, "Fiscal Impacts of Immigration to the United States."

32. Muller and Espenshade, *The Fourth Wave*.

33. Manuel Moreno-Evans, "Impact of Undocumented Persons and Other Immigrants on Costs, Revenues and Services in Los Angeles County," a report prepared for Los Angeles County Board of Supervisors, November 6, 1992.

34. Richard A. Parker and Louis M. Rea, "Illegal Immigration in San Diego County: An Analysis of Costs and Revenues," prepared for the California State Senate Special Committee on Border Issues, San Diego State University, 1993.

35. Kevin F. McCarthy and R. Burciaga Valdez, *Current and Future Effects of Mexican Immigration in California* (Santa Monica: RAND Corporation, 1986).

36. Rebecca L. Clark, Jeffrey S. Passel, Wendy N. Zimmerman and Michael E. Fix, *Fiscal Impacts of Undocumented Aliens: Selected Estimates for Seven States* (Washington, D.C.: Urban Institute Press, 1994).
37. Sidney Weintraub, "Illegal Immigrants in Texas: Impact on Social Services and Related Considerations," *International Migration Review* 18 (1984):733–47.
38. Community Research Associates, *Undocumented Immigrants, Their Impact on the County of San Diego* (San Diego: 1980); Los Angeles County, *Updated Revenues and Costs Attributable to Undocumented Aliens* (Los Angeles: 1991); Parker and Rea, "Illegal Immigration in San Diego County."
39. Borjas and Trejo, "Immigrant Participation in the Welfare System."
40. For a careful presentation of the argument, see Stephen Steinberg, *The Ethnic Myth, Race, Ethnicity and Class in America,* 2d ed. (Boston: Beacon Press, 1989), especially ch. 8.

7

Long-Run Economic Impacts

One could be forgiven for thinking that the perspective of Chapter 6 is a little narrow. The issues of wages, unemployment and public finance are important, but they are short-run issues. The models and the research reviewed in Chapter 6 dealt almost exclusively with current or recent immigration and its immediate effects on the economy. They did not consider how immigration over the last century has affected today's economy, nor how immigration over the next century will affect the country that our descendants inherit.

The short run is important. Most of the political debate about immigration deals with current policy and with the effects that people think they are feeling today. Economists are experienced in modeling short-run behavior and in using statistical methods to estimate short-run impacts. To peer into the distant future seems speculative and uncertain, perhaps illegitimate, certainly unscientific.

It has to be done, however, because the long-run impacts of immigration are likely to differ fundamentally from the short-run impacts, for at least two reasons. First, the demographic consequences of immigration are much greater over decades

The stronger nations, the ones that will outlive the European nation-state, will be those that have successfully adapted to this latest wave of immigration, not those that build latterday Berlin walls to keep immigrants out.

—*The Economist*[1]

We are no longer an empty continent with endless absorptive capacity.
—Richard D. Lamm, former governor of Colorado[2]

164

and generations than they are over a year or even several years. Chapter 2 showed that the current level of immigration, although relatively high by historical standards, amounts to less than half of 1 percent of the U.S. population each year. Chapter 5, however, showed that the current rate, if continued, would increase the American population by almost 30 percent by 2050 and more thereafter. Perhaps one reason that the empirical studies reviewed in Chapter 6 could detect so few effects is that they focused on recent immigration. If economists could conduct studies of immigration taking place over decades and amounting to 30 percent of the population, their conclusions might be different.

The second reason for thinking that the long run may differ from the short is that, over a long period of time, economic adjustments occur, adjustments that are impossible or at least incomplete in a short period. A good example is unemployment. It is possible that, when many immigrants arrive in an area, some of them are unable to find jobs. Over time, however, adjustments in the labor market occur, the immigrants find jobs and the unemployment rate subsides. This is a familiar story in the economic history of capitalist countries like the United States. All sorts of events, including immigration, foreign competition and technological change, have led to short-term job losses but not to permanent increases in unemployment. The U.S. unemployment rate has shown no secular tendency to increase. What is true of unemployment may be true of other effects of immigration as well. Even if immigration causes the wages of natives to decline in the short run, for example, adjustments may occur in the long run that reverse this effect. The long run is, therefore, a separate subject of study; it is not just the summation of a series of short runs.

This chapter looks first at the question of whether and to what extent immigration over a long period of time will change what economists call the "factor proportions" in the country. The factors of production are the inputs into the productive system: land, labor, capital and technology. Immigration automatically increases the amount of labor in the country. If this leads to a change in the ratio between labor and the other factors of production, the economic life of the country may be altered. The sections that follow consider first what might happen if immigration induces a proportionate inflow of capital. They then turn to land and natural resources, asking whether those factors of production can also increase in response to immigration and what the consequences might be of their not increasing. This leads to a consideration of the effect of immigration on the quality of America's natural environment.

After looking at factor proportions, the chapter turns to the quality of labor. If the skills of immigrants continue to be below the skills of natives, will the quality of the labor force deteriorate over time? If deterioration occurs, what will be the consequences for the structure of production in the country?

Immigration and the Size of the Economy

One of the supply-and-demand models of Chapter 6 showed that if all workers have the same skills, if the volume of production depends only on labor and capital and if new capital enters the country at the same rate as immigrants arrive, there will be no downward pressure on the wages and incomes of Americans. The model is so general and unspecific that this conclusion applies to the long run as well as to the short.

It is actually a more appropriate model for the long run. Within a short period, international capital flows probably do not match immigrant flows. Over a long period, however, it is not plausible to imagine immigration continually lowering wages and raising profits in the United States without attracting investment from outside the country. The induced capital flows might be a little greater or a little less than the immigrant flows; a neutral assumption is that they will be equal.

One should be careful how this point is stated. International capital flows are influenced by many factors, including savings rates, fiscal and monetary policy, investment opportunities, trade balances, interest rates and immigration. One cannot claim that in a period in which immigration increases the labor force by, say, 30 percent, international capital flows will necessarily increase the domestic capital stock by 30 percent. The more modest and defensible argument is that capital imports will make the capital stock 30 percent greater than it would have been, had there been no immigration.

If immigration induces an equal proportionate inflow of capital, the scale of the economy will increase, but nothing else: not wage rates, not profit rates, not the incomes of the natives. Nothing will change besides the overall size of the economy.

How should we evaluate such a change? Is bigness, by itself, an advantage to the United States? Do Americans benefit by living in a country that has a lot of people, with a lot of production? The sheer size of the U.S. economy makes it the largest in the world and means that the country is a leader not only in the economy but in much else besides—in international politics, diplomacy and military affairs and perhaps also cultural influence. Sociologist Ben Wattenberg argues that this translates into advantages for the average American citizen. "In the century to come, the population of the planet as a whole will double," he and Karl Zinmeister write. "Is it wise for America to be a no-growth player in a high-growth world?"[3] It is hard, however, to put one's finger on what the advantages of bigness are. It is difficult to say why Americans are better off than the Swiss, for example, who have an equally high or perhaps higher standard of living but a much smaller population and economy. It is more reasonable to think that, if immigration brings no changes to the living standards of the natives, they will be indifferent to it.

The immigrants will not be indifferent, however. They will have moved from a low-wage, low-productivity economy to one marked by high wages and high productivity, and they will be participating in that economy on an equal basis with the natives. This model has pleasant implications over the long run. Immigration can proceed at a high rate, without inconveniencing any natives, while offering the advantages of an American standard of living to an increasing number of people.

The picture may be even more pleasant than that. Suppose that what economists call "economies of scale" exist: when capital and labor increase in the same proportion, output increases in a higher proportion. Suppose, for example, that labor and capital increase by 30 percent by 2050, leading to an increase in production of 50 percent. If so, everyone will be better off.

Are economies of scale like these plausible? Perhaps. Some have argued that economies of scale are an important part of American economic history. As European settlers took over an enormous land mass, they were at first overwhelmed by the magnitude of the task. As more arrived, they were able to differentiate tasks, specialize and cooperate with one another through internal markets and transportation systems, in such a way that they increased their productivity. Moreover, the argument of writers like Julian Simon goes, immigrants brought new energy and efficiency to the country.[4]

Economies of scale may have been important in the economic history of the United States, although it is difficult to verify this through empirical tests. If one is to rely on the sorts of stories the historians tell, however, one must be skeptical that substantial economies of scale remain to be exploited in the future. The United States is not an empty country with too low a density of population for people to cooperate effectively with one another. It has large cities and intensively cultivated rural areas. Efficient communication networks bring people together over long distances for the purposes of work and exchange. It is hard to understand, therefore, how an increase in the size of the economy could by itself create new efficiencies. No doubt many immigrants bring energy, enthusiasm, skills and courage with them, but the question is whether they bring them in ever-increasing amounts, so as to continually raise the average amount of those virtues in the population. This seems improbable. Today's immigrants are not necessarily more motivated and skillful than yesterday's.

Immigration is unlikely, therefore, to make Americans better off in the next generations, at least because of economies of scale. Nevertheless, if this model is a good way of understanding the future economy, immigration will cause no harm to current American residents and their descendants, and it will certainly be of advantage to the immigrants. The model is simple, however, perhaps excessively simple. Has it omitted features that would lead us to reverse this benign conclusion?

Technology and Natural Resources

An obvious problem with the discussion in the previous section is that the United States does not have a two-factor economy, nor does any other country. In addition to labor and capital, the economy depends on technology and natural resources such as land and minerals.

First, consider the role of technology. Technological improvement is the principal engine of economic growth and improvement in the standard of living. Although capital accumulation helps, what really changes our material condition is new ideas, translated into production. Is it possible that, as immigration occurs over a long period of time, and as capital imports keep pace with it, the failure of technology to increase its growth rate simultaneously might limit the growth in production? The simple answer is no.

Technology is critical, but to be useful it must be embodied in the capital stock. As new capital equipment is built, the equipment brings with it the newest technology. It follows that, if immigration generates new capital in the country, that capital will expand the scope of new technology and the economy will expand to match the immigration. Suppose, for example, that a firm develops a new, computerized way to build a better mousetrap with laser optics. In a country that has no immigration, the firm develops new machinery embodying the new technology, builds a new factory and produces and sells a million mousetraps. Now suppose instead that the country welcomes immigrants, who in turn double the population. This poses no problem for the firm. It just produces twice as many machines, builds two factories and puts 2 million mousetraps on the market. The fact that our models do not take explicit account of technology as a separate factor of production should not alter the conclusions they lead to. If immigration produces an equal proportionate increase in the capital stock, technology should present no obstacle to a proportionate expansion of the economy.

Is the same true of natural resources? The literature on this question at a global level is marked by an interesting debate.[5] The pessimists point to the undisputed fact that the earth is a finite body and that the resources it contains are limited. It is a physical impossibility for them to expand at the rate that the population and the world economy are expanding. As minerals and fossil fuels are extracted and transformed, the remaining supplies near the earth's surface become scarcer. Increasingly, they argue, these fixed supplies will become a constraint on our ability to produce at the current level, let alone to increase production.

In contrast, the optimists say that the usable supply of natural resources expands to meet our demands. Perhaps in some ultimate sense natural resources are fixed, but not in any operational sense. Continued exploration and technological development bring new deposits to our attention and increasingly allow us to make use of deposits that were formerly known but were too inaccessible or too dilute to be usable. If a natural resource becomes scarce, its price rises; that, in turn, provides all the incentive that is needed for innovative people to discover new resources.

The debate over natural resources is so fundamental that it cannot be resolved by turning to data or experience. So far, experience seems to favor the optimists. Known reserves of most minerals and fuels have multiplied many times over the course of generations. Furthermore, there has been no long-run trend for the relative price of nonrenewable natural resources to increase over time, as would happen if they were becoming scarcer. But sheer logic favors the pessimists. Even if known reserves and usable supplies of natural resources have increased over time in the past, this must surely come to an end some time in the future, because the earth is finite.

Most of the debate about natural resources has been conducted at a global level and has been directed toward the question of whether the world as a whole can continue to add population and production without running up against a binding constraint. The focus of this chapter is on a single country, however: the United States. From this perspective, it appears that the scarcity of natural resources is a less serious problem than it might be for the world as a whole. The United States can trade with other countries for the resources it lacks. For example, although the United States is one of the major petroleum-producing countries in the world, it produces less than it needs for its domestic consumption, so it is also the world's largest petroleum importer. If immigration increased the scale of the U.S. economy and generated economic growth to such an extent that certain minerals and fuels became scarcer, the United States could trade with other countries for those resources.

It could not, however, trade to expand its scarce supply of land. The most obviously fixed factor of production in any country is its land. Sometimes countries can invest resources to increase the portion of their land that is usable for building or for agriculture, and sometimes they can improve the productivity of their farmland. This has already been done to a large extent in the United States, however, and it is unlikely that further major improvements can be realized. Land really is a fixed factor. It will not expand as immigration continues and as the labor force, capital and production grow.

Strictly speaking, then, immigration cannot lead to economies of scale, because all the factors of production cannot expand at the same rate. Immigration must necessarily reduce the amount of land per worker. In the first model in Chapter 6, we saw that if capital inflows do not match immigration, the reduction in the ratio of capital to labor implies a reduction in output per worker. Is this also the consequence of land being a fixed factor of production that cannot increase to match immigration?

Analytically, there is no difference between land being fixed and capital being fixed, so the answer is yes. In practice, however, land is a minor, almost unimportant factor of production in the U.S. economy. It is critical, no doubt, for agriculture. But the most recent figures show that agriculture accounts for only 1.5 percent of the gross domestic product, and when forestry and fisheries are added, the total rises only to 1.9 percent. All rents taken together are only 1.8 percent of personal incomes, and most of the rental income relates to buildings, not land.[6] Perhaps these figures understate the importance of land to the production process; certainly the country could not get by without land. That is not what is at issue, though. The question is whether a long-run increase in immigration, accompanied by capital and improving technology, would run up against the scarcity of land to such an extent that average incomes would fall. The answer has to be that this is unlikely— or at least that the effect would be so small as to be hardly noticeable.

Fixed factors of production are unlikely, therefore, to constrain economic growth in the presence of immigration, at least in the foreseeable future. Although there is no reason to expect increasing returns to scale, neither is there much fear of declining returns, provided that immigration is matched with the inflow of capital.

Environmental Deterioration

The argument above misses the most important point about land. Some of the strongest arguments against immigration have come from people whose principal concern is the long-run integrity of the natural environment. From the point of view of environmental preservation, land is anything but a "minor" factor of production; it is scarce, fragile and infinitely valuable. So too are the waters and the atmosphere. The environmental case against immigration is really not against immigration at all but against population growth, which is seen as necessarily having negative environmental consequences.

Some environmental problems are global in scope. The danger of an increase in the world's temperature, for example, is one that relates to the globe as a whole and cannot be usefully approached on a country-by-country basis. Many environmental problems are more localized, however. The air quality over Los Angeles, the acid rain in the forests of New England, the pollution in Lake Erie and the crowds in Yosemite National Park are all environmental issues that originate in the United States. The argument can plausibly be made, therefore, that sustained immigration into the United States over decades and generations will create population growth and economic growth that will lead to environmental deterioration or at least make environmental improvements harder to achieve.

The view that population growth and economic growth lead to environmental and resource deterioration is not universally accepted. Economists William Baumol and Alan Blinder argue that environmental quality is a "luxury good," that as societies become richer, they can afford more of it. Medieval London was so filthy, for example, and sanitation so primitive that the population of diseased rats flourished and caused the Black Death. Today London has many more people with much higher incomes in a much cleaner, healthier environment.[7]

Perhaps so. Perhaps in some ways economic growth enhances environmental preservation. This sort of argument does nothing to allay one's concerns about population growth, however. If population B is twice as large as population A but has the same standard of living, it will generate twice the pollution. It will have twice the economic resources to deal with the pollution, but the cleanup problems may be more than twice as difficult. Lake Erie may be large enough to absorb the wastes from A, for example, but not double that amount from B, so population B faces an expensive environmental problem that A can avoid.

Julian Simon is audacious enough to claim that population growth actually increases the usable level of natural resources. Growth in population makes resources scarcer relative to the demands for their use, he says, and therefore raises their price. The price increase gives innovative people an incentive to search for more such resources, to develop alternative resources and to figure out how to use the existing resources more efficiently. The consequence over the long run is that the usable supplies of resources are so expanded that they become more plentiful and their price falls.[8]

It is hard to evaluate this sort of argument. It might have some truth in an intermediate period. In the long run, though, it must come up against the fact that the earth is finite, that the supplies of natural resources simply cannot grow without limit. Ironically, Simon and the other economist-optimists who make these sorts of arguments put their faith in scientists who will make innovative breakthroughs. As demographer Nathan Keyfitz has pointed out, however, the majority of biologists and other scientists are seriously concerned about the physical limits of the globe and are in the forefront of those arguing for restraint in population and economic growth.[9]

Keeping in mind that predictions about the long-term future are speculative, the most responsible prediction about the environmental consequences of immigration is this: Immigration will increase the American population. This, in turn, will increase the size of the economy, but not more than proportionately; immigration by itself will not raise the standard of living in the country. The increased population and the increased level of production will raise the level of environmental damage. Because the economy is larger, the country will have more resources to devote to cleaning up the damage. Immigration will not make people richer, however, so on a per capita basis, they will not have more resources for environmental cleanup. Therefore, if the environmental damage is more than proportional to the growth in population and output, either environmental quality will deteriorate or the country will have to devote a higher proportion of its income to environmental preservation just to stay even, or both. Since the environment—the land, the water and the air—is a fixed resource, the problems of absorbing industrial pollution are likely to grow more than proportionately as the economy grows. It is likely, therefore, that immigration will make environmental improvements more expensive and more difficult over a long period of time. One is certainly hard-pressed to see any environmental benefit from immigration.

Perhaps the most direct environmental problem associated with immigration or any other source of population growth is the pressure on space. Space is absolutely limited; it cannot be increased one iota. People differ in their assessment of the value of open space, of course, but for those who oppose population growth and immigration on the grounds that more people mean more expansion into untouched or lightly touched areas of the United States, there is not much of a rejoinder.

In sum, substantial immigration over the long run can impose all sorts of scarcities in the United States. Human ingenuity is such that many of those scarcities can be compensated for. The most rigid scarcity, however, the one least likely to be expansive in the face of continuing immigration, is the quality of the natural environment.

Quality of the U.S. Labor Force

So far in this tentative exploration of the long-run effects of immigration, labor has been treated as homogeneous: all immigrants and all native members of the labor force are exactly the same. It is time to abandon this assumption and consider whether the heterogeneity of the immigrants may have a lasting effect on the quality of the American economy.

Julian Simon argues that immigration improves the American labor force, because immigrants are motivated to work hard, improve their skills and pass on the opportunity for a better life to their children. This has always been the role of immigrants in the United States, he asserts, and it will continue to be in the future. Immigrants are not ordinary people, he believes. They are a select group, with unusual imagination and foresight, people who have shown themselves willing to take the risk of abandoning what is familiar and to strike out into an unknown future—exactly the qualities the United States needs in its labor force.[10]

This may have been true for earlier waves of immigrants, although most contemporary observers doubted it. It was not necessarily true, however. As Chapters 2 and 4 showed, both in earlier waves and today, many people turned to immigration not as a great opportunity but because their familiar, traditional ways of life had been destroyed and they were forced to move in order to survive. Many were victims as much as they were initiators. The fact that they found themselves on American shores proves nothing, in and of itself, about their vision. In spite of a great deal of rhetoric on the subject, we actually know little in a systematic way about the inner lives of immigrants: about their initiative, enthusiasm and entrepreneurship, to say nothing of their other emotional characteristics. Novels and memoirs paint rich pictures of individual immigrants, but to my knowledge, no social scientist or psychologist has compiled a representative survey. Julian Simon's enthusiasm notwithstanding, therefore, we have no basis for saying that immigrants differ from natives systematically in terms of initiative.

Earlier chapters showed that, in terms of skills, today's immigrants are on average less prepared to contribute to the economy than natives are. Over time, however, they assimilate, at least to a certain degree, into the American labor force, adopting the characteristics and the productivity of the natives. Although a great deal more remains to be learned about this process, it appears that some of the immigrants who begin at a disadvantage, especially those who come to the United States at a young age, adapt so well that they are eventually indistinguishable, in terms of productivity, from members of their ethnic group who are natives. Others, particularly older immigrants, may move somewhat toward the standards of the residents, but they always remain at a disadvantage. Their children, though, have skills similar to those of other Americans of the same group.

At present, however, the ethnic groups to which the immigrants assimilate are different in terms of their wages and overall success in the labor market. Therefore, the question of how immigration will affect the distribution of skills and earnings over the long run dissolves into another, broader question: will America achieve racial justice in earnings and employment?

Most Asian American groups, although not all, earn incomes as high as or higher than the average of all Americans. The incomes of Latinos and African Americans are much lower, however. From the end of the Second World War until the present, the unemployment rate of African Americans and Latinos has been close to double that of whites, with no improving trend.[11] The incidence of poverty is significantly higher than average among the ethnic groups to which most of the immigrants assimilate. If the ethnic structure of economic opportunity remains unchanged in the future, and if the immigrants come from the third world, continued high immigration will lower the skills and productivity of the U.S. labor force.

This is not inevitable. One of the principal challenges facing the United States is the achievement of racial justice in earnings and employment. Although progress in breaking racial barriers has been made over the last decades, a great deal remains to be done. No one can be certain what the twenty-first century will bring, but one would have to be an optimist to predict that racial differences will disappear.

The effect of immigration on the long-term makeup of the U.S. labor force depends partly on social change within the country, but it also depends on the characteristics of the immigrants. Perhaps more highly skilled immigrants can be attracted in the future. Chapter 3 showed, however, that this will be difficult, and perhaps impossible, because the lowest skills are found among undocumented immigrants and refugees, both of which groups would be untouched by changes in immigration priorities.

The pessimistic long-run view is, therefore, that immigration from the third world will have the effect of significantly increasing the proportion of workers in the labor force who are low skilled and relatively unsuccessful in getting stable jobs with decent wages. The optimistic view is that after an initial period of familiarization, immigrants in the twenty-first century will adjust fully to American labor force norms—which by then will be undifferentiated by national origin.

The changes in American social and political life that would help the optimistic scenario come true will be difficult to achieve and should not be counted on. It would be prudent, therefore, to explore the consequences of continuing immigration leading to a deterioration in the productivity of the American labor force.

Long-Run Consequences of Deteriorating Labor Market Skills

Does it matter to Americans whether immigration over the long run increases, reduces or leaves unchanged the skills and productivity of the labor force? This is a surprisingly controversial question.

It is startling how often one hears the argument that a supply of cheap, unskilled labor is good for the American economy and for Americans generally. As has been noted earlier, some people claim that low-paid immigrants do the jobs that natives refuse to do but that need to be done. Some maintain that competition from unskilled immigrants is needed to keep wages from rising too much and threatening profits. The argument is made that a reduction in unskilled labor would be disruptive to the smooth functioning of the industrial system. Employers often predict that the disappearance of menial labor will lead to the collapse of their industries.

There may be some truth in some of the arguments, but none of the claims either separately or together makes a persuasive case that the American economy will be healthier over the long run with a substantial supply of low-skilled labor. Although there are many reasons for this, the fundamental one is that the economy is not something separate from the people. The economy *is* the people, at work producing and consuming. If the people are poor, the economy is necessarily less successful than if the people are prosperous. This may seem like a naive thing to say, but in all the arguments and counterarguments about immigration, it is frequently forgotten.

Certainly, a severe reduction in unskilled labor would be immediately disruptive to an economy that has come to rely on it. It might even lead firms to fail and sectors to be reduced. The focus of this chapter is on the long run, however, and in the long run, a well-paid labor force is an asset, not a liability. The overall wage level in a country is determined largely by the labor force's productivity, as economists use that term: the money value of output per worker.[12] Workers earn their wages by producing. A poorly paid labor force is evidence of a lack of productivity; it is a negative factor, not a positive one.

One might object that this position is not completely relevant in the case of immigration. Suppose immigrants and their descendants do not acquire the labor market skills of other Americans and therefore remain relatively low skilled and low paid. As long as they do not negatively affect the skills and incomes of the natives, this should be of no particular concern to the natives, at least for economic reasons.

We have already reviewed one of the responses to this objection, namely, the possibility that unskilled immigrants harm the employment and income prospects of unskilled native workers and ethnic minority groups. This argument is probably correct, at least to some extent, although empirical verification is hard to come by.

Beyond this, unskilled immigration may have a more complex, systemic effect over the long run, because of the United States' competitive position in international trade.[13] As the world becomes more interconnected, international economic relations will become more important to all countries, and certainly to the United States, which is the world's largest trading country. The competition for international markets is fierce. After the Second World War, the United States had the field pretty much to itself, since its western European allies were devastated and Germany and Japan and their allies were defeated. All that has changed; today, American firms must struggle to maintain their markets, both abroad and at home, against the competition of foreign companies. The competition will probably intensify in future decades.

Trading patterns among nations are determined primarily by their comparative advantages in production, which are influenced largely by differences in their endowments of the means of production. Countries with a relative surplus of natural resources are likely to export goods that make intensive use of those resources, countries with sophisticated technology are likely to export high-tech products and countries with ample supplies of cheap labor are likely to specialize in exports that need a lot of unskilled labor in their production.

The productive endowments of a country can change over the long run. Natural resources can be depleted or, alternatively, new sources of natural resources can be developed. Investment in research and development can increase the level of technology. Education and training can raise the skills of the labor force. As a consequence, the patterns of international trade change continuously.

One of the fears about continued high immigration in the long run, therefore, is that the increased supply of unskilled labor will promote the growth of industries that require cheap labor, to the exclusion of high-productivity, high-technology industries. The United States will increasingly trap itself into a third-world pattern of exports and economic growth.

What is wrong with that, one might ask. What is so bad about the picture of the United States attracting low-skilled immigrants and then growing economically by expanding the industrial sectors that use that kind of labor: textiles and clothing, the picking and packing of fruits and vegetables, component assembly, and so on?

The problem is that this kind of production does not have much future, since it does not lead to innovations and new technology. In sectors where low-skilled labor is easily available and is used intensively, employers have little incentive to invest in the search for better ways of doing things. They invest, rather, in the political process, to ensure that the supplies of their low-cost labor will not be impeded. An example is the Bracero program. This kind of activity will not lead to progress in the U.S. economy, in the way that innovation, research and development will.

One can acknowledge that some American industries are dependent on low-wage labor, much of it supplied by immigrants, and that if the workers were unavailable, those industries would have difficulty surviving. In the long run, however, the United States will not be well served by having a large number of such industries.

If the supply of low-wage labor were to decline, industries that depend on that labor would have several options. One would be to develop labor-saving technology and machinery to substitute for labor. Employment in those industries would decline, but the workers would be better paid and the industries would be on the road to self-sustaining technological development. The American economy has a lot of experience along these lines. Earthmoving equipment replaced strong backs in road building. Computerized equipment replaced armies of men working on assembly lines. As these changes occurred, overall employment in the country rose, not fell, because of the new, higher-paid opportunities that new technology opened up. As long as labor is cheap, however, employers have little incentive to invest in labor-saving, productivity-enhancing technology. Employers will always claim that they need cheap labor to survive and thrive, but those same arguments were once used in defense of slavery and child labor.[14]

Leon Bouvier tells the story of lemon growers in California. From the Second World War until 1964, they were dependent on temporary workers from Mexico under the Bracero program. When the Bracero program ended, and with it the supply of cheap labor, the growers invested in machinery and developed higher-producing dwarf trees. When the immigrant flow resumed in the 1970s, the growers stopped innovating and once again depended on cheap labor. No matter how cheap it was, however, labor in the U.S. fields was still far more expensive than labor in many foreign countries, so the U.S. industry had increasing difficulty competing with imports.[15]

The other option would be to go out of business in the United States and relocate in a country where wages were lower and labor more plentiful. Firms are often criticized for doing just this, for relocating to the third world where labor is cheap. It causes dislocations in the short run, but in the long run, it is usually the best result both for the third world country and for the United States. Third world countries typically lack many of the advantages in production that the United States enjoys—the capital, the technology, the infrastructure, the experience in modern business methods, the highly skilled workers—but they do have one advantage, cheap labor. If they are ever to develop manufacturing processes that can compete on world markets, it will be by making use of their cheap labor. This was the strategy that the United States followed in the nineteenth century in the textile mills of New England, and it is the strategy currently employed throughout much of the less developed world. Even countries like Korea that today export high-technology products began their industrialization with cheap-labor industries such as textiles. Other countries need those industries.

This is not to say that poor countries need the abysmal working conditions, health hazards and abuse that often accompany early industrialization—conditions reminiscent of the industrial revolution in Britain. At the end of the twentieth century, however, cheap-labor industries do not have to bring with them environmental catastrophes and the abuse of workers. The struggle by working people and their allies to improve working conditions and assert their rights is one of the most important causes of social progress. To have any chance for success, however, working people need the industries; without them, they will have no employment at all.

The United States does not need cheap-labor industries. The only disadvantage of reducing the country's reliance on them is the short-run dislocation that may ensue, as companies fail and some workers lose their jobs. This is a serious problem, but it is one to which the country could find solutions if it put its collective mind to it. Economic change always leaves behind a wake of people who have been disadvantaged by it. As mechanization proceeds in agriculture, for example, farm laborers lose their jobs. It may not be much consolation to them that their children will be able to find better-paying jobs in the future. It should be one of the responsibilities of government to help displaced workers make a transition to new firms and new occupations in more promising sectors. The United States has some programs along these lines, and more have been suggested by the Clinton administration, but on the whole, the country does not do nearly as well as some European countries at helping its citizens through periods of occupational transition.

This is the most useful response to economic change: to help workers weather the storm by providing retraining and other assistance. It is not useful for governments to take action to stop the change from low- to high-productivity industries. To take an obvious example, had the U.S. government prevented the development of the internal combustion engine, on the grounds that hundreds of thousands of blacksmiths and horse dealers would be thrown out of work by the automobile, Americans would be far poorer than they are today. In the long run, people are helped by the growth of high-productivity sectors.

In any case, the United States has a great deal of low-skilled labor already, without having to depend on immigrants. "No technologically advanced industrial nation that has 27 million illiterate and another 20–40 million marginally literate adults need fear a shortage of unskilled workers in its foreseeable future," writes Vernon Briggs.[16]

The supply of unskilled labor in the country might be reduced by providing better educational and training opportunities to minority youth and other disadvantaged groups in the country, by reducing immigration or by attracting more highly skilled immigrants. Wages would rise. The American economy would move toward a base of high-technology production and away from low wages. If Americans compete internationally in the future on the strength of their technology, their innovativeness and their brains, they will continually upgrade their industrial and service processes and increase their productivity. If they compete on the strength of their cheap labor, they will garner none of these advantages and they will always be struggling to keep up with countries where wages are even lower.

Earlier, I raised the question: who could object if immigration increases the supply of unskilled labor over the long run but leaves untouched or even improves the incomes of the natives and their descendants? The answer is that this is a false way of putting the question; immigration that leads to declining labor market skills will likely have a negative effect on the economic situations of Americans generally. Moreover, within a generation, the descendants of today's immigrants will be native residents; the distinctions between "them" and "us" will have disappeared.

The consideration of the long-run economic impacts of immigration in this chapter has necessarily been more speculative than the short-run analysis of wages, employment and public finances in Chapter 6. The discussion in the previous chapter was based on a great deal of analytical and statistical research. In the case of long-run impacts, that kind of research is impossible. In the absence of econometrics, all we can do is try to think clearly. The further into the future one peers, however, the greater the danger of being mistaken.

With that caveat, the conclusion of this chapter is that some of the economic effects of immigration that seemed dangerous in the short run will likely evaporate over the long run. In particular, the tendency of immigration to lower the ratio of capital to labor in the country—and therefore to shift the country's income away from labor—will probably not be sustained generation after generation, since new capital will eventually be attracted from abroad. Taking the place of the short-run problems, however, are some new problems.

One of them is the environmental effect of immigration. In spite of the arguments that a number of people have made to the contrary, it is hard to see how population growth, whether caused by immigration or by natural increase, can be anything but harmful to the natural environment. Over a long period of time, the most rigidly scarce natural resource a country has is space, and population growth will impinge upon it.

A second problem is the long-run competitive position of the United States in international trade. The debate in this area hinges on the question of whether immigration will lead to a deterioration in the skills of the labor force. That, in turn, depends on the success of the country in breaking down the racial inequities that have plagued it since its founding. One has to consider the possibility that significant economic gaps will remain between the different American ethnic groups. If so, continuing immigration from the third world will have a long-run negative impact on the productivity of the labor force, and this will skew the direction of American industrial development in a low-wage, low-skill, unprogressive direction. This is not a necessary consequence of immigration, but it is a danger.

Chapters 6 and 7 have dealt with a wide variety of economic issues related to immigration, from wage rates to public expenditures to the natural environment to international competitiveness. One theme that pervades the discussion is uncertainty. Sensible people come down on all sides of the issue. They do so not just for ideological reasons but because, in truth, most of the answers are not obvious. In spite of the sureness with which many of the participants in the debate trumpet their positions, a careful consideration of the arguments and the evidence reveals that a great deal is unknown. Nevertheless, on most of the issues, the arguments in support of the position that immigration helps improve the standard of living of Americans seem unpersuasive. The opposite arguments, that immigration will harm the economic welfare of American residents, seem more likely to bear out in the future. The conclusion of these last two chapters is that, on balance, continued high rates of immigration will probably require some sacrifice from Americans.

One should not assume from this, however, that continued immigration into the United States at roughly the current rate is unwise. Immigration brings benefits, which are the subject of the next two chapters. In the end, the benefits are so important that the economic price is one that the country should consider paying.

Notes

1. "The Stranger at the Door," *The Economist* (December 23, 1989), 9–10.
2. Correspondence, *New Republic* (January 31, 1994), 4.
3. See Ben J. Wattenberg and Karl Zinmeister, "The Case for More Immigration," *Commentary* 89 (1990):20.
4. Julian Simon, *The Economic Consequences of Immigration* (Oxford: Basil Blackwell, 1989), 8–9.
5. For a summary of the debate, see John Isbister, *Promises Not Kept, the Betrayal of Social Change in the Third World*, 3d ed. (West Hartford, Conn.: Kumarian Press, 1995), ch. 8, and Nathan Keyfitz, "Population and Sustainable Development: Distinguishing Fact and Preference Concerning the Future Human Population and Environment," *Population and Environment* 14 (1993):441–61.
6. All figures are calculated from *The Economic Report of the President* (Washington D.C.: U.S. Government Printing Office, 1995), tables B-9, B-11, B-25.
7. William J. Baumol and Alan S. Blinder, *Microeconomics, Principles and Policy*, 6th ed. (Fort Worth: Dryden Press, 1994), ch. 21. See also Simon, *The Economic Consequences of Immigration*, ch. 9.
8. Simon, *The Economic Consequences of Immigration*, ch 9.
9. Keyfitz, "Population and Sustainable Development."
10. Simon, *The Economic Consequences of Immigration*.
11. *Economic Report of the President*, table B-40.
12. Note that I am asserting here only that the overall level of wages in a country is strongly influenced by productivity. I am not making the more controversial assertion, believed by some economists, that each individual's income is a consequence of his or her productivity, or even marginal productivity.
13. Leon F. Bouvier makes a similar argument in Chapter 5 of *Peaceful Invasions, Immigration and Changing America* (Lanham, Md.: University Press of America, 1992).
14. See Elizabeth K. Koed, "The Loss of Cheap Labor and Predictions of Economic Disaster: Two Case Studies," in *Immigration 2000: The Century of the New American Sweatshop*, ed. Dan Stein (Washington, D.C.: Federation for American Immigration Reform, 1992), 139–47.
15. Bouvier, *Peaceful Invasions*, 93.
16. Vernon M. Briggs Jr., "Immigration Policy: Political or Economic?" *Challenge* 34 (September–October 1991):17.

8
Making a Multicultural Society Work

The consequences of immigration into the United States are not limited to the economy. Just as important, perhaps more important, are the social and cultural impacts of immigration, particularly those resulting from changes in the ethnic composition of the population. As Chapter 5 showed, if immigration continues at its current rate, the time will come, a couple of generations hence, when Anglos will be a minority of the population and Latinos, not African Americans, will be the next largest group.

Many Americans oppose these changes, believing that their country is turning into something they do not like and did not agree to. Journalist Peter Brimelow writes, "The onus is on those who favor the major change in the ethnic balance entailed by current immigration levels to explain exactly what they have against the American nation as it had evolved by 1965 (90 per cent white, primarily from Italy, Germany, Ireland and Britain). While they're at it, they can explain just what makes them think that multi-racial societies work."[3]

This chapter provides a response to Brimelow's challenge, arguing that the changes in the U.S. population caused by

You can go to France, but you will never be a Frenchman. You can go to Germany but you will never be a German. Today you are all Americans, and that is why this is the greatest country on the face of the earth.
—former Rep. Silvio Conte (R-Mass.), speaking at a citizenship ceremony for immigrant children, 1990[1]

Multicultural is not good. It divides. . . . We have so many groups wanting to be in America, but not wanting to be American.
—Bette Hammond, president of STOP IT (Stop the Out-of-Control Problems of Immigration Today)[2]

immigration are positive, constructive changes, that most Americans will benefit from living in a more multicultural society and that the tension between the different ethnic groups can be alleviated.

The Mosaic of American Life

American culture is based on a multitude of different nationalities and ethnicities. "It never happened that a group of people called Americans came together to form a political society called America," writes political philosopher Michael Walzer. "The people are Americans only by virtue of having come together."[4] American culture does not derive from a single folk tradition; it is not based on a particular religion or a single race. It embodies many folkways, many religions, many races.

The principal metaphor for how the various traditions came together in America used to be the melting pot. The groups were thought to have mixed together so thoroughly that they created a new culture, one that was common to most Americans and that erased the immigrant past. The ideology of the melting pot is still alive, but at the end of the twentieth century it is weak. It is now apparent that the nineteenth-century immigrant groups did not assimilate as thoroughly as was once thought, that the melting pot never worked with African and Native Americans and that the latest waves of immigrants show few signs of disappearing into an undifferentiated brew. Replacing the melting pot is the pluralist, multicultural image of the mosaic, in which immigrants and their descendants are understood as retaining important parts of their ethnic identities, and together constituting a varied, diverse nation.

Some of the insights of the melting pot ideology are valid, to be sure. Perhaps the most important example is the American political ideology of democratic liberties constrained by a constitution. It is a common ideology that serves to bind the disparate pieces of the American mosaic together. It is an ideology that was created on these shores, not imported from abroad. The American Revolution, with its Declaration of Independence and the Constitution that followed, established a democratic republic with a balance of powers and constitutional protection for individual and minority rights. The American system was different from any governmental system in existence elsewhere at the end of the eighteenth century. Although its architects were of English background, and although many of the ideas it embodied were based on English writings (particularly those of John Locke), it was not an English constitutional form. It was uniquely American. Successive waves of non-English immigrants have adopted its rules and pursued their interests within its framework, the consequence being that the shape of the Constitution has not changed much in over two centuries, despite Americans' disagreements about political issues. With the one notable exception of the Civil War, Americans have largely accepted the Constitution and the doctrine of individual but constrained liberties that it embodies.

The melting pot also has some validity in terms of Americans' identities. The question of identity is complicated. Some people think of themselves primarily as adjectivally qualified Americans—African American, Irish American, Mexican American, and so on—and some simply as Americans. Many ethnic groups have struggled to become "American," to become fully integrated into the social, cultural and political life of the country. To a certain extent, ethnic groups have been required to abandon their cultural roots, as the price for social and economic advancement.[5] Most Americans are patriotic; regardless of whether they use an adjective to qualify their American-ness, they love their country and are prepared to make at least some sacrifices for it. Moreover, many Americans marry across ethnic lines. As the generations pass, it becomes difficult for them to maintain an identity with their immigrant past, because that past is too complex.

The metaphor of the melting pot misses, however, the essence of American culture. To be sure, the experience of being in America has changed people. African Americans are not Africans; neither, however, are they just Americans. They are African Americans, and their experience of the United States is strongly influenced by that fact. This is also true for the Jews, the Puerto Ricans, the Mexicans, the Chinese and many other groups that have come in large numbers to the United States. In their seminal 1963 study *Beyond the Melting Pot*, Nathan Glazer and Daniel Patrick Moynihan rejected the idea of a uniform American culture, at least in the neighborhoods of New York.[6] Scholarly work since that time has expanded their ideas. In his 1993 book *A Different Mirror*, for example, Ronald Takaki interprets the full sweep of American history as being dominated by the interactions of immigrant and ethnic groups.[7]

To the extent that the melting pot is a valid idea at all, its contents are white. The melting pot brought together English, Irish, Swedes, Italians, Hungarians, Russians and other European groups and made a country out of them. In the first part of the twentieth century, this seemed a remarkable achievement, because the history of immigration had been fraught with suspicion, disdain and discrimination. The English once thought of the Irish immigrants as scruffy and papist; at a later date, the English and Irish together thought that the Italians and Greeks were barbarian. Yet by the first half of the twentieth century, the distinctions between the European groups were blurring. They retained ethnic organizations, with the Jews being perhaps the strongest in maintaining their communities. They cooperated together in business and in politics, however; they sometimes moved into the same suburbs, and their children intermarried. The ethnic identities did not disappear, but they were on the road to becoming footnotes to an American identity.

If that sort of description rings true for some Irish and Poles, however, it does not for African and Native Americans. One can take the melting pot seriously as the central process of American civilization only if one thinks that non-white groups were not really part of that civilization. Many people have exactly that opinion. For example, Brimelow's popular book on immigration, *Alien Nation*, overflows with observations that the United States is properly a white nation and should stay that way. "The American nation has always had a specific ethnic core. And that core has been white," he writes. Later, he writes, "And—if only for my son Alexander's sake—I'd like it to stay that way."[8] In spite of Brimelow's protestations that his views are not racist, the words speak for themselves.

Like it or not, non-whites have always been a fundamental component of American culture, since the first day a settler encountered a Native on the shore of the Atlantic, and since the first docking of a slave ship. Today, there are many more non-white groups. The majority of Latinos and Asians in the United States are the descendants of fairly recent immigrants, or immigrants themselves, so it is early to judge how those groups will assimilate into mainstream culture, or if mainstream culture will be there when they do. So far, however, they are not melting with other Americans nearly as completely as the different European groups did. They face racial discrimination that is different from and deeper than anything the Europeans faced. Their ethnic organizations and ethnic identities seem to be stronger.

If immigration continues at its current pace, therefore, and if third world countries of origin still predominate, so that non-Anglo ethnic groups continue to grow as proportions of the population, each passing decade will make it more obvious that the United States is a plural and not a unicultural society.

The alternative to the melting pot metaphor is the mosaic, or the idea of a multicultural society. The benign side of the multicultural vision is that which sees many ethnic groups retaining a strong sense of identity, generation after generation, and at the same time moving across the ethnic divides to participate in the common life of the country. Separation and cooperation are seen as complements, not contradictions.

In their family lives and voluntary associations, many American ethnic groups maintain cultures that are distinctive. These cultures do not necessarily become weaker with the passing generations or with the affluence of the members. Sometimes distance from an immigrant past makes people all the more determined to maintain their ethnic connections, and in some cases, affluence gives them the resources to develop the institutions to support their cultures. When the Japanese American community was poor and weak during the Second World War, for example, it was vulnerable to the hysteria that led to its members being placed in concentration camps as suspected enemies. Today, Japanese Americans have a more secure place in the business life of the country and have some political representation. They can maintain their own cultural institutions and are less likely to be attacked again in such a devastating way. Although immigration from Japan is only a trickle, Japanese cultural influence is growing, not receding. What is true for the Japanese is more true for groups that are continuously renewed by fresh immigration: for example, the Mexicans, the Chinese and the Vietnamese.

A good vantage point for viewing the multicultural mosaic is the campus of the public university in California where I teach.[9] Significant numbers of students come from almost every ethnic and immigrant group in the country. They are at a stage in their lives and in an environment in which the exploration of ethnic roots seems urgent. Many of the students are most comfortable associating with others of the same ethnicity: they walk around together, go to the same parties, share tables in the dining hall, paint murals with ethnic themes, form organizations and write for their own publications.

The role of music in shaping the ethnic communities on the campus is particularly interesting. One might think that music would break barriers, that people could enjoy one another's ethnic music and that a common American popular music, rock and roll, would bring young people of all backgrounds together. Often that is not what happens, however. Music seems to be culturally specific. The African Americans play rap and soul at their events, the Latinos play salsa and the Anglos play heavy metal. They do not go to one another's events, at least not very much, because they do not understand the music and think that they would feel awkward and look silly trying to dance to it. At an annual college-wide, day-long mural painting event, the biggest conflicts are apt to arise over who controls the stereo system.

Some observers of student life are troubled by this picture, seeing in it ethnic separatism and the disintegration of American culture. Some liberals are especially upset at the sight of ethnic tables in the dining hall. Isn't racial segregation what the civil rights movement was struggling against? they ask. This response is overly alarmist. Students tend to feel insecure in an environment in which they know few others, so they cling naturally to the people who at least look familiar. If they can become comfortable in that restricted social situation, they are often able to branch out across ethnic lines, make friends with different kinds of people and participate in broader social and intellectual activities. University administrators make a mistake when they try to stifle ethnic groupings, because then the students take their social organizations underground and infuse them with a spirit of hostility. If they are helped to be secure in their own culture, they can share it with others. The fact of a stable home base makes wider multicultural activity possible. There is no necessary conflict, therefore, between a certain degree of separatism, on the one hand, and a vibrant multicultural community, on the other.

This is the optimistic pluralist paradigm for the country as a whole, not just for an isolated college campus. The different ethnic groups are what give the United States its character. The groups need to keep separate so that the cultures are retained and reinforced, but they interact with one another too, to create the distinctively American society.

This is a controversial vision of American society that is at odds, for example, with the views of the distinguished liberal historian Arthur M. Schlesinger Jr. In his passionate book *The Disuniting of America*, Schlesinger argues that modern ethnic separatism is transforming the essence of what it means to be an American: "Instead of a nation composed of individuals making their own free choices, America increasingly sees itself as composed of groups more or less indelible in their ethnic character. The national ideal had once been *e pluribus unum*. Are we now to belittle *unum* and glorify *pluribus*? Will the center hold? or will the melting pot yield to the Tower of Babel?"[10]

This fear is off the mark. At the Tower of Babel, the different language groups could not understand one another. The promise of the emerging American society, in contrast, is that the different groups will interact and communicate; as a consequence, all Americans will be able to benefit by living in a national community that is broadening and stimulating.

This is the optimistic multicultural vision, but a troubling one exists too—one of racial conflict, discrimination and oppression. At the heart of American cultural life is racism: an unending process of exclusion, of dominant groups protecting their privilege against the claims of the excluded and the newcomer. The European settlers took over the land by killing the Natives. Until the 1860s, the social system of half the country was based on the slavery of Africans. For a century after slavery, the Jim Crow system persisted in the South. The civil rights movement revealed that racism was just as entrenched in the North. As Chapter 2 showed, immigration into the United States was unchecked as long as only whites came, but when the Chinese arrived in large numbers, the Chinese Exclusion Act of 1882 was passed, and its prohibitions were later extended to other Asians.

Racism persists today. In spite of the legal victories in the civil rights movement, African Americans are still overrepresented in the worst jobs, when they have them, and earn the lowest incomes. So too Latinos, Native Americans and some Asian groups are at a disadvantage in terms of income, education and opportunity. Personal racism and prejudice seem almost beside the point in American life today; what matters is systematic disadvantage, systematic oppression that maintains a wide gulf between the different ethnic groups. Racial tensions are frequently at the flash point, as shown, for example, during the 1992 uprising in Los Angeles when the white police officers who had attacked Rodney King, an African American motorist, were acquitted. That uprising showed that the antagonisms were complex; some of the victims of the violence were not Anglos but immigrant Korean shopkeepers.

Ethnic and immigrant groups have had to defend themselves against racism in order to secure their place in America. Their struggles are central to the strength of their ethnic identities. The experience and the memory of the fights are in part what keep the identities alive. Many people have only a dim concept of what life is like in the old country, but they are all too aware of what their struggles in this country are. If they have experienced discrimination on account of their race, language or nationality, they develop the conviction that their ethnic group matters a great deal. The natural response to being discriminated against is to claim pride in one's identity. If the rest of America is telling you that you are of no account, your survival as a healthy person requires you to counter with the assertion that you and your group matter.

Immigration as a Threat to the Dominant Culture

The majority of white Americans think of themselves as Americans, not any particular kind of Americans. They often think of themselves as people without any particular culture, just "people." The truth, however, is that they have merged not into a common American culture but into the dominant American culture, so dominant that they can be blinded into thinking of it as the only culture. Thus Bette Hammond, in the quotation at the beginning of this chapter, complains that today's immigrants want to be in America but they do not want to be American. She means, presumably, that they do not want to be part of the predominantly white, Anglo, middle-class culture that the melting pot has produced. The non-white groups tend to see it differently. They cannot be part of that dominant culture, they believe, because they are excluded from it and oppressed by it.

Anglos who fear the new immigration understand this on some level. They know, and fear, that the forces of the melting pot are not strong enough to assimilate the latest wave of newcomers completely. They may, of course, be wrong. It is possible that the dominant American culture will incorporate the descendants of today's Latin American and Asian immigrants without changing very much. This is far from a sure bet, however. Today's immigrants look different, they speak differently, they have different values, different family structures, different commitments, different heritages. Mainstream-culture Americans often fear that this new multiculturalism is altering the life to which they are accustomed. They fear that the newcomers are bringing poverty and crime into their neighborhoods, guns to the schools and drug deals to the playgrounds. They complain that immigrants bring too many new languages, the consequence being that Americans are in danger of not being understood in their own country and not understanding many of their fellow Americans. Where once the American cultural landscape was familiar and comfortable to the great majority, now it seems to them jarring, uncomfortable, unfamiliar.

These are strongly held views, but to a large extent they are romantic and ahistorical. They refer back to a lost golden age of consensus and universal culture that never existed. American cultural values have never been uniform, and American residents have always feared immigrants. Still, the fears about immigration are real. Today's and tomorrow's immigration is certain to challenge the dominant American culture, and that is what is troubling to the critics. Although it is true that yesterday's European immigrants did not assimilate completely, the new non-Europeans will in all likelihood assimilate even less, because of the racial differences. Chinese and Haitians will always look distinct from whites, many generations down the road. Some Latinos resemble southern Europeans (although some do not), but their assimilation may be impeded by a different factor, geographical proximity to the source countries. Add to this traditional white American racism, which has been altered in the last generation but not disposed of, and the critics of immigration are right to perceive that their country is changing under their noses, without their endorsement.

The doctrine of the melting pot may not be good history, but it is powerful ideology. Newcomers would be welcome if they were willing to merge their identities into the dominant culture, but they cannot do so and, for the most part, they do not want to do so. They therefore pose a threat to that culture.

Immigration Seen through Multicultural Lenses

Those who see the country as pluralist, myself included, do not share the fears of the uniculturalists. The essence of American life is that it is composed of different groups, different cultures, races, religions, attitudes, folkways and ideologies, differences that give the country its distinctiveness. Current immigration is sure to change the mixture, but change is not new; the cultural mixture of America has been changing continuously.

Brimelow's question was: what was wrong with the American nation as it was in 1965, 90 percent white? The answer is that there were serious problems, as the civil rights movement and the explosions in the central cities revealed. America has always been multicultural, but it has been a peculiar kind of multiculturalism: not equally powerful cultures enriching one another on a reciprocal basis, but a dominant culture set against subservient cultures fighting to secure places for themselves. Today's immigration creates the possibility that the United

States may become a country without a dominant race and without a dominant culture. If Anglos become a minority by the second half of the twenty-first century, and if the different ethnic groups achieve political representation, they will have the power to protect their interests and their cultures. As the sizes of the different racial and ethnic groups become more comparable, the likelihood of one group dominating the others will become correspondingly less.

The alternative to an egalitarian, reciprocal, multicultural society is not the single culture imagined by the uniculturalists. The implication of Brimelow's description ("90 per cent white, primarily from Italy, Germany, Ireland and Britain") is that the United States really could be a country with a single culture, much like some imagine France or Japan to be. It never has been, however, and it cannot be. The most important theme in American cultural history, since the seventeenth century, has been racial conflict. The conflicts have been marked by slavery, unequal power, widely disparate economic statuses, personal prejudice and institutional discrimination. Although the terms of the confrontation have shifted, whites and non-whites are still unequal in status. The alternatives before the country, therefore, are not a single culture versus many cultures, but multiculturalism marked by dominance, subordination and conflict versus multiculturalism marked by equality of status and reciprocity.

How can the first kind of country be transformed into the second? There is no single answer. I am enough of an optimist, however, to think that I have been living in the United States during a generation of change—through the civil rights movement, through political action, through education, through the assertion of legal rights, through cooperation by people of good will and through immigration. The shift in immigration legislation from a racist to a nondiscriminatory basis in 1965 has allowed and will continue to allow the relative numbers of the different ethnic groups to change in such a way that they confront one another on a more equal basis.

Numbers matter. In order for the different groups to relate to one another on an equal basis, without the members of one group feeling that they have to suppress their values and their interests, all the groups need to be not equal in size but well represented. As Anglos move toward minority status, and as Latinos and Asian Americans grow proportionately and African Americans retain their current relative representation, the interactions among the different groups may become more direct, clearer, more reciprocal, more equal. The United States will not become multicultural because it always has been, but its multiculturalism will become healthier, its citizens less constrained by structures of discrimination.

For centuries, the United States has been a model to the world of one sort or another, sometimes a constructive model, sometimes harmful, sometimes ambiguous. Although the United States' relative power has slipped toward the end of the twentieth century, it is still the strongest, most influential country in the world. As a consequence, what happens internally in the United States has an impact on other societies.

As the cold war recedes into memory, it is being replaced as the globe's principal problem with nationalism, coupled with racism and cultural conflict. Without the discipline of the great-power rivalry to keep antagonistic groups from each other's throats, warfare between ethnic groups has broken out in many areas of the world. People who are engaged in nationalist, ethnic conflict often hold the illusion that self-determination, or even "ethnic cleansing," will solve their problems. It cannot solve their problems; it only transforms them into something else. There is no geographical area, or at least no area large enough to constitute a viable national state, that is populated by an ethnically pure population. In the former Yugoslavia, for example, once the ethnic cleansing is over and the borders are redrawn, Croats, Muslims and Serbs will still have to coexist, their relationships made difficult to the point of impossibility by the memory of the atrocities of the mid-1990s. So too the Hutus and the Tutsis in Rwanda. Even French Canadians, were they to separate Quebec from the rest of Canada, would find themselves in a country with significant minorities of Natives, English speakers, Chinese and other groups, none of whom would be prepared to abandon their identities. There is no avoiding the fact that the world is multicultural, as are its various communities.

Since we cannot be separate, it follows that we must live together. Communities both small and large throughout the world will be characterized by a mixture of ethnic, racial and religious groups as well as by all sorts of other differences: in family structures, political opinions, incomes, interests and other features. In other words, the choice available to the world is the same as America's choice—not one culture versus many, but many cultures in conflict with one another versus many cultures cooperating with and enriching one another.

What will be distinctive about the United States is that the mix of cultures will be so rich. Even today, the representation of different groups in the United States is broader than in any other country; as immigration proceeds, the combination of ethnic groups will approach that of the world as a whole. Anglos will probably continue to be over-represented and Asians underrepresented, in comparison to their proportions in the world's population, but the former will be less than half and the latter will constitute a substantial number.

One of the reasons that it is important for America to become a country in which different cultural groups encounter one another on the basis of equality and respect is that America could become a model to the world. The world needs models of cultural respect.

An Agenda for Peaceful Multicultural Integration

The hopes expressed in the previous section may seem pious and unrealistic. The history of race relations in the United States is anything but harmonious. And we have not yet dealt with Brimelow's second question: what makes the advocates of immigration think that multiracial societies work?

Left to their own devices, they frequently do not. If peace, reciprocity and good will are to obtain in a culturally plural country, public policy has to be active and constructive. An agenda of programs can be developed that, although not guaranteeing peaceful coexistence, would make it more likely. The agenda includes at least the following: immigration, health and welfare, education, employment policy, the political and legal rights of immigrants, transition assistance and tolerance of diversity.

Immigration Policy

The question of what immigration policies the country should adopt, were it to base those policies on defensible ethics, is left to Chapter 9. Here we consider what sort of immigration policy would best serve the promotion of a decent, egalitarian, multicultural society.

The current policy serves quite well. It permits a fairly large flow of immigrants, and those immigrants enhance the cultural diversity of the country. At the same time, immigration is restricted below the level that would occur in the absence of border controls, keeping the flow within the limits of the country's absorptive capacity, loose and uncertain as those limits are.

At a time when many are calling for both a severe reduction in immigration and a reimposition of racial bias against non-Anglos, we need to recall that continued immigration from every part of the world benefits not just the immigrants themselves and their immediate communities but also the entire country as it moves toward the stimulating, challenging future of a plural society.

Health and Welfare

Immigrants have more difficulty establishing eligibility for public benefit programs than do residents. Undocumented immigrants are barred from almost all programs, even in the absence of California's Proposition 187. Legal, nonrefugee immigrants are barred from many for a period of five years after entry. Their sponsors' incomes—whether their employers' or their families'—are construed as being available to them, so by definition, they are regarded as not being in need of public support. The fact that their sponsors' income is often not available to them is not taken into account. Throughout the twentieth century, American law has forbidden the entry of people likely to become a public charge; in principle, immigrants who are forced to turn to public welfare for survival are subject to deportation. Americans who complain that immigrants come to the United States because they want to share in the culture of entitlement are apparently unaware of how hard it is for a newcomer to become entitled.

The country faces a conflict in this area. On the one hand, Americans do not want to be so generous with their benefit programs that foreigners move to the country solely or principally for the purpose of obtaining those benefits. On the other hand, if the country denies immigrants benefits for which other residents can qualify, it creates a category of underprivileged people who may negatively affect the lives of Americans. A balance has to be struck; at present, the balance weighs heavily in the direction of exclusion from benefits. Survey after survey has shown that immigrants come to the United States to work, not to qualify for public benefits. Once here, however, some of them find themselves in need but are unable to turn to public agencies for help.

The policy of keeping immigrants away from the public benefits system is based at least partly on the assumption that immigration is a privilege and that, once having obtained such a privilege, immigrants should not be able to ask for any further generosity from the American people. Generosity is not the foundation of the American welfare system, however. To the extent that American taxpayers are willing to support welfare (and their willingness has increasingly come into question), it is not because of their benevolence but because of their self-interest. Transfer payments to the poor, aid to dependent children, medical benefits and all the other forms of welfare support in the country are in place mostly to benefit the population at large. The American people have decided that their own society and their own personal lives would be worse off if they were marred by the presence of a large group of destitute people whose very survival was in danger. In *The Great Transformation*, Karl Polanyi demonstrated the organic nature of Britain and, by extension, most other societies; the privileged cannot simply cut themselves off from the plight of the poor, lest the quality of their own lives be crippled.[11] Advanced industrial societies like the United States provide welfare and health services to their citizens who are in greatest need, lest they pay a steeper price in terms of social disorder.

Since this is the principal reason for the system of health and welfare services, eligibility should not be based on the distinction between citizen and noncitizen immigrant status. Legal immigrants, and even to some extent the undocumented, are people who are wanted in the country, who contribute and who constitute part of the social fabric. They are here to stay, and they cannot be wished away by denying them basic benefits. Their needs should be assessed, just as citizens' needs are.

Education

Good, accessible public education is essential to immigrants' integration into American life. The latest wave of immigration is occurring at a time when the nation's educational system is shaky, in some places in crisis. This as much as any other obstacle stands in the way of a successful transformation of American society. Three factors are particularly important: the quality of the elementary and secondary schools in the central cities, access to higher education and the curriculum.

Immigrants, as we have seen, tend to move disproportionately to several large cities, where they join a concentration of native-born ethnic minority groups. The cities are the areas of the country where poverty and social breakdown are most concentrated and where public schools have had the most difficulty maintaining their standards, as they have had to cope with gangs, drug abuse, many different primary languages, disintegrating families and the whole litany of modern social problems. The traditional story of immigrants and other poor people in the United States is that they or their children have used the public education system to advance themselves. If the schools are incapable of providing a good educational foundation, this avenue of progress is weakened. One of the important tasks before people who are concerned that the ethnic differences in the country will congeal into permanent class differences, therefore, is to support basic education in the cities.

At present, all resident children in the country have the right to attend public elementary and secondary schools. The right of undocumented immigrants to send their children to public schools was affirmed by the U.S. Supreme Court in 1982 in *Plyler v. Doe*, which reversed an exclusionary policy in Texas. This decision is under attack by Proposition 187, but to date, it still stands. It is important that universal access be maintained; otherwise, a large class of uneducated, low-skilled and dependent people will be generated. In the long run, any savings to the public purse resulting from excluding undocumented children from the public schools will be more than reversed because of the perpetuation of poverty, which will require continuing welfare expenditures.

At the level of higher education, access is a present and increasing problem. In previous generations in the United States, a college education was reserved for the few, but even those without it had many opportunities to advance, both economically and socially. This has changed, since the employment base has changed from blue collar to white collar. Although a college degree is not absolutely essential in some walks of life, its absence frequently confines people to relatively low-paying jobs.

This is one reason that the current financial problems of colleges and universities are so distressing. Costs are rising faster than inflation, because such a large portion of educational budgets consists of salaries and because class sizes cannot be increased significantly without harming quality. In an era of stringent budgets, tax support is not keeping pace. Student fees are therefore rising continually, and financial aid cannot match the increasing costs. A greater share of the burden is imposed on the students and their families; this is a burden that many low- and moderate-income people are unable to meet. These trends will probably get worse in the future. The crisis in access is occurring in the midst of the latest great wave of immigration, and it is impacting immigrant families disproportionately because of their limited financial resources. The student bodies are becoming increasingly multicultural, but not to the extent that they would be if all the groups were represented in proportion to their numbers in the population. Increased financial aid for deserving students is therefore of the highest priority, if the members of all ethnic groups are to take their rightful places in American life.

The curriculum has become a controversial topic. Some minority spokespeople complain that their stories and their cultures are not taken seriously in the curriculum and that they are therefore devalued. Critics on the other side say that the contrary is true, that a fashionable or "politically correct" commitment to dealing with every ethnic group in a positive and even congratulatory way has diverted education from both basic skills and its historical function of integrating diverse groups into a single American culture. Critics of the curriculum call on the one hand for multicultural awareness and on the other hand for basic literacy.

The battles in the curriculum war have been excessive and unnecessary. Young people are in school so many hours of their lives that all the goals can be met, provided that the teachers are adequately supported. This is not the place to discuss curriculum reform in detail, but a few principles are worth expressing. Schools are where young people first develop a sense of the broader community and of citizenship, so it is important, if the United States is to be a genuinely multicultural country, that students learn how different ethnic and cultural groups have contributed and continue to contribute to their country. It is possible to do this in a critical way, so that young people develop their independent creative faculties. At the same time, there is much more to American and world history: it would be an impoverished American education, for example, that did not deal seriously with the Constitution and the Bill of Rights. In literature, the study of the writings of some of the "dead white males" can coexist with an awareness of writings that come from other cultures. Many of the important school topics proceed outside the realm of the multicultural disputes: math and science, for example. The point is that dealing with a multitude of cultures is important in school curricula, and it can proceed without hijacking education away from its other essential goals.

One of the strangest disputes has to do with bilingualism. Some critics of the multicultural approach complain that bilingual programs encourage immigrants to stay separate from mainstream American society. This is not, however, the purpose of bilingual programs. Bilingual education is intended to help immigrant children make the transition into American culture. The goal is to allow them to succeed at school in their own languages—rather than fail in a language that they do not understand—and, at the same time, help them learn English well enough to eventually be successful in that language as well.

That is not how the programs work, charge the critics. Instead, they keep the immigrants mired in a linguistic trap from which they cannot escape. English-language instruction may be traumatic at first for immigrant children, but it is what they need, some critics argue. "Monolingual education opens doors to the larger world," writes Arthur Schlesinger. "A common language is a necessary bond of national cohesion in so heterogeneous a nation as America. . . . Institutionalized bilingualism remains another source of the fragmentation of America, another threat to the dream of 'one people.'"[12]

This is a subject about which the critics of multiculturalism and immigration are egregiously wrong. One of the most useful things the immigrants bring to American life is an appreciation of bilingualism. To be bilingual is to open doors, not close them. Americans typically rank at the bottom of the world in language facility, and they are the poorer for it. An educated European almost by definition is fluent in several languages (with the notable exception of the British). In much of the third world, people speak a local or tribal language plus the national language. Businesspeople on every continent speak English with one another. People who are bilingual or multilingual can communicate with more people than can those who are simply monolingual, but this is only the beginning of the advantages that knowing another language brings. A language includes within it ways of thinking and cultural patterns. If you learn French well, you learn a little of what it means to think like a French person, to be a French person.

Part of the image of the "ugly American," or the typical "American tourist" abroad, is the boorish, loud, self-satisfied person who lives in his or her protected shell and is unaware of the surrounding nuances. Doubtless it is an exaggerated and sometimes false stereotype. It is based partly, however, on the fact that the Anglo American is usually monolingual and therefore lacks the tools to understand what is going on around him or her. In a world that is increasingly interconnected, monolingualism is a handicap for Americans.

It is a handicap that immigration helps to remedy. Immigration increases English-speaking residents' exposure to foreign languages, and this helps accustom them to the idea of bilingualism. In almost every area of the country now, one can hear Spanish being spoken, and in the West, one often hears Chinese, Vietnamese and other Asian languages. Increasingly, educated Americans are coming to the view that a working knowledge of Spanish can be useful to them in their lives and careers.

Anything that can be done to increase the teaching of foreign languages in American schools, and the teaching of other subjects in foreign languages, will not only improve the multicultural climate of the

United States but also enhance the ability of Americans of all backgrounds to function effectively in the world. Foreign language teaching cannot possibly threaten the position of English as the common American language.

Employment Policy

Social peace is always easier to attain when the unemployment rate is low and the economy is booming. It is no coincidence that the expansive Immigration Act of 1990 was passed at the end of a decade of steady economic growth, increasing prosperity for many Americans (although not all) and falling unemployment. The overall civilian unemployment rate had risen at the beginning of the 1980s to a peak of 9.7 percent of the labor force but had fallen to 5.3 percent by 1989. At the end of the decade, there was little effective opposition to immigration, even though the numbers admitted had risen steadily and the Immigration Reform and Control Act of 1986 (IRCA) had permitted the legalization of millions of the undocumented. There was little reason to doubt that the American labor market could absorb the newcomers.

In the early 1990s, recession hit, and the mood of the country turned sharply. The unemployment rate rose to 7.4 percent in 1992.[13] The recession was responsible for President Bush's defeat at the end of 1992, and it coincided with a major backlash against immigration. The opposition to immigration reached its height in California not just because that state was the major recipient of new immigrants but also because, for the first time, California's economy lagged behind the rest of the country. People were looking for someone to blame for their troubles, and immigrants were an easy target.

As Chapter 6 showed, careful economic research has difficulty identifying just what impact immigration has on the wages and employment of residents. Popular opinion is not slow to come to conclusions, however; in times of economic hardship, politicians can advance their careers by striking out against immigrants.

Although much of the opposition to immigration is doubtless based on ignorance of the actual economic impacts, the changing of the ethnic structure of the U.S. population and the achievement of some kind of multicultural balance are sure to create frictions and require sacrifices. All this can be borne more easily in an expanding, healthy economy. Part of the political strategy for the new American society, therefore, is to encourage the growth of the economy and the creation of jobs, so as to ease the sometimes painful change.

Political and Legal Rights of Immigrants

Compared with citizens, noncitizen immigrants and potential immigrants have many fewer rights. In part, this is inevitable; one of the purposes of becoming an American citizen is to secure equal rights with Americans. A lot could be done, however, to protect and enhance the rights of immigrants. According to legal scholar Peter Schuck, American law relating to immigrants has been torn between two ideologies: "the one denying that a society owes aliens any obligation to which it does not consent, the other affirming the existence of certain obligations to aliens simply by reason of their humanity."[14]

In the mid-1990s, the rights of immigrants came under severe attack. California's Proposition 187 threatened to remove access to all public services (except emergency medical care) from undocumented immigrants and required everyone in a position of public authority to report people they suspected of being in the country illegally. The measure was immediately challenged in the courts. But even if it is found unconstitutional in its totality—and that is uncertain—it will remain important as an indicator of anti-immigrant sentiment in at least one area of the country. In the aftermath of the passage of Proposition 187, a number of suggestions were made for similar measures at the national level, perhaps drafted more skillfully to survive constitutional challenge. One suggestion was to make legal as well as illegal immigrants ineligible for most public services.

These sorts of policies are not only offensive and immoral; they are counterproductive as well. Immigrants, both legal and undocumented, are going to be a permanent part of American society. As long as the United States places any restrictions at all on immigration, it will automatically have undocumented immigrants. Some foreigners will be willing to violate the border restrictions, and some American residents will be willing to welcome the violators.

That fact creates an almost impossible dilemma. The policy of acquiescing to the presence of millions of undocumented immigrants and yet denying them political, legal and civil rights has the effect of creating an exploited, abused class of people. They are subject to exploitation because they cannot publicly protest unfair treatment without making themselves visible to American authorities and thereby subjecting themselves to deportation.

The problem of the unequal rights accorded to the undocumented cannot be wished away, but the trend could be shifted in the opposite direction from Proposition 187, to accord them greater protection. The federal government could decline to deport anyone who brought legal action on account of exploitative treatment, whether by an employer, a spouse or anyone else. If an undocumented immigrant knew that he or she could bring a complaint against an employer for violating the laws relating to minimum wages, health and safety or sexual harassment, or against a spouse or companion for physical assault, without being vulnerable to deportation, the incidence of such abuses might be reduced. Such a rule would not reduce the number of deportations, because at present these crimes are hardly ever reported, and it would demonstrate Americans' conviction that no one should be illegally exploited, whatever his or her status.

Among the many proposals that have been made to take rights away from undocumented immigrants, the most insidious is a proposal by several anti-immigration groups, as well as the governor of California, to change the Fourteenth Amendment to the Constitution so that the American-born children of illegal immigrants would not automatically be citizens. The Fourteenth Amendment begins, "All persons born or naturalized in the United States, and subject to the jurisdiction thereof, are citizens of the United States." Proposed in 1866 and ratified in 1868, it is the constitutional provision by which slaves were accorded citizenship after the Civil War. A change in it would have grave consequences for the meaning of American society. It would create a situation such as currently exists in Germany, Italy, Sweden and Japan, where some people can trace their ancestry within the country back for generations but have no legal claim to citizenship.[15] It would set up a permanent category of second-class residents—people completely connected to the United States, who know no other home, yet who are not recognized as equals before the law.[16]

Transition Assistance

Little is done by the federal or state governments to help immigrants with their transition to American life after arrival.[17] The programs are few in number, poorly funded and subject to cutbacks. The principal transition policy of the United States is that immigrants should be either self-sufficient or supported by people in the private sector, and that the public bears no responsibility for them.

The one group of immigrants for whom the government recognizes a responsibility is refugees. Federal programs help them travel to places where jobs are available, find accommodations and learn English. The refugee programs have been cut back drastically, however. For example, expenditures for the Refugee Resettlement Program fell from $7,300 per refugee in 1982 to just $2,200 in 1993.[18]

Moreover, the fact that funds are available to refugees and not to other immigrants raises questions about the arbitrary use of the refugee category. For decades, Cuban immigrants were almost automatically classified as refugees and were therefore eligible for support, whereas immigrants from El Salvador were generally not able to obtain the status of refugees, even though their lives were often in greater danger.

Few other programs exist to assist immigrants in their transition. The policies of the states are uneven. In the states of highest immigration, the backlash has been most severe, and it is there that assistance is being cut back the most. The federal government had a program to compensate states for their expenditures on people legalized under IRCA, but the funds were minimal, they were deferred frequently and they terminated in 1995.

The basic problems with transition programs are two: they are skimpy at best, and they are arbitrary in coverage because the awarding of refugee status is based on political considerations. Eligibility for transition assistance should be separated from immigrant status and awarded instead on the basis of need.

Tolerance of Diversity

The U.S. Constitution provides protection for minority views, personal privacy and free association, and it does so more strongly than almost any other country. Although the country's founders did not envision an American society that embodied most of the world's cultures, the framework they established makes such a society possible. Government under the American Constitution is to be neutral with respect to cultural values, even when the majority of the population might wish otherwise. Consequently, minority groups are granted the space to preserve and enhance their own cultures.

This understanding of the American system of government needs constant protection and reinforcement, because it is vulnerable to attack from majorities. Sometimes the Constitution fails, as evidenced by the forced internment of Japanese Americans during the Second World War for no crime other than their Japanese heritage. The members of the Supreme Court are political appointees; although the Court's record is generally commendable, the justices cannot always be counted on to resist the will of the majority when the Constitution demands it.

Today, the most serious threat to an open, diverse society comes from the fundamentalist Christian right. Fundamentalist Christians have and should have the same rights as anyone else to organize, associate, worship and in other ways enhance their culture. They are free to take part in the political life of the country, as are all other groups. Increasingly, however, the agenda of the Christian right has become to impose its cultural views on the rest of the population. By taking over the apparatus of the Republican Party in some communities and states, it has increased its power and created a danger that its views may prevail. Those views are antithetical to the traditions of tolerance and diversity that are embodied in the Constitution and that are essential if a multicultural society is to thrive.

Although the fundamentalists have many policy proposals that are offensive to a variety of groups in the country, their most dangerous assertion is that the United States is a Christian nation. The Constitution bars the government's establishment of any religion, in the first words of the Bill of Rights. Americans have reasonable disagreements about just how this constitutional provision should be interpreted and where the boundary between public and private exercise of religion should be drawn. By asserting that the United States is a Christian nation, however, the fundamentalist right automatically relegates to a marginal status all non-Christians, be they Jews, Muslims, Buddhists, Hindus, atheists or anything else. Moreover, their interpretation of Christianity is one with which many other Christians take issue.

Abraham Foxman, national director of the Anti-Defamation League, writes, "The aversion to church/state separation is bound up with the movement's broader hostility toward a society premised on diversity and dissent. Its efforts to impose its own religious identity on the soul of the state erodes public goodwill and flaunts the ideals of a pluralistic democracy."[19] Were the views of the Christian fundamentalists to become the law of the land, the hope of the United States' being a tolerant, multicultural, open society would be lost. Protection of tolerance is therefore a matter of general concern, one that cannot be left only to the courts.

The Primacy of Politics

Something like the agenda outlined in the previous section would help immigrants become fully integrated into American life and would help the country proceed in the direction of an open, respectful, multicultural society with a minimum of acrimony and conflict. None of the agenda will be achieved easily. Particularly in an era of skepticism and hostility toward immigration, progress on any front will require well-thought-out political engagement. People have to fight for their rights; the most effective way to carry out that fight is through political representation.

The history of American social struggles demonstrates this clearly. When African Americans were denied the vote, they had few effective ways to argue for redress of grievances. The civil rights movement of the 1960s took the struggle to the streets and to the jails, but that kind of action could not be sustained year after year. Fortunately, the movement put at the top of its agenda the securing of the vote. The Voting Rights Act of 1965 led to a transformation in the political landscape of the country; a generation later, African American officials are found at all levels of government, elected largely by African American constituencies and working in the interests of those who elected them. They are a critical part of the Democratic Party coalition. Within a generation they have not transformed the condition of African Americans, but their presence ensures that their interests will be dealt with seriously. So too with women. When they lacked the vote and lacked political representation, they could not deal in a public way with their disadvantage in American society. With the vote, and with the creative use of political action, they have been able to raise concerns of women to the forefront. On the negative side, the fact that poor people and racial minorities are less likely to vote than other Americans means that their interests are less fully represented than they could be.

The optimism I have about the possibility of the United States' using continued immigration to develop into a country in which different cultures cooperate with one another in an open and equal way is based largely on a faith in the American political system. All the immigrant streams from Europe—Irish, Poles, Jews, Italians and others—found a way to participate fully in politics, from the local to the national levels. They used their positions in government to protect their communities, to advance their interests and to fight against the discrimination that they faced from other groups. One of the legacies of the civil rights movement is that the same opportunity is now open to people of non-European origins. Because of the victories of the 1960s, the vote cannot be denied to any group of citizens just because it is perceived as a threat to a dominant group.

The immigrant groups must, however, exercise the vote if they are to have an effective political strategy. If they do not, their numbers will still influence electoral districting, since it is based on census enumerations, but they cannot influence their representation. Immigrants must go through the naturalization process and become citizens, they must register to vote and, once registered, they must vote.

This is where the position of Latin American immigrants is weak. Since so many move back and forth across the borders and maintain an active presence in both the United States and their home countries, they are less apt than other immigrants to develop the sort of commitment to the United States that would make naturalization seem important. Furthermore, Latinos are the highest proportion of undocumented immigrants, a group that has no possibility of voting. This is one of the most serious problems connected with illegal immigration. It creates a subset of the population that is vulnerable to exploitation not simply because the migrants are in danger of deportation but because they cannot achieve political representation. These handicaps notwithstanding, Latinos are gaining ever-increasing representation at all levels of American government, and together with other immigrant and non-Anglo ethnic groups, they are able to exert some influence over public policy.

With representation comes the power to take action to protect ethnic and immigrant communities and to work for an agenda of change on behalf of a pluralist community. The new immigration inevitably leads to conflict, but if that conflict can be focused in the political sphere, it can be channeled in ways that are productive. Without a political forum, the conflict may take the form of discrimination, exploitation and violence, as the country has seen too often. Vigorous political debate of the issues and passage of appropriate legislation are the best ways of moving the country in the direction of meeting its next great challenge.

The overall conclusion of this chapter is optimistic. Today's immigrants have a great deal to contribute to America. They bring with them the hope—and the reasonable expectation—that the United States is on the road to becoming a dynamic multicultural society in which representatives of all the world's peoples will interact in ways that are peaceful and respectful and that have the effect of enriching all the parties to the interactions. To achieve this will not be easy, and it is not inevitable. It is a worthy goal for the country, however. If it can be achieved, America will be a model to the world.

Notes

1. Quoted in Albert R. Hunt, "Demagoging the Immigration Issue," *Wall Street Journal* (July 7, 1994), A13.
2. Quoted in "Divided We Stand, the Immigration Backlash," *San Francisco Chronicle* (March 29, 1994), A6–7.
3. Peter Brimelow, "Response," *National Review* (February 1, 1993), 33.
4. Michael Walzer, *What It Means to Be an American* (New York: Marsilio Publishers, 1992), 27. In writing this section, I have been strongly influenced by Walzer's essays.
5. Stephen Steinberg's interpretation of the melting pot is much more conflictual and oppressive than the usual account. See *The Ethnic Myth, Race, Ethnicity and Class in America*, 2d ed. (Boston: Beacon Press, 1989), ch. 1.
6. Nathan Glazer and Daniel Patrick Moynihan, *Beyond the Melting Pot, the Negroes, Puerto Ricans, Jews, Italians and Irish of New York City* (Cambridge, Mass.: MIT Press, 1963).
7. Ronald Takaki, *A Different Mirror, a History of Multicultural America* (New York: Little, Brown, 1993).
8. Peter Brimelow, *Alien Nation, Common Sense about America's Immigration Disaster* (New York: Random House, 1995), 10, 221.
9. My personal observations have been informed, and are confirmed, by a study of the student body at the University of California, Berkeley, *The Diversity Project: Final Report* (Berkeley, Calif.: Institute for the Study of Social Change, 1991).
10. Arthur M. Schlesinger Jr., *The Disuniting of America, Reflections on a Multicultural Society* (Knoxville, Tenn.: Whittle Direct Books, 1991). For an equally passionate attack on current American race relations, see Jared Taylor, *Paved with Good Intentions, the Failure of Race Relations in Contemporary America* (New York: Carroll and Graf, 1992).
11. Karl Polanyi, *The Great Transformation* (New York: Farrar and Rinehart, 1944).
12. Schlesinger, *The Disuniting of America*, 62.
13. The unemployment rates in this and the previous paragraph are from *The Economic Report of the President* (Washington, D.C.: U.S. Government Printing Office, 1995), 320.
14. Peter H. Schuck, "The Transformation of Immigration Law," *Columbia Law Review* 84 (1984):7.
15. Rosemary E. Jenks, "Immigration and Nationality Policies of Leading Migration Nations," *Population and Environment* 14 (1993):567–92.
16. For a thoughtful exposition of an opposing viewpoint, see Peter H. Schuck and Rogers M. Smith, *Citizenship without Consent, Illegal Aliens in the American Polity* (New Haven, Conn.: Yale University Press, 1985).
17. For a review of what analysts at the Urban Institute call "immigrant policies," see Michael Fix and Wendy Zimmermann, "After Arrival: An Overview of Federal Immigrant Policy in the United States," and Wendy Zimmermann and Michael Fix, "Immigrant Policy in the States: A Wavering Welcome," both in *Immigration and Ethnicity, The Integration*

of America's Newest Arrivals, ed. Barry Edmonston and Jeffrey S. Passel (Washington, D.C.: Urban Institute Press, 1994), 251–85, 287–316.

18. Fix and Zimmermann, "After Arrival," 258.

19. Abraham Foxman, letter to the editor, *Wall Street Journal* (July 21, 1994), A15.

9

Interests and Ethics in Immigration Policy

American immigration policy is a hodgepodge of diverse regulations, the result of political compromises among narrow interest groups. If one were to try to discern the purposes of the country's immigration policy by reading the relevant legislation and by examining the statistical record, one would conclude that Americans' principal goal in the area of immigration is family reunification.[3] Although Americans care about family reunification, they have many other pressing concerns related to immigration: jobs, wages, economic growth, public finance, cultural diversity, language acquisition, responsibility to refugees, even fairness. Yet these concerns are translated into policy either obscurely or not at all.

This final chapter turns therefore to the question of how American immigration policy should be formulated. It argues that a national interest exists, beyond the often conflicting particular interests, and that an ethical approach can be identified—and that these should be the bases of American immigration policy.

The two approaches—national interest and ethics—are in some tension with each other. Those who base their views

In a truly liberal polity, it would be difficult to justify a restrictive immigration law or perhaps any immigration law at all.
—Peter H. Schuck[1]

If you love everybody, you love nobody. And that's the bottom line. And we've got to love our own people first.

—Rep. Dana Rohrabacher, R-Calif.[2]

on national interest believe that Americans have a responsibility only to themselves. They believe that Americans should think in terms that are broader than just their personal interests but that the standard for judging immigration policy should be to maximize the welfare of all Americans taken together. From this point of view, the benefit to the potential immigrants has no standing: if their entry helps American residents, let them in; if it hurts, keep them out.

I would like to argue, however, along with others, that the criteria for evaluating immigration policy should include not just interest but morality. Interest is inward looking and self-serving; morality looks outward to the rights and welfare of others. To pursue the national interest may be more ethically defensible than simply to pursue one's personal interest, but the national interest has its moral limitations. It would be a curious ethical system that accorded moral worth to some people and denied it to others solely on the grounds of whether their legal residence fell within a particular geographical boundary.

Interests

Let us start with the interests of Americans. Exclude for now their altruism, their identity with foreigners, their ethical sense, their preference at times for outcomes that benefit others even at a cost to themselves. Looked at narrowly, what immigration policy will best serve Americans?

As the previous chapters have shown, no clear answer exists to this question, for a number of reasons. The answers to many of the factual questions remain cloudy. We are not sure of the effect of immigration on wages and unemployment, on environmental quality and international competitiveness, on the plight of the least fortunate Americans and on the profits of the wealthiest. All these questions and more have been studied extensively, and the studies have narrowed our range of ignorance, but they have not brought us to a consensus. We are even less certain about the effects of immigration on political and community values in the United States, on social cohesiveness, public safety, intellectual stimulation and other less quantitative variables. People often speak as though the cause-and-effect relationships were transparent, but the research of social scientists has shown that they are not.

The national interest is also complicated by the conflict among the various interests of individuals and groups. One cannot find the national interest simply by adding individual interests, since they are in contradiction with one another. Politicians and columnists are fond of ascribing views to "the American people," but the American people are divided on most issues of public policy. If the national interest has any meaning, it can only be as a result of value judgments that some people's interests are more compelling than others. What follows, therefore, is a personal, although I hope reasoned, assessment of the national interest in immigration policy.

Columnist George Will argues that in spite of the fact that immigration helps the economy, it disrupts the social fabric to such an extent that it should be reduced.[4] My view is the opposite. Immigration probably harms Americans economically but helps them socially and culturally. The multicultural future of the United States is so important that the national interest lies in the continuation of fairly high levels of immigration.

Economically, as earlier chapters showed, immigration affects different people differently. For the most part, one group's gain is another's loss. Immigration may increase the scale of the U.S. economy and it may benefit employers and capital, but it probably harms working people, particularly the unskilled, and it increases pressure on the environment and on nonrenewable resources. The reason that my judgment differs from Will's is not, I suspect, a difference in our assessment of the facts. Rather, I give more weight to the harm imposed on unskilled and minority Americans by immigration, whereas Will values the improved business climate and the generation of profits.

The United States is a country of terrible inequalities. It is one of the world's richest lands, yet it is marred by a legacy of racism, by a growing underclass and by an ever-widening gap between rich and poor. One of its pressing tasks is to narrow that gap and give new hope to people who are hopeless.

Immigration is one factor among several that worsens the prospects of the poor in the United States. Although the studies reviewed in Chapter 6 are contradictory, as that chapter argued, the weight of the evidence is that the wages and employment of Americans fall in response to immigration—and this surely impacts most heavily on the poor. Immigration also probably helps a number of businesses by keeping their labor costs low.

The fiscal impacts of immigration are in doubt, with the preponderance of the evidence indicating a net fiscal benefit at the national level along with significant fiscal costs for some states and local jurisdictions where immigrants have settled in disproportionate numbers.

Averaged across the entire economy and the entire population, however, the national benefit is so small as to be virtually undetectable, whereas the net costs in some smaller areas are large enough to impose hardships.

In terms of long-run economic impacts, as shown in Chapter 7, a case can be made that immigration will have negative effects on both the environment and the international competitive position of the United States in world trade. These effects are not firmly established—long-run effects seldom can be—but it is telling that they are not balanced by persuasive arguments on the other side.

Taking the pieces of the economic analysis together, it is not in the overall economic interest of Americans to continue the type of immigration that the country has seen in recent years. There may be some negative effects, and there are unlikely to be positive effects, with the exception of improved business profits that come at the expense of the economic welfare of poor Americans. The economy is not everything, however—Bill Clinton's 1992 presidential campaign to the contrary notwithstanding. The character of the American people may be more important.

Chapter 8 outlined the case that America is a multicultural society; it always has been, it is now and it will be in the future. The first generations of settlers had to grapple with the complex problems created by the "others": by the Indians, by Europeans with different religious sensibilities and by African slaves. Over the centuries, the interactions of cultures became more complicated as the national sources of the different immigrant waves changed and as the slaves were freed.

From time to time, including at the present, a movement has arisen in the United States to assert that a unified American culture is threatened by the new immigrants who do not share that culture. This movement is mistaken. There is no single American culture; the melting pot has had some effect, but it has not obliterated the principal ethnic and cultural distinctions among Americans. The United States is not a European country; it is a country rooted in many areas of the world. It is not a white country, but a country composed of many races. It is not a Christian country, but a country in which many faiths (and the absence of faith) coexist. It is the mixture of all these elements, not their absence, that gives the United States its character.

The multicultural nature of American society should not be at issue. What is reasonably in contention is whether the many cultures can live in harmony, preserving what is important to each while stimulating and enriching one another—or whether racism, oppression, suspicion and hostility will be the themes of American public life. In all probability, the answer will never be completely clear; American cross-cultural life will likely continue to be marked by some cooperation and good will combined with some tension and conflict. It is important to shift the balance toward the former.

Immigration can help with the process of cultural accommodation. The continual arrival of new people will help renew the different American cultures; it will keep them alive and vibrant and remind Americans of their many origins. Because current immigration is predominantly from the third world, the ethnic balance in the country is shifting. Eventually, whites will be in a minority, and no single group will have a preponderant position. As the various groups participate in the political process at all levels of government, they will face one another on a more equal basis than they do now. Immigration is helping to bring about this change from a majority confronting several minorities that are struggling to achieve a foothold, toward many different groups that are equivalent in terms of status.

Immigration by itself will not accomplish this. Chapter 8 outlined an agenda of policies that could help the transition to a reciprocal multicultural society; doubtless that list could be lengthened. Continued immigration is a central part of the strategy, but not unrestricted immigration.

No one knows how many people would choose to come to the United States if border controls were abolished and the country returned to the immigration policy of the nineteenth century. Certainly the number of entrants would be larger than it is today. The absorptive capacity of the United States is not unlimited. If the flow of immigrants were much greater than it is today, the transition mechanisms—the processes by which the newcomers acquire labor market and language skills and learn how to function efficiently in their new country—might well deteriorate. A large increase in unskilled labor would probably have a negative impact on low-income and unskilled American residents, many of them recent immigrants or members of minority groups themselves, and this would increase, not reduce, the tension among the different cultures. It is impossible to be precise about what amount of immigration is "just right," but unrestricted immigration would likely create more social problems within the country than it could solve efficiently.

Where, then, does the national interest lie? If the national interest were strictly economic, a reduction in the current level of immigration would be called for. But since the national interest is much broader than just economic, and since multicultural relations are so central to American life and immigration can help improve those relations, a continued relatively high rate of immigration is justified. A consideration of the national interest leads to the conclusion that something like the current rate of immigration is optimal: not a reduction and not a great deal more.

The next sections broaden the inquiry by considering the morality of U.S. immigration policy.

An Ethical Argument for Open Borders

Americans typically express their opinions about immigration with certainty and moral outrage. I would like to argue, however, that most Americans are in an ethically fraught position with respect to immigration. We have deeply held convictions about the equality of all people. At the same time, though, we use immigration policy to perpetuate a privileged lifestyle at the expense of foreigners. We are not prepared to abandon either this use of immigration policy or the ideology of equality. At the very least, therefore, our moral stance should be one of humility, not outrage.

This section outlines an argument, grounded in ethics, against the very existence of immigration controls.[5] The next section considers a series of rejoinders to this argument.

The moral validity of border controls is drawn into question if we believe in the moral equality of all human beings. If only Americans have moral standing, or if Americans are more worthy than non-Americans, we do not need to take into account the rights of others on an equal basis. If all people are equally valuable, however, a policy that favors one group at the expense of another—such as apartheid, Jim Crow laws or immigration controls—seems on its face to be invalid.

Moral worth is not the same as merit. As philosopher Gregory Vlastos stated, "It differs from every kind of merit, including moral merit, in respect to which there are vast inequalities among persons."[6] People earn merit by their behavior, talent and skills and may be judged quite differently. They are equally worthy, however, simply by virtue of being human beings.

Philosophers have made many attempts to demonstrate the equal worth of all people.[7] For the most part, though, those of us who believe in equality treat it as an assumption, an axiom, not something to be proved. The axiom of equal worth is at the core of the two most important statements of political philosophy in American history, the Declaration of Independence and the Gettysburg Address.

In the Declaration of Independence, Thomas Jefferson wrote, "We hold these Truths to be self-evident, that all Men are created equal." He did not argue the point; it was "self-evident." The importance of equality was that equal rights accrue to all people: "They are endowed by their Creator with certain unalienable Rights, that among these are Life, Liberty, and the Pursuit of Happiness."

Neither Jefferson nor his Virginian compatriots conducted their lives in accordance with these "Truths," for they were slaveholders. Similarly today, most people do not base their actions on a commitment to the equality of all people. Nevertheless, for the most part, we believe in equality not because we have reasoned it out and considered the arguments pro and con but because it is "self-evident."

The radical equality of the Declaration of Independence was restricted sharply by the more conservative Constitution of 1789, a document that, among other things, protected slavery. As Gary Wills has argued, however, Abraham Lincoln's Gettysburg Address of 1863 had the effect of subverting the Constitution by restoring equality as the central American value.[8] It began, in words now as familiar to Americans as those of the Declaration, and more familiar than any in the Constitution, "Fourscore and seven years ago, our fathers brought forth upon this continent a new nation, conceived in liberty and dedicated to the proposition that all men are created equal."

Neither document says "all Americans are created equal." Jefferson and Lincoln may or may not have implied "people" by their use of the word "men," but in our current reading we do. These most formative of American documents assume the equality of all human beings.

People are equally valuable and therefore have equal rights. It does not follow from this that they have unlimited rights. Rights often conflict with one another, and when they do, the liberal state (that is, the state based on the presumption of equal worth) is justified in restricting some rights in order to protect others. Whenever it restricts rights, however, the state must be able to give morally justifiable reasons why it has done so—otherwise it forfeits its claim to liberalism and descends into despotism.

Immigration controls restrict free movement by establishing groups that have unequal rights. Among those people in the world who wish to live in the United States, the favored are allowed to, and others are not. Can one successfully argue that immigration controls that infringe on some people's liberties are justified because they protect more important rights and liberties? Or does their allocation of unequal rights to people who are of equal worth make them morally impermissible?

Freedom of movement is a facet of the "Liberty" that the Declaration of Independence takes to be an inherent right of equal human beings. Countries that systematically restrict the movement of their people are rightly criticized. In recent years, the clearest example of the morally unjustified restriction of internal movement was in South Africa, which enforced its apartheid system with pass laws.

As a mental exercise, one could ask how a law passed by the residents of New York City that restricted the permanent entry of Americans who were not city residents would be judged. Leaving aside the fact that it would be unconstitutional, would it be morally justified? The people of New York could offer some good reasons for the law. New York is already crowded and cannot tolerate further population growth, they might argue. The sanitation system is close to breaking down, the schools are crowded, the welfare system is bankrupt, the homeless shelters are inadequate and the unemployment rate is rising.

These sorts of arguments would not prove convincing to most Americans, who would find the restriction on personal freedom too onerous. Every day people migrate into (and out of) New York for compelling reasons. They move in order to accept jobs or to look for jobs or because their jobs have been relocated to New York. They could not have the same jobs in Boston or Chicago because New York is unique (as are Boston and Chicago). They move to New York to be with their families or to care for friends or for any number of other reasons. The decision to migrate to New York is seldom taken lightly; people have good reasons. The interests that New Yorkers have in restricting entry, although perhaps meritorious, are not of sufficient weight to permit such massive violations of the rights and interests of outsiders. New York cannot justify its own immigration policy, morally.

If this argument is accepted, how can one accept immigration restrictions in the United States? What makes the United States different from New York? Nothing much, except sovereign power. If New York were a sovereign state it might well have an immigration policy, notwithstanding the fact that the policy violated the rights of non–New Yorkers. New York's laws would not have to conform to the laws and constitution of a broader entity, so its government would not be compelled to take into account the rights of people outside its jurisdiction. This would not, however, make a restrictive immigration policy ethical, unless one could somehow argue that by virtue of their sovereignty New Yorkers abandoned their moral connections to people outside their border.

Reasoning by analogy, it is hard to find an ethical justification for the United States' restricting entry across its borders. In fact it is harder, since the people of the United States are privileged, vis-à-vis the rest of the world, in a way that the residents of New York are not, in comparison to other Americans. New Yorkers could argue plausibly that among American cities their city is not so special, that people denied entry into it could find comparable amenities in other cities. The United States occupies a unique position in the world, however, or at least the long lines of potential immigrants would so indicate. The great majority of immigrants and potential immigrants hope to enjoy a significantly higher standard of living in the United States than they experienced in their home countries. Immigration controls on the U.S. border therefore restrict access to privilege.

It is the protection of privilege that is so damaging, ethically, to the country's immigration laws. It makes U.S. border controls even less justifiable than New York's would be. The purpose and effect of American immigration controls are to maintain a state of inequality in the world between the haves (the Americans) and the have-nots (the foreigners, especially the potential immigrants). Americans maintain immigration laws because they fear that unrestricted entry would lead to a major influx of people, that the newcomers would compete for scarce resources and jobs in the United States and that they would drive down the standard of living of residents. No doubt it is in the interest of the privileged to protect their privileges, but it cannot be ethical if that protection has the effect of further disadvantaging the unprivileged.

The ethical case against immigration controls is based, therefore, not just on the fact that they convey unequal rights to morally equal people but that they do so in a particularly damaging way, so as to protect advantage and deepen disadvantage. To understand the importance of this, one can consider the argument that some types of unequal treatment are morally justified. For example, a system of preferential hiring in which race is taken into account treats different groups of people unequally, but it may be fair if it is designed to benefit people who have been exploited or to dismantle a system of racial injustice.[9] Unequal treatment is clearly unjust, however, when it is used to perpetuate rather than break down a system of privilege and disadvantage. This is just what American immigration controls do. They violate the equal worth and equal rights of people in an egregious way, by sheltering already advantaged Americans at the expense of relatively disadvantaged potential immigrants.

A second ethical argument against border controls is that they automatically create a class of people in the United States who have fewer rights, the undocumented. The undocumented are branded as illegal; police forces arrest and deport them. Border controls will never eliminate this group, as long as foreigners who are denied entry see some advantage in being in the country. As earlier chapters have shown, undocumented immigrants are part of American society; they work, pay taxes, contribute to their communities and have personal relationships with American citizens and legal residents. Yet many rights that legal residents take for granted are denied to them.

The argument was made in Chapter 8 that their rights should be enhanced. At bottom, however, the dilemma cannot be resolved as long as border controls remain. The very meaning of border controls is that some people are denied entry. The denial must be enforced if the border controls are to exist. Consequently, the undocumented must have rights that are inferior to those of other residents. The only way to avoid the unequal treatment of American residents is to remove the restrictions on immigration.

Arguments for Immigration Controls

This section considers six ethical arguments that are made in favor of immigration controls, in ascending order of persuasiveness. They are not the only arguments made in the academic literature and the political discourse, but they seem to me to be the strongest. In the end, I find that the first five are rationalizations used to perpetuate a structure of advantage and disadvantage in the world while allowing Americans to avoid this truth, and that their moral logic fails. The sixth argument, however, has merit and leaves us with a conflict of rights.

"Immigration Is Theft"

It is argued that the United States, with all its wealth, is the property of Americans, to treat as they wish. Immigrants want to share in the country's wealth, but they have no right to it unless Americans willingly offer it to them. People have the legal and moral right to protect their property against theft. They are under no obligation to give it away.

Is the country the private property of Americans? Can one say that Americans own the United States, just as an individual owns a house? Or would a better analogy be to a public beach? Whoever arrives first on a secluded beach would perhaps like to claim title and keep others from gaining access to it, but the first-comer has no right to do so, because the beach is common property. International law gives Americans the legal right to treat the country as their private house, but I think that morally the United States has more of the characteristics of a public beach.

The United States is both a land area and the society that has been built on it. As to the land itself, Americans are in a weak position to claim exclusive ownership of it, since they are such recent arrivals themselves. Most Americans are only a few generations removed from immigration. If they were to take seriously the claim of prior ownership, they would have to return the land to the descendants of the Native Americans whom their forebears pushed aside and slaughtered. They are not prepared to do this. They cannot successfully claim, therefore, that a new wave of entrants has fewer rights of access to the land than their immigrant predecessors did.

The United States is more than the land, however; it is the improvements as well. Today the United States is far different from the place the settlers wrested from the Native Americans. It is now a rich country—and it is because of its standard of living, not its land mass, that it is a mecca for immigrants. Can Americans claim that they created the wealth they enjoy and that they therefore have the sole right to decide whether and which foreigners have access to it? I think not.

For the most part, Americans now living did not create the wealth; they inherited it. At the time they were born, the United States was already one of the world's richest countries, and its wealth was growing rapidly. If anything, the collective actions of Americans over the last quarter century have diminished their inheritance. By living beyond their means, both personally and publicly, Americans have actually lowered the standard of living of a good many people. They are living off their inheritance.

In other words, Americans now living found a lovely beach; they did not build or buy a new house. Since they are not responsible for their good fortune, they do not have the moral right to deny other people the opportunity to share in it.

Not so, Americans might reply. We have a right to our inheritance. Our ancestors built this country not just for their own pleasure but for the well-being of their children. If one could ask them who has a claim to the riches they built up, they would reply that it is we, their descendants.

This argument is not silly, but it is not transparently valid either. Inheritance presents ethical difficulties. Small inheritances are certainly morally justifiable, since they represent a simple expression of family love. Just as a mother cares for her baby, so does she want to pass some of her gains on to her child after her death. To want to do so is not wrong; indeed, to fail to do so would be thought by most people to exhibit a lack of parental love. When inheritance is so substantial that it perpetuates a system of privilege and disadvantage, however, it lacks moral justification, since it violates the norms of equal access, equal opportunity and equal treatment—the norms that follow from the axiom of equal worth. Americans would reject as immoral the rigid class system of medieval Europe or the caste system of India, in which one's prospects in life were completely determined by the accident of birth. That sort of inheritance is immoral. And it is just the sort of inheritance that Americans as a whole have received from their ancestors, an inheritance that gives them enormously greater privilege than most of the rest of humankind. It does not give them the right to exclude others from their country.

One cannot, therefore, defend immigration restrictions as protection against theft. Immigrants are not burglars.

"Open Immigration Would Destroy Important American Values"

The second argument for border controls is that unrestricted immigration might destroy institutions or values in the United States that are of transcendent importance. Open immigration might destroy something that is vital not only to Americans but to foreigners and potential immigrants as well.

What might such institutions or values be? Political scientist Frederick Whelan argues that liberal values—equal moral worth, democracy, equal access and so on—are scarce and precious in the world and need protection. It is a mistake to use liberal principles to argue for open access, if open access would diminish liberal values and institutions in the world.[10]

The concern is one of absorptive capacity and the assimilative powers of the United States. A massive influx of foreigners who were unfamiliar with and uncommitted to American political values might use the democratic procedures of the country to destroy the institutions that support those procedures, before they had the opportunity to adopt as their own the principles of freedom and self-government. Under such circumstances, Whelan and others argue that the state is morally justified in restricting immigration. A closely related argument made by political scientist Michael Walzer is that the citizens of a community have the right to protect their values and culture from disruption by outsiders.[11]

These arguments may have theoretical merit, but no evidence exists that they relate to a real danger in the United States. Native groups have often opposed the political positions taken by immigrants, regarding them as inimical to their interests, but this is simply evidence that the immigrants have adapted to the political norms of the country and have used the political process to their own benefit. Disagreement over political goals is not the same as rejection of basic political philosophy. During the entire period before the twentieth century, when the United States maintained open borders, the principal threat to a liberal political system in the country came not from recent immigrants but from the slaveholders who were descended from the first white settlers.

"We Have Better Ways of Helping the World's Disadvantaged"

The third argument in favor of immigration controls is that although Americans may be morally obliged to redress the imbalance of privilege in the world, they can do so more effectively by implementing policies to improve standards of living in poor countries than by allowing a few residents of those countries to immigrate. Immigration focuses the benefits of American resources on just a few people. Action to improve the entire economies of poor countries would affect far more people. The policy tools available to the U.S. government are innumerable, including not only foreign aid, loans and technical assistance but also trade, investment and fiscal and monetary policies designed to benefit poor countries. In addition, individuals can contribute best to world justice by making personal charitable contributions.[12]

An effective rejoinder to this argument is that although rich countries and their citizens may have a duty to assist in the economic development of poor countries, fulfillment of this duty does not relieve them of the obligation to allow immigration. The two policies are not alternatives; they can be thought of rather as complements with different sorts of effects. Foreign economic aid, though never enough and often ineffective, is normally designed to facilitate small improvements in the lives of large numbers of people. Immigration enables a relatively small number of people, the immigrants, to make a radical change in their living situations. One would like to find a policy that combines the merits of both—one that lifts the economic disadvantage of a large fraction of the world's people in a short period of time. No such policy exists. In its absence, therefore, the residents of the world's richer countries have a duty to do what they can on all fronts. The case for open borders is not refuted just because other ways exist for Americans to redress injustice.

"Americans Have a Special Obligation to Their Fellow Citizens"

The fourth argument for immigration controls is that Americans have greater obligations to their fellow citizens than to foreigners. If there is a reasonable possibility that immigration may hurt some U.S. citizens, Americans are justified in restricting entry, even though restrictions may violate the rights of foreigners.[13]

Consider a parallel case that is clearer. A middle-class couple has enough savings to provide either a basic education for a poor orphan or supplementary educational enrichment for their own child. The orphan has the greater disadvantage and the greater need, but few would criticize the parents for deciding that their priority was to provide the best possible education for their own child. Can Americans not make a similar case relating to their fellow citizens?

Perhaps they can. Perhaps one can posit a series of widening circles, and outside of each circle our obligations diminish. Our greatest obligation is to our family, then perhaps to our friends, then to our neighbors, then perhaps to our ethnic group, then to our fellow citizens and finally to all people. No doubt a great many people think this way. To test yourself, think back to the spring and summer of 1994, when hundreds of thousands of innocent Rwandans were murdered, and ask whether that event occasioned as much moral anger in you as did a smaller, more local violation of rights, such as the burglary of a neighbor's home. Most Americans had some sympathy for the Rwandans, but not as much as they would have, had they been neighbors.

People think this way, but that does not mean that this kind of thinking is morally justified. Before accepting this view as the proper basis for immigration policy, it is important to understand how devastating it is to the proposition with which this inquiry into ethics began: that all people are morally equal and as a consequence have equal rights. The fourth argument denies this "Truth" of the Declaration of Independence. If the argument is accepted, Americans have greater moral standing than foreigners and more rights, at least as seen through the eyes of Americans.

I think that we must concede that kin have greater standing than nonrelatives in the moral considerations of most people and that this is natural and good. In all likelihood, it is an evolutionary necessity. But further departures from the norm of equal moral worth seem to me to be unjustified. The failure to recognize the full humanity of people who are different from oneself—people who have different ethnic backgrounds, languages, religions, citizenships and so forth—is at the root of much of the warfare and suffering in the world today. We may feel a more natural connection to people who are like us in some ways, but if we act on that feeling, we are in danger of creating terribly unjust situations, such as those in Rwanda and Bosnia.

I do not mean to disparage patriotism. Love of one's country can be an affirming, healthy sentiment. An ethical patriot recognizes, however, that his or her patriotism does not diminish the rights of others. Patriotism and other kinds of group identity must be grounded in the understanding that everyone else has equal rights and that one's own group is not justified in reducing the rights of other groups in any way.

Although it is tempting, the fourth argument for immigration controls fails. If we develop public policy on the presumption of unequal worth, we are heading down a path toward conflict and selfishness, not moral clarity.

"Americans Are Not Obliged to Be Heroic"

The fifth argument for immigration controls is that although people may have an obligation to come to the aid of other people in distress, that obligation holds only if it can be done without undue sacrifice. The idea is sometimes called the "principle of mutual aid," or the "cutoff for heroism." To incur or risk great sacrifice for someone else's benefit is commendable because it is heroic, but because it is heroic, it is not required. Ordinary people have an obligation to take ordinary care for their fellow humans, but not to be saints.[14] Andrew Shacknove describes the principle this way:

In its classic form, the principle of mutual aid envisions a passer-by who encounters a drowning child. If the passer-by can easily save the child, she is morally obligated to do so, even if the child is a complete stranger. Failure to save the child under such conditions would be universally condemned as callousness. If, to the contrary, the passer-by could hope to rescue the child only at great personal risk, no one would chastise her for not acting. The passer-by is not expected to sacrifice life or limb because of a chance encounter with a stranger. Doing so is heroic, but heroism by its nature is voluntary; it exceeds the limits of obligation.[15]

The analogy to immigration policy is obvious. If the cutoff for heroism is a valid principle, and if it takes precedence over other moral principles—if we are required to help our fellow human beings only when doing so is not very difficult or dangerous—we may be rescued from the obligation to open our borders to all comers. In the long run, at least, open borders would probably entail a real sacrifice for many Americans. Immigrants come to the United States partly because of its high standard of living; they would likely continue to come until they had driven down wages and driven up unemployment to such an extent that immigration was no longer so attractive.

Perhaps we can say, then, that morality does not require such a heroic sacrifice. Americans are obligated to do what they can to alleviate suffering in the world, as long as they do not have to pay a significant price.

The argument is respectable, but it is too comforting to the rich and privileged to stand unmodified. It is a justification for continued injustice. If it is applicable to Americans, why is it not equally applicable to anyone in a position of privilege? Could it not be used by any reactionary to justify keeping his status and income: by the King of France before the Revolution, by southern slaveholders before the Civil War, by South African whites before the transfer of power? Any readjustment of a privilege-disadvantage relationship calls for sacrifice on the part of the privileged. If the principle of the cutoff for heroism is dominant, if it holds greater weight than the principle of the equal moral worth of all people, the privileged are morally justified in maintaining their privilege.

Attractive though the fifth objection is, it fails as an ethical justification for immigration controls. The cutoff for heroism may be a valid principle when a passerby is considering saving a drowning child, because in that case the two people are not connected by a relationship of privilege and subordination. When it is used as an argument for protecting privilege, however, it does not have greater moral weight than the principle of equal worth or even the Golden Rule.

"Immigration Controls Protect the Disadvantaged"

The sixth and strongest argument against open borders is that immigration controls may not protect the privileged at all, but rather the unprivileged. The discussion in this and the previous section tacitly assumes that all Americans are the same, but they are not. Some are privileged, and some are severely disadvantaged: the poor, the unskilled and many members of minority groups.

The research that has been conducted so far on the impact of immigration on the prospects of disadvantaged Americans is not definitive. Nevertheless, an increased and unending supply of low-wage labor from third world countries would likely keep the earnings of unskilled workers low and profits high, thereby increasing the gap between the poor and the rich in the United States. If so, it is argued, immigration should be curtailed.

Sometimes this argument is mixed with either the fourth or the fifth argument, but those arguments can be refuted, as we have seen. The sixth argument should not depend on the assertion that Americans are more worthy than foreigners; they are not. Neither should it depend on the assertion that immigration should require no sacrifice from Americans; sacrifice may be morally required.

Can the sixth argument be refuted successfully? One way of attempting to do so would be to say that immigration policy need not bear the burden of reducing the inequities among Americans. Many other policy tools are available, among them welfare, education, social insurance programs and job training. In the conservative political atmosphere of the mid-1990s, these policies are being deemphasized, but if the country had a commitment to reducing poverty, it could reverse those trends. If it did, it could promote social justice at home and still allow increased immigration. Put differently, the obligation to rectify the imbalances of privilege in the world rests on the shoulders of the privileged in the rich countries, not everyone in those countries. Morality requires them to transfer resources to their less fortunate brethren at home and to allow immigrants from the third world to enter their country.

This refutation is valid, but only up to a point. Certainly rich and middle-class Americans cannot ethically argue that the welfare of their poor fellow citizens requires them to discriminate against poor foreigners when they are actually reducing their help to their own people. Still, it is likely that, even if the United States made a massive good-faith effort to reduce domestic poverty, it could never be successful if completely open immigration were permitted. Whatever advances were made in the welfare of the American poor would be negated by new immigrants from poor countries who were seeking to take advantage of American generosity.

A second possible refutation is to assert that the needs of foreigners are more pressing than the needs of even disadvantaged Americans. The relative gap between the rich and the poor in the United States is substantial and shameful, but it is far from the largest in the world; the gap in many third world countries, including the largest senders of immigrants to the United States, is greater. The standard of living of most poor Americans is higher than the *average* standard of living in most poor countries and certainly higher than the standard of living of most immigrants. Many Mexicans, for example, enter the United States in order to earn wages that, although low by American standards, are several multiples of what they could earn at home. In the hierarchy of advantage, therefore, poor Americans occupy an intermediate position—much worse off than other Americans, but still better off than many immigrants. Therefore, one might maintain that it is morally permissible to harm poor Americans if this is the price that must be paid to improve the lot of poor immigrants.

This refutation is not persuasive. Poor Americans are genuinely needy and unfairly impoverished. It simply cannot be right to take conscious, public action to worsen their plight. Morality obliges us to protect the welfare not just of the most disadvantaged people in the world but of all who suffer disadvantage.

The sixth argument in favor of border controls is therefore valid. So, however, is the argument in the previous section for open borders. We are left with an ethical conflict. On the one hand, disadvantaged foreigners have a moral right to enter the world's most privileged country, in an attempt to improve their position. On the other hand, poor Americans have the right to be protected against so much competition from low-income newcomers that their own circumstances deteriorate. The conflict cannot be resolved completely; in the end, the best solution may be a compromise.

Although the conflict of rights cannot be resolved completely, it can be resolved partially. Recall the point made above that as long as the United States is a rich country, with a majority of its people very well off or at least comfortable, it is not ethical to depend on immigration restrictions alone to improve the position of poor Americans. Such a policy would put the burden of sacrifice on even poorer foreigners rather than on comfortable Americans—the truly privileged among equally worthy human beings—where it rightfully belongs.

The sixth argument is therefore a valid justification for immigration restrictions only if (1) the restrictions are accompanied by a major national commitment to improve the quality of life of the U.S. poor and (2) in the absence of restrictions, the flow of immigrants would be too great to allow that program to be successful.

An Ethical Immigration Policy

An ethically defensible immigration policy, based on the principle of equal moral worth, would be just one component of an integrated program in which rich and middle-class Americans fulfilled their obligations to people who are of equal moral worth but through no fault of their own are in less fortunate circumstances. The policy would harm no one who was in an already disadvantaged position, would help as many disadvantaged people as possible and would require sacrifice on the part of the privileged. The program would consist of at least the following:

1. Privileged Americans (the majority in the United States) would greatly increase their commitment to improving the well-being of the American poor by transferring such a significant portion of their resources to them that they bore a real sacrifice.

2. The United States would increase its commitment to foreign aid and other ways of improving the standard of living in poor countries.

3. The United States would raise the flow of immigrants, in order to increase the number of foreigners who had a chance of participating in the advantages of American life. This could be done without hurting the domestic poor, if the country really did increase its commitment to the poor, as stipulated above.

4. The United States would maintain some quantitative limit on immigration, or at least the stand-by authority to impose a limit if the flow of immigration became too great to be absorbed without sacrifice by the U.S. poor.

ble to live—even if this meant cutting back on immigrants who4were admitted for reasons of employment or family reunifica-he next section returns to this point.

In the end, the case for completely open borders can probably not
be sustained; some limits on immigration may be required. Note,
however, how different this argument is from the usual discourse. The
usual view is that American immigration policy should maximize the
interests of American residents. The argument I am making is that
privileged Americans have a moral obligation to redress the balance
of privilege in the world, through immigration and other policies. How
exactly to do this is complex, because the structure of privilege and
disadvantage in the world is not straightforward. Any adjustment of
that relationship in the direction of greater equity, however, will require
sacrifice by those who currently have the advantage, not the enhancement of their own self-interest.

This conclusion is troubling because it is so completely at variance
not only with U.S. immigration policy but also with every country's
policy and with the opinions of almost every American. Faced with such
overwhelming rejection of one's reasoning, a prudent person should
consider the possibility of being in error.

Of course, I may be. I think, however, that what has been uncovered is
a fundamental dilemma. Americans are not about to admit so many immigrants that they bear a significant cost. For those who are comfortable
simply with the pursuit of self-interest, the immigration restrictions will
not cause any sleepless nights. Those Americans who are genuinely
altruistic, however, those who try to think out their positions from an ethical perspective and who believe in the equal worth of all people, those
most admirable of Americans need to come to terms with the fact that
they are among the world's privileged, that immigration controls protect
their privilege and that they are not going to abandon that protection.

It is a dilemma familiar to thoughtful people, though not necessarily in the context of immigration. Who has not, at least momentarily,
compared his or her life to Mother Teresa's and concluded that it is
wanting in courage and ethics? Can those of us who are not willing to
abandon our worldly goods and devote our lives completely to the
service of the poor claim to live moral lives?

This investigation into the ethics of immigration policy has concluded that, even if completely open borders are not required, Americans should still welcome immigrants to their country in such large numbers that they sacrifice and that their position of privilege in the world is reduced. We can be certain that this conclusion is not going to be translated into policy. Almost no American would stand for it. We are up against the uncomfortable realization, therefore, that our actions to maintain our standard of living through our immigration policy are inherently immoral. If this understanding does not change Americans' behavior, it may at least clarify where we stand.

Priorities

If immigration policy is developed solely with regard to the interests of Americans, the number of entrants will be restricted. If policy is developed with an eye toward global ethics, the number may also be restricted, although more loosely. In either case, Americans will be in the position, as they are now, of choosing among applicants. How should they make the choices?[16]

Currently, as Chapter 3 showed, immigrants are admitted in a complex series of priority categories. The largest number of entries is reserved for relatives of American citizens and residents. Lesser provision is made for people with labor market skills that are in short supply in the United States, for refugees, for people willing to make a financial investment in the U.S. economy and for a certain number who are not covered in the above groups (the so-called diversity category).

Reunification of families is an important goal, but the overwhelming priority it is given in U.S. law is unjustified in terms of either interests or ethics. It creates a set of immigrants that is less defensible than several different criteria would generate, among them a random lottery.

The criterion of family reunification has some merits. It serves two sorts of interests of Americans. First and most obviously, it meets the needs of a small number of residents, those wishing to be reunited with their kin. For them, the interest is exceptionally strong. Second, the emphasis on family reunification helps ease the transition of new immigrants into American society. The immigrants' family members are their sponsors and are legally required to provide at least some material support to the immigrants, if needed. They often provide much more, including a home, help with finding a job and orientation and information about their new surroundings. The networks that Chapter 4 showed to be central to immigration patterns are often closely connected to kinship. The result is that other Americans bear less of the burden of helping the newcomers adjust to their new country. Beyond the interests that American residents have in family reunification, such immigration is also a benefit to foreigners who want to be reunited with their family members in the United States.

Immigration of family members achieves some valid goals, and by itself it is worthwhile. The problem is that since so many of the scarce immigrant slots are allocated to family members, a severe shortage of slots exists for other types of immigrants. When such weight is accorded to family reunification, the number of eligible people tends to expand, pressing out other important claims. Each immigrant has the right to sponsor many additional immigrants, and each one of those people who takes advantage of the right to immigrate creates additional legitimate claims, and so on. Although some early dire predictions of "explosive" chain reactions have not been confirmed by the data, the tendency of family-reunification immigration to expand is well documented.[17]

The goal of family reunification could be honored without having this consequence. The law could state, for example, that only people who are legally resident in the country as of a certain date—such as the date of passage of the law—are eligible to sponsor immigrants for the purpose of family reunification. Immigrants who entered after that date would be perfectly welcome, but by virtue of arriving they would not automatically create new claims for family reunification, except for very close family members: spouses and minor children. Although such an amendment would eventually lead to discrimination against more recent immigrants, it would accord with the goals of legislators at the time of passage of the law. At that time, the lawmakers would be more interested in the needs of their actual constituents than in the potential needs of people who are not in the country and, for the most part, are not even identified.

Such a restriction in the provisions for family reunification could be justified ethically. As just noted, it would be discriminatory, and discrimination is an ethical concern. When entry into a country is restricted, however, all legal immigration is discriminatory. Everyone who enters takes the place of another who is not allowed to enter. Given the strong claims that many people have to immigrate for reasons other than family reunification (to be outlined below), it is hard to maintain that reduction of the family category is impermissible.

Furthermore, it is not necessary that the United States bear the entire burden for the reunification of families whose members are found in different countries. Families can be reunified through emigration from the United States as well as immigration. Those who object that this is too high a price to pay for family reunification are really saying that reunification is not an overwhelming priority.

If open borders are not a possibility—that is, if overall immigration into the United States must be restricted—the priority given to family reunification should be reduced.

What should replace family reunification as the leading purpose of American immigration policy? Many critics of current policy argue that the interests of Americans would be better served by admitting a higher proportion of people based on their labor market skills, or that the moral responsibility of Americans would be better met by admitting a higher proportion of refugees.

Let us consider first the expansion of categories related to labor market needs. This would speak to the interests of at least some Americans, but not very much to ethics. The recommendation has frequently been made, for example, that the country give greater weight to education and skills in selecting its immigrants, much as Canada and Australia do. Priority could be given to occupations in particularly short supply in the United States.[18]

The problem with such a strategy is that, although it would be in the interest of some Americans, it would be to the disadvantage of others. As noted in Chapter 6, labor shortages have some good effects. They encourage employers to economize on labor and raise productivity, and they also encourage employers to provide training to people who are not qualified at present. An ample supply of labor is an enemy of rising wages and rising standards of living.

The immigration of any particular category of workers has complex effects. A predominance of unskilled immigrants keeps the costs of manual labor low, with the consequence that it allows some labor-intensive industries to survive, keeps some consumer prices relatively low and hurts the incomes of relatively poor Americans. But as we have seen, it may also lead to an expansion of the economy and an increase in the overall demand for labor, with the result that new job opportunities are opened up for some Americans. The same sort of contradictory results occur at the upper end of the scale. The immigration of doctors, for example, increases competition in the medical sector, helping to keep doctors' incomes and the costs of medical care in check. American doctors are injured, and so are Americans aspiring to be doctors who find their way blocked by the newcomers. In each case, one can identify different groups of Americans who are helped or hurt by the immigration, but since these interests are in conflict with one another, it is all but impossible to identify the national interest.

Furthermore, an emphasis on labor market skills has no relationship to the ethical goals of immigration. The United States will not do more good in the world by giving greater priority to people with more education or more skills. If anything, the contrary is true, since higher-skilled people are likely to have better opportunities in their home countries and elsewhere. Expansion of the labor market categories would not, therefore, generate a better profile of immigrants than a random lottery or an emphasis on family reunification would, from the point of view of either interest or ethics.

Expansion of the refugee category would be neutral or perhaps somewhat harmful to the economic interests of Americans. Refugees need not be unskilled, but they tend to be. In contrast to family members of current U.S. residents, they often lack networks and ties in the country that can help them find jobs, get settled and learn the ropes. Refugees are more likely than other immigrants to require state assistance during the transition period while they become accustomed to the United States. The experience of some Southeast Asian refugees has shown that the transition period may be quite long. More than other groups of immigrants, refugees impose a fiscal burden.

Yet the moral obligation of the United States lies in the admission of refugees, particularly when their status as refugees is a consequence of American actions in the world. The United States recognized this when it admitted Southeast Asian refugees whose lives had been disrupted by the Vietnam War. I would like to argue, however, that Americans have a moral obligation to admit refugees even when their status has no relationship to American foreign policy.

Recall that the strongest moral objection to any restriction on immigration is that it harms people who are, on average, disadvantaged. For no group of foreigners is this truer than for refugees. Refugees are people who cannot return to their countries of origin because of a well-founded fear of persecution, and that persecution sometimes includes death. They are people without homes. Their numbers are growing quickly. The United Nations High Commissioner for Refugees estimated that at the beginning of 1995, 23 million refugees were living outside the borders of their countries, and an additional 26 million were displaced inside their countries—a total amounting to one out of every 115 people in the world.[19] The United States cannot, of course, take all or even a significant fraction of refugees, but the greatest good that American immigration policy can do in the world is to permit the entry of some.

An objection to an emphasis on refugee immigration is that it is sometimes impossible to tell who the legitimate refugees are. According to both U.N. conventions and current U.S. law, refugees must be people who reasonably fear persecution as a consequence of their status. People who are poor and who reasonably fear destitution, if not starvation, in their home countries are not viewed as refugees. As the newspapers make clear on an almost daily basis, however, it is often nearly impossibile for the immigration authorities to make the distinction fairly. A related problem has been the unwillingness of the American government to recognize people as refugees if such recognition implies the censure of a friendly government.

These are serious practical problems. They call for a commitment by the United States to reconsider its refugee policy, to define eligibility more clearly and to adhere to its regulations in a principled way. The practical problems of defining refugee status in no way gainsay the importance of increasing the immigration of refugees. Refugees can be victimized by any regime, whether that regime is on good terms with the United States or not. American immigration policy could have no higher purpose than helping to find a permanent home for victims of oppression.

This book began with the observation that Americans are divided over all questions relating to immigration: whether current immigration is typical in terms of American history or extraordinary; whether it helps Americans or threatens them; whether it should be cut off, reduced, maintained, increased or deregulated; whether the qualifications and the national origins of immigrants should be shifted; whether further actions should be taken against undocumented immigrants or whether their rights should be enhanced and many other issues. The disagreements cut across most normal political boundaries: conservatives argue against conservatives and liberals against liberals. As immigration has increased over the last generation, so too has the backlash against it. Politicians are increasingly taking stands on immigration—mostly con, but occasionally pro—and the issue seems likely to become a major one in American public discourse in the future. This book is an attempt to make sense of the debate and to formulate a defensible position about American immigration policy.

Opponents of immigration are apt to view the current wave as an unusual if not unprecedented phenomenon in American life, whereas defenders generally picture it as normal, of the magnitude that Americans have dealt with successfully for generations and even centuries. Yet in some ways, today's immigration is extraordinary: if it proceeds into the twenty-first century, it will become the principal source of population growth, and it will transform the ethnic structure of the country. To be persuasive, therefore, defenders of immigration such as myself must be able to argue that the changes produced by immigration, far-reaching as they will be, are desirable.

Can that argument be made? Yes, although it will not be persuasive to everyone, since some people will be hurt and others helped by continued high immigration. The economic impacts of high immigration, surveyed in Chapters 6 and 7 and reviewed briefly at the beginning of this chapter, are uncertain and various, but on the whole, they are probably harmful to Americans. The social consequences of continued immigration from the third world are probably positive in terms of helping Americans develop decent, reciprocal, multicultural communities. Most important, immigration is helpful to the immigrants, especially those whose life prospects in their home countries are dim.

The national interest in immigration is ambiguous, but the importance of encouraging constructive cross-cultural relationships in the United States is so central that it calls for at least maintaining the current rate of immigration. Moreover, the demands of morality on a global scale are at variance with the national interest, since they call on Americans to open their borders wider than they have thus far been willing to open them, in order to help break down the international structure of privilege and disadvantage. Americans will certainly not allow this vision of morality to drive their immigration policy, but at the very least, the arguments based on ethics rather than interest can help buttress the case against closing the gates.

Americans are not accustomed to thinking of immigration policy in the context of human rights, but this is actually the most important perspective from which to view it. Each immigrant and each potential immigrant is a human being, a person of equal worth with every other human being, and many are vulnerable to serious violations of their rights. Two measures in particular are called for.

The first relates to the rights of unauthorized immigrants. Americans are divided about whether the undocumented should be in the United States in the first place; the laws say no, but many residents depend on them. The fact is that they are in the United States and will continue to be, as long as any restrictions on immigration are retained. They are of equal worth, and although they cannot have equal rights with legal American residents, they should be accorded more rights than they have now. Most urgently, they should be protected against being exploited in ways that are in violation of American laws, whether in the workplace or in the home.

The second measure relates to refugees. They are the most needy of all potential immigrants. It is true that they often have more transition problems than other immigrants, since they usually lack either resident families or employer sponsors, and since their decisions to leave their homes are frequently involuntary. It is incumbent upon Americans, however, who are among the most privileged people on earth, to use their immigration policy in the most effective way possible to respond to exploitation and to alleviate suffering. The best way of doing this would be to increase greatly the number of openings for refugees and to pay the price of assisting them with the transition to their new home.

The pressure for immigration to the United States is not going to lessen; if anything, it will increase. As the immigrants arrive, they will remake America. That is the American tradition, to be remade by wave after wave of newcomers. This time, they will change the face of the country so that it looks more like the face of the world as a whole: a rich mixture of every ethnic group, every national background, every faith, every conviction that can be found in the world. Although it is not certain, one hopes that they will do so in a constructive, peaceful manner, expressing their disagreements openly within the framework of the Constitution and the rule of law, continually learning from and enriching one another. If so, the immigrants can help America become a model to the world of diverse, plural interaction.

Notes

1. Peter H. Schuck, "The Transformation of Immigration Law," *Columbia Law Review* 84 (1984):85.
2. Quoted in "Divided We Stand, the Immigration Backlash," *San Francisco Chronicle* (March 31, 1994), A16.
3. This argument is made in Otis L. Graham Jr., *Rethinking the Purposes of Immigration Policy* (Washington, D.C.: Center for Immigration Studies, 1991).

4. George Will, "Assimilation Is Not a Dirty Word," *Los Angeles Times* (July 29, 1993), B7.
5. In thinking about the ethics of immigration, I have been influenced by the stimulating collection of papers in Mark Gibney, ed., *Open Borders? Closed Societies? The Ethical and Political Issues* (Westport, Conn.: Greenwood Press, 1988). For a comprehensive survey of philosophical thinking about immigration, see Myron Weiner, *The Global Migration Crisis, Challenge to States and to Human Rights* (New York: HarperCollins, 1995), ch. 8.
6. Gregory Vlastos, "Justice and Equality," in *Social Justice*, ed. Richard B. Brandt (Englewood Cliffs, N.J.: Prentice-Hall, 1962), quoted by Andrew E. Shacknove, "American Duties to Refugees, Their Scope and Limits," in Gibney, *Open Borders? Closed Societies?* 131–49.
7. Carens bases the case for open borders explicitly on three philosophical traditions: those of Robert Nozick and John Rawls, and utilitarianism. See Joseph H. Carens, "Aliens and Citizens: The Case for Open Borders," *Review of Politics* 49 (Spring 1987):251–73. His arguments are extended in a number of other writings, including "Immigration and the Welfare State," in *Democracy and the Welfare State*, ed. Amy Gutmann (Princeton, N.J.: Princeton University Press, 1988), 207–30; "States and Refugees: A Normative Analysis," in *Refugee Policy, Canada and the United States*, ed. Howard Adelman (Toronto: York Lanes Press, 1991), 18–29; and "Migration and Morality: A Liberal Egalitarian Perspective," in *Free Movement, Ethical Issues in the Transnational Migration of People and of Money*, ed. Brian Barry and Robert E. Goodin (London: Harvester Wheatsheaf, 1992), 25–47.
8. Gary Wills, *Lincoln at Gettysburg, the Words That Remade America* (New York: Simon and Schuster, 1992).
9. Richard Wasserstrom, "One Way to Understand and Defend Programs of Preferential Treatment," in *The Moral Foundations of Civil Rights*, ed. Robert K. Fullinwider and Claudia Mills (Totowa, N.J.: Rowman and Littlefield, 1986), 46–55.
10. Frederick G. Whelan, "Citizenship and Freedom of Movement, an Open Admission Policy?" in Gibney, *Open Borders? Closed Society?* 3–39.
11. Michael Walzer, *Spheres of Justice, a Defense of Pluralism and Equality* (New York: Basic Books, 1983).
12. For an argument supporting the obligation of individuals in rich countries to contribute charitably to the world's poor, see Peter Singer, *Practical Ethics*, 2d ed. (New York: Cambridge University Press, 1993), ch. 8.
13. This seems to be the main argument in Peter Brimelow's chapter on the morality of immigration. *Alien Nation, Common Sense about America's Immigration Disaster* (New York: Random House, 1995).
14. See Susan Wolf, "Moral Saints," *Journal of Philosophy* 79 (1982):419–39.
15. Shacknove, "American Duties to Refugees," 147.
16. For a thoughtful answer to this question, which is quite different from the one offered here, see Vernon M. Briggs Jr. and Stephen Moore, *Still*

An Open Door? U.S. Immigration Policy and the American Economy (Washington, D.C.: American University Press, 1994), 57–67.
17. The state of the research on this topic is reviewed in John M. Goering, "The 'Explosiveness' of Chain Migration: Research and Policy Issues," *International Migration Review* 23 (Winter 1989):797–812.
18. See, among many others, Gary S. Becker, "Opening the Golden Door Wider—to Newcomers with Knowhow," *Business Week* (June 11, 1990), 12.
19. Barbara Crossette, "There Is No Place Like Home," *New York Times* (March 5, 1995), E3.

Bibliography

Acevedo, Dolores, and Thomas J. Espenshade. "Implications of a North American Free Trade Agreement for Mexican Migration into the United States." *Population and Development Review* 18 (1992):729–44.

Ad Hoc Committee for Immigrant Rights of the Monterey Bay Region. "Immigration and Immigrants: The Issues." Santa Cruz, Calif.: 1993.

Aldrich, Thomas Bailey. "The Unguarded Gates." *Atlantic Monthly* (1882).

Aleinikoff, Thomas A., and David A. Martin. *Immigration, Process and Policy.* 2d. ed. St. Paul: West Publishing, 1991.

Altonji, Joseph G., and David Card. "The Effects of Immigration on the Labor Market Outcomes of Less-skilled Natives." In *Immigration, Trade, and the Labor Market,* edited by John M. Abowd and Richard B. Freeman, 201–34. Chicago: University of Chicago Press, 1991.

Arnold, Fred. "International Migration: Who Goes Where?" *Finance and Development* 27 (1990), 46–47.

Arnold, Fred. *Revised Estimates and Projections of International Migration, 1980–2000.* Washington, D.C.: World Bank, Population and Human Resources Department, 1989.

Associated Press. "Immigrant Furor Kills School Promo." *Santa Cruz Sentinel.* July 27, 1994, A8.

Auster, Laurence. *The Path to National Suicide, an Essay on Immigration and Multiculturalism.* Monterey, Va.: American Immigration Control Foundation, 1990.

Bartel, Ann P. "Where Do the New U.S. Immigrants Live?" *Journal of Labor Economics* 7 (1989):371–91.

Baumol, William J., and Alan S. Blinder. *Microeconomics, Principles and Policy.* 6th ed. Fort Worth: Dryden Press, 1994.

Bean, Frank D., Jorge Chapa, Ruth R. Berg and Kathryn A. Sowards. "Educational and Sociodemographic Incorporation among Hispanic Immigrants to the United States." In *Immigration and Ethnicity, the Integration of America's Newest Arrivals,* edited by Barry Edmonston and Jeffrey S. Passel, 73–100. Washington, D.C.: Urban Institute Press, 1994.

Bean, Frank D., Barry Edmonston and Jeffrey S. Passel, eds. *Undocumented Migration to the United States, IRCA and the Experience of the 1980s.* Washington, D.C.: Urban Institute Press, 1990.

Bean, Frank D., Mark A. Fossett and Kyung Tae Park. "Labor Market Dynamics and the Effects of Immigration on African Americans." In *Blacks, Immigration and Race Relations,* edited by Gerald Jaynes. New Haven, Conn.: Yale University Press, 1993.

Becker, Gary S. *Human Capital, a Theoretical and Empirical Analysis, with Special Reference to Education,* 2d ed. Chicago: University of Chicago Press, 1975.

Becker, Gary S. "Opening the Golden Door Wider—to Newcomers with Knowhow." *Business Week.* June 11, 1990, 12.

Berry, R. A., and R. Soligo. "Some Welfare Aspects of International Migration." *Journal of Political Economy* 77 (1969):778–94.

Blau, Francine. "The Use of Transfer Payments by Immigrants." *Industrial and Labor Relations Review* 37 (1984):222–39.

Borjas, George J. "The Economic Benefits from Immigration." *Journal of Economic Perspectives* 9 (Spring 1995):3–22.

Borjas, George J. "The Economics of Immigration." *Journal of Economic Literature* 32 (1994):1667–1717.

Borjas, George J. *Friends or Strangers, the Impact of Immigrants on the U.S. Economy.* New York: Basic Books, 1990.

Borjas, George J. "Immigrants, Minorities, and Labor Market Competition." *Industrial and Labor Relations Review* 40 (1987):382–92.

Borjas, George J. "National Origin and the Skills of Immigrants in the Postwar Period." In *Immigration and the Work Force, Economic Consequences for the United States and Source Areas,* edited by George J. Borjas and Richard B. Freeman, 17–47. Chicago: University of Chicago Press, 1992.

Borjas, George J., and Richard B. Freeman, eds. *Immigration and the Work Force, Economic Consequences for the United States and Source Areas.* Chicago: University of Chicago Press, 1992.

Borjas, George J., Richard B. Freeman and Lawrence F. Katz. "On the Labor Market Effects of Immigration and Trade." In *Immigration and the Work Force, Economic Consequences for the United States and Source Areas,* edited by George J. Borjas and Richard B. Freeman, 213–44. Chicago: University of Chicago Press, 1992.

Borjas, George J., and Stephen J. Trejo. "Immigrant Participation in the Welfare System." *Industrial and Labor Relations Review* 44 (1991):195–211.

Boswell, Richard A. *Immigration and Nationality Law, Cases and Materials.* 2d ed. Durham, N.C.: Carolina Academic Press, 1992.

Bouvier, Leon F. *Fifty Million Californians?* Washington, D.C.: Center for Immigration Studies, 1991.

Bouvier, Leon F. *Peaceful Invasions, Immigration and Changing America.* Lanham, Md.: University Press of America, 1992.

Briggs, Vernon M. Jr. "Immigrant Labor and the Issue of 'Dirty Work' in Advanced Industrial Societies." *Population and Environment* 14 (1993):503–14.

Briggs, Vernon M. Jr. "Immigration Policy and Work Force Preparedness." *ILR Report* 28 (Fall 1990).

Briggs, Vernon M. Jr. "Immigration Policy: Political or Economic?" *Challenge* 34 (September–October 1991):12–19.

Briggs, Vernon M. Jr. *Mass Immigration and the National Interest.* Armonk, N.Y.: M. E. Sharpe, 1992.

Briggs, Vernon M. Jr. and Stephen Moore. *Still an Open Door? U.S. Immigration Policy and the American Economy.* Washington, D.C.: American University Press, 1994.

Brimelow, Peter. *Alien Nation, Common Sense about America's Immigration Disaster.* New York: Random House, 1995.

Brimelow, Peter. "Response." *National Review.* February 1, 1993, 33.

Butcher, Kristin, and David Card. "Immigration and Wages: Evidence from the 1980's." *American Economic Review* 81 (1991):292–96.

Californians for Population Stabilization. *Newsletter* (Sacramento). Published quarterly.

Card, David. "The Impact of the Mariel Boatlift on the Miami Labor Market." *Industrial and Labor Relations Review* 43 (1990):245–57.

Carens, Joseph H. "Aliens and Citizens: The Case for Open Borders." *Review of Politics* 49 (Spring 1987):251–73.

Carens, Joseph H. "Immigration and the Welfare State." In *Democracy and the Welfare State,* edited by Amy Gutmann, 207–30. Princeton, N.J.: Princeton University Press, 1988.

Carens, Joseph H. "Migration and Morality: A Liberal Egalitarian Perspective." In *Free Movement, Ethical Issues in the Transnational Migration of People and of Money,* edited by Brian Barry and Robert E. Goodin, 25–47. London: Harvester Wheatsheaf, 1992.

Carens, Joseph H. "States and Refugees: A Normative Analysis." In *Refugee Policy, Canada and the United States,* edited by Howard Adelman, 18–29. Toronto: York Lanes Press, 1991.

Chiswick, Barry R. "Is the New Immigration Less Skilled than the Old?" *Journal of Labor Economics* 4 (1986):168–92.

Chiswick, Barry R. "The Effect of Americanization on the Earnings of Foreign-Born Men." *Journal of Political Economy* 86 (1978):897–921.

Clark, Rebecca L., Jeffrey S. Passel, Wendy N. Zimmerman and Michael E. Fix. *Fiscal Impacts of Undocumented Aliens: Selected Estimates for Seven States.* Washington, D.C.: Urban Institute Press, 1994.

Coale, Ansley J. "Demographic Effects of Below-Replacement Fertility and Their Social Implications." In *Below-Replacement Fertility in Industrial Societies, Causes, Consequences, Policies,* edited by Kingsley Davis, Mikhail S. Bernstam and Rita Ricardo-Campbell. Supplement to *Population and Development Review* 12 (1986):203–16.

Coale, Ansley J. "How a Population Ages or Grows Younger." In *Population, the Vital Revolution,* edited by Ronald Freedman, 47–57. Garden City, N.Y.: Doubleday, 1964.

Collins, Nancy. "Do Immigrants Place a Tax Burden on New Jersey Residents?" Senior thesis, Princeton University, Department of Economics, 1991.

Community Research Associates. *Undocumented Immigrants, Their Impact on the County of San Diego.* San Diego: 1980.

Crossette, Barbara. "There Is No Place Like Home." *New York Times.* March 5, 1995, E3.

Daniels, Roger. *Coming to America, a History of Immigration and Ethnicity in American Life.* New York: HarperCollins, 1990.

DeFreitas, Gregory. "Hispanic Immigration and Labor Market Segmentation." *Industrial Relations* 27 (1988):195–214.
de la Garza, Rodolfo O., Angelo Falcon, F. Chris Garcia and John A. Garcia. "Attitudes toward U.S. Immigration Policy, the Case of Mexicans, Puerto Ricans and Cubans." *Migration World* 21 (1993):13–16.
Deveny, Kathleen. "Immigrants: Still Believers after All These Years." *Wall Street Journal.* July 12, 1994, B1, B9.
The Diversity Project: Final Report. Berkeley, Calif.: Institute for the Study of Social Change, 1991.
"Divided We Stand, the Immigration Backlash." *San Francisco Chronicle.* March 29–April 1, 1994.
Duleep, Harriet Orcutt, and Mark C. Regets. "The Elusive Concept of Immigrant Quality." Policy Discussion Paper. Washington, D.C.: Urban Institute, 1994.
Durand, Jorge, and Douglas S. Massey. "Mexican Migration to the United States: A Critical Review." *Latin American Research Review* 27 (1992):3–42.
The Economic Report of the President. Washington, D.C.: U.S. Government Printing Office, 1995.
Edmonston, Barry, and Jeffrey S. Passel. "Ethnic Demography: U.S. Immigration and Ethnic Variations." In *Immigration and Ethnicity, the Integration of America's Newest Arrivals,* edited by Barry Edmonston and Jeffrey S. Passel, 1–30. Washington, D.C.: Urban Institute Press, 1994.
Edmonston, Barry, and Jeffrey S. Passel. "The Future Immigrant Population of the United States." In *Immigration and Ethnicity, the Integration of America's Newest Arrivals,* edited by Barry Edmonston and Jeffrey S. Passel, 317–53. Washington, D.C.: Urban Institute Press, 1994.
Edmonston, Barry, and Jeffrey S. Passel, eds. *Immigration and Ethnicity, the Integration of America's Newest Arrivals.* Washington, D.C.: Urban Institute Press, 1994.
Espenshade, Thomas J. "Can Immigration Slow U.S. Population Aging?" *Journal of Policy Analysis and Management* 13 (Fall 1994):759–68.
Espenshade, Thomas J. "Does the Threat of Border Apprehension Deter Undocumented US Immigration?" *Population and Development Review* 20 (1994):871–92.
Espenshade, Thomas J., Leon F. Bouvier and W. Brian Arthur. "Immigration and the Stable Population Model." *Demography* 19 (1982):125–33.
Estrada, Richard. "Myth of Labor Shortage Is Harmful." In *Immigration 2000: The Century of the New American Sweatshop,* edited by Dan Stein, 129–30. Washington, D.C.: Federation for American Immigration Reform, 1992.
Filer, Randall K. "The Effect of Immigrant Arrivals on Migratory Patterns of Native Workers." In *Immigration and the Work Force, Economic Consequences for the United States and Source Areas,* edited by George J. Borjas and Richard B. Freeman, 245–69. Chicago: University of Chicago Press, 1992.
Fix, Michael, and Jeffrey S. Passel. "Immigrants and Welfare: New Myths, New Realities." Testimony before the U.S. House of Representatives, Committee on Ways and Means, Subcommittee on Human Resources. November 15, 1993.

Fix, Michael, and Jeffrey S. Passel. *Immigration and Immigrants, Setting the Record Straight.* Washington, D.C.: Urban Institute Press, 1994.

Fix, Michael, and Wendy Zimmermann. "After Arrival: An Overview of Federal Immigrant Policy in the United States." In *Immigration and Ethnicity, the Integration of America's Newest Arrivals,* edited by Barry Edmonston and Jeffrey S. Passel, 251–85. Washington, D.C.: Urban Institute Press, 1994.

Foxman, Abraham. Letter to the editor. *Wall Street Journal.* July 21, 1994, A15.

Franklin, Benjamin. *Observations Concerning the Increase of Mankind, Peopling of Countries, &c.* Boston: S Kneeland, 1775.

Friedberg, Rachel M., and Jennifer Hunt. "The Impact of Immigrants on Host Country Wages, Employment and Growth." *Journal of Economic Perspectives* 9 (Spring 1995):23–44.

Friedman, Dorian, Mary C. Lord, Dan McGraw and Kukula Glastris. "To Make a Nation." *U.S. News and World Report.* October 4, 1993, 47–54.

Fuchs, Lawrence H. *The American Kaleidoscope: Race, Ethnicity, and the Civic Culture.* Hanover, N.H.: Wesleyan University Press, 1990.

Fuchs, Lawrence H. "The Search for a Sound Immigration Policy: A Personal View." In *Clamor at the Gates, the New American Immigration,* edited by Nathan Glazer, 17–48. San Francisco: Institute for Contemporary Studies, 1985.

Galloway, Lowell, and Stephen Moore. "Do Immigrants Increase Unemployment or Reduce Economic Growth?" *Congressional Record.* September 26, 1990.

Gibney, Mark, ed. *Open Borders? Closed Societies? The Ethical and Political Issues.* Westport, Conn.: Greenwood Press, 1988.

Gibson, Campbell. "The Contribution of Immigration to the Growth and Ethnic Diversity of the American Population." *Proceedings of the American Philosophical Society* 136 (1992):157–75.

Glazer, Nathan, ed. *Clamor at the Gates, the New American Immigration.* San Francisco: Institute for Contemporary Studies, 1985.

Glazer, Nathan. "The Closing Door." *New Republic.* December 27, 1993, 15–20.

Glazer, Nathan, and Daniel Patrick Moynihan. *Beyond the Melting Pot, the Negroes, Puerto Ricans, Jews, Italians and Irish of New York City.* Cambridge, Mass.: MIT Press, 1963.

Goering, John M. "The 'Explosiveness' of Chain Migration: Research and Policy Issues." *International Migration Review* 23 (Winter 1989):797–812.

Graham, Otis L. Jr. *Rethinking the Purposes of Immigration Policy.* Washington, D.C.: Center for Immigration Studies, 1991.

Greenwood, Michael J., and John M. McDowell. "The Factor Market Consequences of U.S. Immigration." *Journal of Economic Literature* 24 (1986): 1738–72.

Grossman, Gene M., and Elhanan Helpman. "Endogenous Innovation in the Theory of Growth." *Journal of Economic Perspectives* 8 (Winter 1994):23–44.

Grossman, Jean Baldwin. "The Substitutability of Natives and Immigrants in Production." *Review of Economics and Statistics* 64 (1982):596–603.

Hamilton, Alexander, James Madison and John Jay. *The Federalist Papers,* edited by Clinton Rossiter. New York: New American Library, 1961.

Handlin, Oscar. *The Uprooted, the Epic Story of the Great Migrations that Made the American People.* Boston: Little, Brown, 1951.

Hardin, Garrett. "Zero Net Immigration as the Goal." *Population and Environment* 14 (1992):197–200.

Harris, John R., and Michael P. Todaro. "Migration, Unemployment and Development: A Two-Sector Analysis." *American Economic Review* 60 (1970):126–42.

Hatton, Timothy J., and Jeffrey G. Williamson. "What Drove the Mass Migrations from Europe in the Late Nineteenth Century?" *Population and Development Review* 20 (1994):533–59.

Hondagneu-Sotelo, Pierrette. *Gendered Transitions: Mexican Experiences of Immigration.* Berkeley: University of California Press, 1994.

Huddle, Donald. "The Costs of Immigration." Unpublished typescript, Rice University, Houston, 1993.

Huddle, Donald. "Give Us Your Tired Masses." In *Immigration 2000: The Century of the New American Sweatshop*, edited by Dan Stein, 53–57. Washington, D.C.: Federation for American Immigration Reform, 1992.

Huddle, Donald, Arthur Corwin and Gordon MacDonald. *Illegal Immigration: Job Displacement and Social Costs.* Alexandria, Va.: American Immigration Control Foundation, 1985.

Hunt, Albert R. "Demagoging the Immigration Issue." *Wall Street Journal.* July 7, 1994, A13.

Hutchinson, E. P. *Legislative History of American Immigration Policy 1798–1965.* Philadelphia: University of Pennsylvania Press, 1981.

Isbister, John. "Immigration and Income Distribution in Canada." In *Essays in Labor Market Analysis, in Memory of Yochanan Peter Comay*, edited by Orley C. Ashenfelter and Wallace E. Oates, 147–77. New York: John Wiley and Sons, 1977.

Isbister, John. *Promises Not Kept: The Betrayal of Social Change in the Third World.* 3d ed. West Hartford, Conn.: Kumarian Press, 1995.

Jasso, Guillermina, and Mark R. Rosenzweig. *The New Chosen People: Immigrants in the United States.* New York: Russell Sage Foundation, 1990.

Jenks, Rosemary E. "Immigration and Nationality Policies of Leading Migration Nations." *Population and Environment* 14 (1993):567–92.

Johnson, Hans. "A Socioeconomic and Demographic Overview of Women Immigrants in California." Testimony presented to the California Select Committee on Statewide Immigration Impact. Sacramento, June 19, 1994.

Johnson, Steve. "Half Would Deny Illegal Immigrants Schools, Citizenship." *San Jose Mercury News.* June 10, 1994, 1A, 24A.

Johnson, Steve. "Hispanics Aim Campaign at Anti-Immigration Advocates." *San Jose Mercury News.* May 29, 1994, B1.

Kennedy, Paul. *Preparing for the Twenty-First Century.* New York: Random House, 1993.

Keyfitz, Nathan. "Population and Sustainable Development: Distinguishing Fact and Preference Concerning the Future Human Population and Environment." *Population and Environment* 14 (1993):441–61.

244 / THE IMMIGRATION DEBATE

Koed, Elizabeth K. "The Loss of Cheap Labor and Predictions of Economic Disaster: Two Case Studies." In *Immigration 2000: The Century of the New American Sweatshop*, edited by Dan Stein, 139–47. Washington, D.C.: Federation for American Immigration Reform, 1992.

"Kon-Tikis Go Home." *The Economist*. September 2, 1989, 32–33.

Kossoudji, Sherrie A. "Playing Cat and Mouse at the U.S.-Mexican Border. *Demography* 29 (1992):159–80.

LaLonde, Robert J., and Robert H. Topel. "The Assimilation of Immigrants in the U.S. Labor Market." In *Immigration and the Work Force, Economic Consequences for the United States and Source Areas*, edited by George J. Borjas and Richard B. Freeman, 67–92. Chicago: University of Chicago Press, 1992.

LaLonde, Robert J., and Robert H. Topel. "Immigrants in the American Labor Market: Quality, Assimilation, and Distributional Effects." *American Economic Review* 81 (1991):297–302.

LaLonde, Robert J., and Robert H. Topel. "Labor Market Adjustments to Increased Immigration." In *Immigration, Trade, and the Labor Market*, edited by John M. Abowd and Richard B. Freeman, 167–99. Chicago: University of Chicago Press, 1991.

Lamm, Richard D., and Gary Imhoff. *The Immigration Time Bomb, The Fragmenting of America*. New York: New American Library, 1985.

Lee, Sharon M., and Barry Edmonston. "The Socioeconomic Status and Integration of Asian Immigrants." In *Immigration and Ethnicity, the Integration of America's Newest Arrivals*, edited by Barry Edmonston and Jeffrey S. Passel, 101–38. Washington, D.C.: Urban Institute Press, 1994.

Legomsky, Stephen. *Immigration Law and Policy*. Westbury, N.Y.: Foundation Press, 1990.

Los Angeles County. *Updated Revenues and Costs Attributable to Undocumented Aliens*. Los Angeles: 1991.

Lowell, B. Lindsay, and Zhongren Jing. "Unauthorized Workers and Immigration Reform: What Can We Ascertain from Employers?" *International Migration Review* 28 (Fall 1994):427–48.

Martin, Philip. *Illegal Immigration and the Colonization of the American Labor Market*. Washington, D.C.: Center for Immigration Studies, 1986.

Martin, Philip. "The Missing Bridge: How Immigrant Networks Keep Americans Out of Dirty Jobs." *Population and Environment* 14 (1993):539–65.

Martin, Philip. "Proposition 187 in California." *International Migration Review* 29 (Spring 1995):255–63.

Martin, Philip, and J. Edward Taylor. "Immigration Reform and Farm Labor Contracting in California." In *The Paper Curtain: Employer Sanctions' Implementation, Impact and Reform*, edited by Michael Fix, 239–61. Washington, D.C.: Urban Institute Press, 1991.

Massey, Douglas S. "Economic Development and International Migration in Comparative Perspective." *Population and Development Review* 14 (1988):383–413.

Massey, Douglas S., Joaquin Arango, Graeme Hugo, Ali Kouaouci, Adela Pellegrino and J. Edward Taylor. "An Evaluation of International Migration Theory: The North American Case." *Population and Development Review* 20 (1994):699–751.

Massey, Douglas S., Joaquin Arango, Graeme Hugo, Ali Kouaouci, Adela Pellegrino and J. Edward Taylor. "Theories of International Migration: A Review and Appraisal." *Population and Development Review* 19 (1993):431–66.

Massey, Douglas S., Luin Goldring and Jorge Durand. "Continuities in Transnational Migration: An Analysis of Nineteen Mexican Communities." *American Journal of Sociology* 99 (1994):1492–1533.

McCarthy, Kevin F., and R. Burciaga Valdez. *Current and Future Effects of Mexican Immigration in California.* Santa Monica: RAND Corporation, 1986.

McManus, Walter S., William Gould and Finis Welch. "Earnings of Hispanic Men: The Role of English Language Proficiency." *Journal of Labor Economics* 1 (1983):101–30.

Miles, Jack. "Blacks vs. Browns." *Atlantic Monthly.* October 1992, 41–68.

Moreno-Evans, Manuel. "Impact of Undocumented Persons and Other Immigrants on Costs, Revenues and Services in Los Angeles County." A report prepared for Los Angeles County Board of Supervisors. November 6, 1992.

Morganthau, Tom. "America: Still a Melting Pot?" *Newsweek.* August 9, 1993, 16–23.

Muller, Thomas, and Thomas J. Espenshade. *The Fourth Wave, California's Newest Immigrants.* Washington, D.C.: Urban Institute Press, 1985.

Mydans, Seth. "At the Border with Mexico, Agents Push against a Tide." *New York Times.* February 19, 1994, A1.

Neuman, Kristin E., and Marta Tienda. "The Settlement and Secondary Migration Patterns of Legalized Immigrants: Insights from Administrative Records." In *Immigration and Ethnicity, the Integration of America's Newest Arrivals,* edited by Barry Edmonston and Jeffrey S. Passel, 187–226. Washington, D.C.: Urban Institute Press, 1994.

North, David, and Marion Houstoun. *The Characteristics and Role of Illegal Aliens in the U.S. Labor Market, an Exploratory Study.* Washington, D.C.: Linton and Company, 1976.

Pack, Howard. "Endogenous Growth Theory: Intellectual Appeal and Empirical Shortcomings." *Journal of Economic Perspectives* 8 (Winter 1994):55–72.

Parker, Richard A., and Louis M. Rea. "Illegal Immigration in San Diego County: An Analysis of Costs and Revenues." Prepared for the California State Senate Special Committee on Border Issues, San Diego State University, 1993.

Passel, Jeffrey S., and Barry Edmonston. "Immigration and Race: Recent Trends in Immigration to the United States." In *Immigration and Ethnicity, the Integration of America's Newest Arrivals,* edited by Barry Edmonston and Jeffrey S. Passel, 31–71. Washington, D.C.: Urban Institute Press, 1994.

Pear, Robert. "Change of Policy on U.S. Immigrants Is Urged by Panel." *New York Times.* June 5, 1995, A1.

Pear, Robert. "Clinton Embraces a Proposal to Cut Immigration by a Third." *New York Times.* June 8, 1995, A9.

Perotti, Rosanna. "IRCA's Antidiscrimination Provisions: What Went Wrong?" *International Migration Review* 26 (Fall 1992):732–53.

Piore, Michael J. *Birds of Passage, Migrant Labor in Industrial Societies.* Cambridge: Cambridge University Press, 1979.

Piore, Michael J. "Illegal Immigration to the U.S.: Some Observations and Policy Suggestions." In *Illegal Aliens, an Assessment of the Issues.* Washington, D.C.: National Council for Employment Policy, 1976.

Polanyi, Karl. *The Great Transformation.* New York: Farrar and Rinehart, 1944.

Portes, Alejandro, and Ruben G. Rumbaut. *Immigrant America, a Portrait.* Berkeley: University of California Press, 1990.

Ramos, Fernando A. "Out-Migration and Return Migration of Puerto Ricans." In *Immigration and the Work Force, Economic Consequences for the United States and Source Areas,* edited by George J. Borjas and Richard B. Freeman, 49–66. Chicago: University of Chicago Press, 1992.

Ravenstein, E. G. "The Laws of Migration." *Journal of the Royal Statistical Society* (1889):241–301.

"Return of the Huddled Masses." *The Economist.* May 7, 1994, 25–26.

Rivera-Batiz, Francisco L., and Selig L. Sechzer, "Substitution and Complementarity between Immigrant and Native Labor in the United States." In *U.S. Immigration Policy Reform in the 1980s: A Preliminary Assessment,* edited by Francisco L. Rivera-Batiz, Selig L. Sechzer and Ira N. Gang, 89–116. New York: Praeger, 1991.

Romer, Paul M. "The Origins of Endogenous Growth." *Journal of Economic Perspectives* 8 (Winter 1994):3–22.

Rothman, Eric S., and Thomas J. Espenshade. "Fiscal Impacts of Immigration to the United States." *Population Index* 58 (Fall 1992):381–415.

Salins, Peter D. "Take a Ticket." *New Republic.* December 27, 1993, 13–15.

Sassen, Saskia. *The Global City, New York, London, Tokyo.* Princeton, N.J.: Princeton University Press, 1991.

Sassen, Saskia. *The Mobility of Labor and Capital, a Study in International Investment and Labor Flow.* Cambridge: Cambridge University Press, 1988.

Sassen, Saskia. "Rebuilding the Global City: Economy, Ethnicity, and Space." *Social Justice* 20 (Fall–Winter 1993):32–50.

Sassen, Saskia. "U.S. Immigration Policy toward Mexico in a Global Economy." *Journal of International Affairs* 43 (Winter 1990):369–83.

Sassen, Saskia. "Why Immigration?" *Report on the Americas* 26 (1992):14–19.

Sassen, Saskia, and Alejandro Portes. "Miami: A New Global City?" *Contemporary Sociology* 22 (1993):471–80.

Schlesinger, Arthur M. Jr. *The Disuniting of America, Reflections on a Multicultural Society.* Knoxville: Whittle Direct Books, 1991.

Schuck, Peter H. "The Transformation of Immigration Law." *Columbia Law Review* 84 (1984):1–90.

Schuck, Peter H., and Rogers M. Smith. *Citizenship without Consent, Illegal Aliens in the American Polity.* New Haven, Conn.: Yale University Press, 1985.

Shacknove, Andrew E. "American Duties to Refugees, Their Scope and Limits." In *Open Borders? Closed Societies? The Ethical and Political Issues,* edited by Mark Gibney, 131–49. Westport, Conn.: Greenwood Press, 1988.

Simon, Julian. *The Economic Consequences of Immigration.* Oxford: Basil Blackwell, 1989.

Simon, Julian. "What Immigrants Take from and Give to the Public Coffers." In *U.S. Immigration Policy and the National Interest, Appendix D to Staff Report of the Select Commission on Immigration and Refugee Policy*. Washington, D.C.: 1981.

"The Simpson Curtain." *Wall Street Journal*. February 1, 1990, A8.

Singer, Peter. *Practical Ethics*. 2d ed. New York: Cambridge University Press, 1993.

Singer, Peter, and Renata Singer. "The Ethics of Refugee Policy." In *Open Borders? Closed Societies? The Ethical and Political Issues*, edited by Mark Gibney, 111–30. Westport, Conn.: Greenwood Press, 1988.

Smith, Michael, and Bernadette Tarallo. *California's Changing Faces, New Immigrant Survival Strategies and State Policy*. Berkeley: California Policy Seminar, 1993.

Solow, Robert M. "Perspectives on Growth Theory." *Journal of Economic Perspectives* 8 (Winter 1994):45–54.

Sontag, Deborah. "Politicians Treating Illegal Immigration Softly in New York." *New York Times*. June 10, 1994, A1–A12.

Sontag, Deborah. "3 Governors Take Pleas on Aliens to the Senate." *New York Times*. June 23, 1994, A10.

Sorensen, Elaine, and Maria E. Enchautegui. "Immigrant Male Earnings in the 1980s: Divergent Patterns by Race and Ethnicity." In *Immigration and Ethnicity, the Integration of America's Newest Arrivals*, edited by Barry Edmonston and Jeffrey S. Passel, 139–61. Washington, D.C.: Urban Institute Press, 1994.

Stacey, Palmer, and Wayne Lutton. *The Immigration Time Bomb*. Monterey, Va.: American Immigration Control Foundation, 1988.

Stark, Oded, and David E. Bloom. "The New Economics of Labor Migration." *American Economic Review, Papers and Proceedings* 75 (1985):173–78.

Stark, Oded, and D. Levihari. "On Migration and Risk in LDCs." *Economic Development and Cultural Change* 31 (1982):191–96.

Stein, Dan, ed. *Immigration 2000: The Century of the New American Sweatshop*. Washington, D.C.: Federation for American Immigration Reform, 1992.

Steinberg, Stephen. *The Ethnic Myth, Race, Ethnicity and Class in America*. 2d ed. Boston: Beacon Press, 1989.

Stevens, Gillian. "Immigration, Emigration, Language Acquisition, and the English Language Proficiency of Immigrants in the United States." In *Immigration and Ethnicity, the Integration of America's Newest Arrivals*, edited by Barry Edmonston and Jeffrey S. Passel, 163–85. Washington, D.C.: Urban Institute Press, 1994.

"The Stranger at the Door." *The Economist*. December 23, 1989, 9–10.

"Study Sees Disaster If Population Isn't Cut by Two-Thirds." *San Jose Mercury News*. February 22, 1994.

Takaki, Ronald. *A Different Mirror, a History of Multicultural America*. New York: Little, Brown, 1993.

Takaki, Ronald, ed. *From Different Shores, Perspectives on Race and Ethnicity in America*. 2d ed. New York: Oxford University Press, 1994.

Takaki, Ronald. "Reflections on Racial Patterns in America." *Ethnicity and Public Policy* 1 (1982):1–23.

Taylor, Jared. *Paved with Good Intentions, the Failure of Race Relations in Contemporary America.* New York: Carroll and Graf, 1992.

Thernstrom, Stephan. "The Minority Majority Will Never Come." *Wall Street Journal.* July 26, 1990, A16.

Tienda, Marta, and Leif Jensen. "Immigration and Public Assistance Participation: Dispelling the Myth of Dependency." *Social Science Research* 15 (1986):372–400.

Todaro, Michael P. *Economic Development.* 5th ed. New York: Longman, 1994.

Tyson, Ann Scott. "Ethnic, Economic Divisions of U.S. Growing." *Christian Science Monitor.* July 7, 1994, 3.

U.S. Bureau of the Census. *Population Projections of the United States, by Age, Sex, Race, and Hispanic Origin: 1992 to 2050.* Washington, D.C.: U.S. Government Printing Office, 1992.

U.S. Immigration and Naturalization Service. *Statistical Yearbook of the Immigration and Naturalization Service.* Washington, D.C.: U.S. Government Printing Office, annual.

Vedder, Richard, Lowell Galloway and Stephen Moore. "Do Immigrants Increase Unemployment or Reduce Economic Growth?" *Congressional Record.* September 26, 1990.

Vlastos, Gregory. "Justice and Equality." In *Social Justice,* edited by Richard B. Brandt, 31–72. Englewood Cliffs, N.J.: Prentice-Hall, 1962.

Walzer, Michael. *Spheres of Justice, a Defense of Pluralism and Equality.* New York: Basic Books, 1983.

Walzer, Michael. *What It Means to Be an American.* New York: Marsilio Publishers, 1992.

Warren, Robert. "Estimates of the Unauthorized Immigrant Population Residing in the United States, by Country of Origin and State of Residence: October 1992." Washington, D.C.: Statistics Division, Immigration and Naturalization Service, 1994.

Wasserstrom, Richard. "One Way to Understand and Defend Programs of Preferential Treatment." In *The Moral Foundations of Civil Rights,* edited by Robert K. Fullinwider and Claudia Mills, 46–55. Totowa, N.J.: Rowman and Littlefield, 1986.

Wattenberg, Ben J., and Karl Zinmeister. "The Case for More Immigration." *Commentary* 89 (1990):19–25.

Weiner, Myron. *The Global Migration Crisis, Challenge to States and to Human Rights.* New York: HarperCollins, 1995.

Weintraub, Sidney. "Illegal Immigrants in Texas: Impact on Social Services and Related Considerations." *International Migration Review* 18 (1984):733–47.

Weissbrodt, David. *Immigration Law and Procedure in a Nutshell.* St. Paul: West Publishing, 1992.

Whelan, Frederick G. "Citizenship and Freedom of Movement, an Open Admission Policy?" In *Open Borders? Closed Society? The Ethical and Political Issues,* edited by Mark Gibney, 3–39. Westport, Conn.: Greenwood Press, 1988.

White, Michael J., and Yoshie Imai. "The Impact of U.S. Immigration upon Internal Migration." *Population and Environment* 15 (1994):189–209.

Will, George F. "Assimilation Is Not a Dirty Word." *Los Angeles Times.* July 29, 1993, B7.

Wills, Gary. *Lincoln at Gettysburg, the Words That Remade America.* New York: Simon and Schuster, 1992.

Winegarden, C. R., and Lay Boon Khor. "Undocumented Immigration and Unemployment of U.S. Youth and Minority Workers: Econometric Evidence." *Review of Economics and Statistics* 73 (1991):105–12.

Wolf, Susan. "Moral Saints." *Journal of Philosophy* 79 (1982):419–39.

Woo Morales, Ofelia. "Undocumented Migrant Women Migrating to the United States." Testimony presented to the California Assembly Select Committee on Statewide Immigration Impact. Sacramento, July 19, 1994.

Woodrow, Karen A. "A Consideration of the Effect of Immigration Reform on the Number of Undocumented Residents in the United States." *Population Research and Policy Review* 11 (1992):117–44.

World Bank. *World Development Report 1994, Infrastructure for Development.* New York: Oxford University Press, 1994.

Zabin, Carol, Michael Kearney, Anna Garcia, David Runsten and Carole Nagengast. *Mixtec Migrants in California Agriculture.* Davis, Calif.: California Institute for Rural Studies, 1993.

Zimmermann, Wendy, and Michael Fix, "Immigrant Policy in the States: A Wavering Welcome." In *Immigration and Ethnicity, the Integration of America's Newest Arrivals,* edited by Barry Edmonston and Jeffrey S. Passel, 287–316. Washington, D.C.: Urban Institute Press, 1994.

Index

196-97; social problems in, 159, 191, 196; in third world, 100-101
Citizenship, 50, 51, 55, 206
Civil conflicts, 127
Civil Rights Act (1964), 56
Civil rights movement, 56, 159, 188, 189, 191, 205
Civil War, 32, 185
Clinton, Bill, 6, 212
Clinton administration, 179
Cold War, 63, 72, 74, 193
College students, 187-88, 197
Collins, Nancy, 155-56
Colonial American immigrants, 6-7, 32, 45, 50, 212
Colonial European powers, 105, 124
Commerce *see* International trade
Commission on Immigration Reform, 6, 70
Communist countries (*see also* Cold War), 74
Competitiveness, 16-17, 68, 176-77, 181, 212
Conflicts *see* Civil conflicts; International conflicts
Construction laborers, 46
Conte, Silvio, 183
Criminals, 50, 51, 52, 202
Croats, 193
Crop insurance, 115
Cross-sectional studies, 150-51, 152
Cuba, 113, 120n24
Cuban Americans, 6
Cuban immigrants, 64, 72, 74-75, 112, 151-52, 203
Cultural diversity *see* Multiculturalism
Cuomo, Mario M., 60
Curricula, 198

Daniels, Roger, 59n26
Death rate: age distribution and, 131, 132; European, 45; population growth and, 40, 41; projections of, 129-30; of resident population, 39
Debt crisis, 101
Declaration of Independence, 6, 184, 215, 216, 223
Democracy, 184-85, 220-21
Democratic Party, 205
Demographic growth *see* Population growth

Dependency ratio, 131
Deportation, 55; employer sanctions and, 65; exploitation and, 201, 202; indigency and, 195; probability of, 66; reduced grounds for, 67
Depression era, 122, 125, 126
Despotism, 215
A Different Mirror (Takaki), 185
Disadvantaged Americans *see* Poor Americans
Disasters, 63
Discrimination (*see also* Racism), 230
Displaced persons *see* Refugees
The Disuniting of America (Schlesinger), 188
"Diversity" visas, 67, 229
Doctors, 231
Domestic workers, 117
Dropouts, 147-48, 150
Dual labor market theory, 108-10, 147
Duleep, Harriet, 84
Durand, Jorge, 94, 107

Earnings *see* Wages
Earthmoving equipment, 109
East Asia, 100
East Asian immigrants, 10
East Indian immigrants, 72, 97, 105
East Los Angeles, 72
Eastern Europe, 123
Eastern European immigrants, 33, 47-48, 53, 54
Eastern Hemisphere immigrants, 53-54, 55, 56
Economic growth, 16-17, 126; environmental impact of, 171-73; in foreign countries, 15; in Harris-Todaro model, 96; high immigration rate and, 99-100; NAFTA and, 103; in third world, 100-101, 102-3, 122-23, 125; in U.S., 125, 166-68, 171, 200
Economic impacts, 10-17, 18, 70, 200; long-term, 164-82, 212; short-term, 138-63
Economic models, 139, 140
Economic refugees *see* Poor immigrants
Economic status *see* Standard of living
Economies of scale, 167-68, 170
The Economist, 164
Edmonston, Barry, 121

Educational attainment (*see also*
Dropouts; Public schools): admission based on, 21, 232; enhancement of, 22; international trade
and, 177; of Puerto Ricans, 113; of
recent immigrants, 79-81; residential concentration and, 77; wages
and, 97, 112, 180; Walter-McCarran
Act amendments and, 55
Egalitarianism: commitment to, 228;
heroism and, 224; illegal immigration and, 235; inheritance and, 220;
open-border issue and, 214-16, 217-
18; in political process, 213; rights
violations and, 234; self-interest and,
223
Electoral districting, 206
Emergency medical care, 201
Emigration, 36, 37, 38
Empirical research, 149, 152-53
Employees *see* Labor supply
Employers, 8; exploitation by, 202;
global competitiveness of, 16-17, 68,
176-77, 181, 212; political process
and, 177; profits of, 13, 141-42, 212;
sanctions against, 55, 65, 66; in
third world, 100
"Employment creation" preference, 68
Employment identity cards, 66
Enchautegui, Maria, 85, 87
English immigrants, 32-33, 45, 51, 52,
92, 186
English language, 81-83, 84, 105, 198-
99
English political philosophy, 184-85
Entitlement programs *see* Human ser-
vices; Public welfare
Entrepreneurship, 11-12, 14
Environmental impacts, 17-18, 41-42,
123, 171-73, 181, 212
Espenshade, Thomas J., 137n17, 155,
156
Ethical issues, 24-26, 27, 209-37
"Ethnic cleansing," 193
Ethnic quotas *see* Quotas
Ethnicity (*see also* Multiculturalism):
10, 42-49; earnings and, 85; labor
quality and, 174-75; in 1990s, 70-76;
in 19th century, 51; political representation and, 192; projections of,
132-36, 183, 213; residential concen-

tration and, 77; student life and,
187-88; Walter-McCarran Act
amendments and, 56
Europe: citizenship in, 202; class system in, 220; colonies of, 105, 124;
economies in, 117-18, 123, 179; language facility in, 199; taxation in,
112
European Americans (*see also* Anglo
Americans), 42, 56, 183, 192
European immigrants (*see also*
Colonial American immigrants):
Chinese immigrants and, 47; eastern European, 33, 47-48, 53, 54;
educational levels of, 112; in late
20th century, 49;
"melting pot", and, 19, 185-86, 191;
motivation of, 99; Natives and, 189;
networks of, 115; in 19th century,
46, 92; northwestern European, 32-
33, 45, 53, 58n15, 68; political
process and, 205; productivity of,
167; southern European, 33, 47-48,
53, 54, 99; urban residence of, 71;
U.S. ethnic composition and, 10
Exploitation, 25, 26, 201, 235

Factor proportions, 165
Family reunification, 21; "diversity"
visas and, 68; economic goals and,
69-70; female immigration and, 39;
networks and, 116; in 1920s, 54; priority of, 209, 229-31; restrictions on,
61; Truman commission on, 55;
Walter-McCarran Act amendments
on, 56, 57
Family services, 157
Family strategies, 113-15, 222
Farmers *see* Agricultural laborers
Federal government: deficit of, 145;
economic responsibilities of, 125,
179; exploitation cases and, 202; foreign aid from, 221, 222, 227; foreign
policy of, 63, 64, 74, 75-76; origins
of, 184-85; state aid from, 14, 203;
transition assistance from, 202-3
Federal legislation (*see also specific
acts*), 21, 49-57, 62-68; justification
for, 209, 217; networks and, 116;
reform of, 5, 192; restrictive, 6, 48,
51-55, 122

About the Author

John Isbister was raised in Ottawa, Canada, where his father was, for a period, Deputy Minister of Citizenship and Immigration for the Government of Canada. He studied History at Queen's University in Kingston, Ontario, and Economics at Princeton University where he specialized in demography and earned his Ph.D. in 1969. He immigrated to the United States in 1968 to join the Economics faculty at the University of California, Santa Cruz, where he is now Professor and Provost of Merrill College. His interest in immigration has been stimulated largely by the experience of working with immigrant students who have come to the United States from all parts of the world. He is the author of *Promises Not Kept: The Betrayal of Social Change in the Third World,* published by Kumarian Press and now in its third edition, and also of *Thin Cats: The Community Development Credit Union Movement in the United States* (1994). He teaches courses on immigration, the economic development of low-income countries and social change in the third world.